CARNIVORE

Appetite
4 Destruction

CARNIVORE

Appetite
4 Destruction

❧

CHRONICLES

Destructive Appetite 4 Sex

C Ellis Chase

Jeremiah 31:34." The living Bible Paraphrased
Facebook chase007
Twitter @chase0079
Now available on Kindle

Thank you's

⤜⧂⧏

God

Sherly Ellis - Mom

Family & Friends

Brianna Ellis

Jasmine Davis

Theresa Kilpatrick

Karen

Laura Gordon

Book Club Chase007

Everyone supporting my career

⤜⧂⧏

A portion of the proceeds will be donated to LEMATA Leaving Everlasting Memories As Time Advances Cancer Survivor Fashion Show "Models for the Cure"

www.lemata.org

CHRONICLES

It would be minutes before her secret lover arrived tonight. This would make the third time this week his wife wouldn't have a clue about their affair. Paulette stood in front of the mirror, marveling her creamy skin tone, running her fingers through the thick coarse strands of her bleached, damaged, light brown hair. Slowly she sprayed a light scent body perfume, layering her skin from head to toe, all the while envisioning the anger his wife would feel after getting a whiff of it. He insisted she lay off the perfume. Paulette had other tempting pleasures in mind; she could care less. Paulette knew all she needed was a little distraction to take his mind off her scent with the sexy outfit she was going to wear. He would forget all about it. His manhood seemed to control his mind.

Paulette glanced over at the clock—it was 11:00 o'clock at night; it was almost time. Her heart raced, she couldn't wait to spend that little time with the lucky guy. Paulette slipped into a sexy outfit she purchased with the money he had given her earlier this week. Paulette stood mesmerized at the flashback running through her mind. The muscles in her face suddenly went slack. Another side of her revealed a horrifying thought, momentarily sending chills down her spine. Paulette quickly shook the thought from her mind into something pleasing. *He was going to love it*, she thought, taking a look at her backside in the mirror. *His wife had nothing on me, her money can't make him happy, I can.* She couldn't wait. Every moment, Paulette envisioned the two of them wrapped around each other, hot and sweaty in bed. Paulette wanted to give him the best sex before heading home to his wife but for now, all she could do was focus on the last time she had seen him. She wanted to leave something with him, anything that would reveal their affair to his wife. The strong perfume smell left on Chad would be enough.

Paulette quickly threw the sheets off the bed, ignoring the fresh soil marks, balling them up and tossing them into the closet hamper. She avoided the interrupted memories of her recent lover. Leaping from end to end she spread the corners of the clean sheet over, smoothing out the wrinkles, rubbing her body over the tops of the sheet, leaving behind her pungent perfume. Paulette rushed around putting the last finishing touches on her make-up. Everything was set; she stood on the side taking one last look at the bed.

It was after midnight. Paulette was nervous. For some reason, the butterflies that had been dancing around in her stomach had stopped. Paulette glanced at the land line and then her cell phone. He hadn't called yet. Frantically, she searched through her messages but there was nothing. *He promised to be here at twelve, he'd never been late,* she thought. She quickly dialed his cell phone and was disappointed when it went straight to voicemail. Out of anger, she hung up, pacing the floor, and quickly dialed again. *He's always been early, at least ten to twenty minutes.* Each time, she hung up after hearing the voice mail. Paulette continued dialing, over and over. She plopped down on the side of the bed, furious. Her eyes darted from the clock back to the phone; her next thought was dialing his home number.

Mr. Right had no idea I had his home phone number. If he did, he'd probably shit bricks. After a night of hot sex, he decided to go to the bathroom leaving behind his wallet and cell phone on my nightstand. His dumb ass had no idea I was the pro at scamming and still doesn't. He always carried a lot of money. That night I stole a few extra dollars. He must not have known because he never mentioned it. Besides, what the hell could he say anyway?

Paulette's first thought was to call and have a friendly conversation with his wife, then laying it on her. *He had no excuse not to phone me. How dare he, I don't give a damn about his wife and unborn child. Ever since his wife became pregnant, he's been trying to be Mr. Do Right! He claimed it was an accident, and that he never wanted to have a child.* The disappointing factor was his wife was still getting sex. *I thought I was taking care of all his needs!*

Paulette became so angry she could feel her blood starting to boil. Slowly her fingers pressed the number keys, only getting up enough nerve to dial four numbers. She stopped.

"Forget him!"

Paulette stood in front of her closet door. It was still early enough to make a catch. Most of the important people at the bar were still in VIP. She pulled out the shortest backless dress, slipping it on along with a pair of four-inch slingback heels.

"This bed is going to have some more action tonight," she said aloud, taking a last look at the bed before walking out.

Paulette drove around hoping to find Mr. Right, searching every place she thought he might be before going to the club. She thought her luck might pay off, but it didn't; he was nowhere in sight. Paulette's disappointment turned into rage. She knew where his wife was located.

❦

"The call from Valerie can as a shock, more so disappointment to learn that my wife was in the hospital for over three hours without my knowledge. Why was I the last to find out! Those damn Crawford's! I don't care what I do; I'll never be good enough for them!"

Chad drove recklessly over the speed limit through town. The disturbing phone call from Valerie, Christine's mother, replayed like a broken record in his head. Each thought drove him to push down on the accelerator more, weaving in and out of traffic like a bat out of hell. Chad rushed into the parking lot, slowing down just a bit to find the first empty parking spot. The hospital was packed this time of night; Friday seemed to draw more tragic incidents in after midnight. Chad pulled his custom-painted SUV into a faraway spot, giving him enough room on each side for other car doors to swing open. Christine paid for the SUV and she hated door dings. Chad swung open the door, darting out of the car. A look of worry hung on his face. Paulette was nowhere in his thoughts tonight. Chad rushed into the emergency room through the double doors, out of breath. He waited impatiently for an elderly couple in front, still breathing hard.

"Is there a patient by the name of Christine Crawford-Stone here?" Chad's eyes zoomed in on her name tag. As Sheila searched the computer, he observed her intense expression.

Chad's heart raced a mile a minute. He impatiently tapped his fingers on the desk top. The agony was practically over. Within seconds the receptionist pulled up her name.

"Sir, she's still in with the doctors."

"What! I need to know something about her; she was rushed in not too long ago!"

"She's still in surgery, sir."

"Surgery! What the hell happened?"

"Sir, I need you to calm down."

Chad paced the floor, angry and confused, running his hand across the top of his head. Before turning to the receptionist's desk, he heard a familiar voice calling from behind him. It was deep and masculine. The voice instantly gave Chad a sense of fear that could be seen by the naked eye. Mr. Crawford was intimidating; there was something about him. Chad made it a point to avoid Christine's family if there any way possible, but tonight there was no way to avoid something this tragic without being ridiculed. Chad changed his composure quickly, instantly straightening up his slouchy posture.

"Chad."

He hesitated, turning to face Donny.

It was a change seeing Christine's dad in a pair of jeans and a polo shirt, looking like the average Joe. Chad reflected back to the day he and his daughter married. It took years of approval. He remembered the long talks and the threats Mr. Crawford made before Chad become his son-in-law; they would make any man walk away. Mr. Crawford spoke by hinting around in so many words, but his actions spoke louder while cleaning off his pistol. He always made a point to express how important Christine was to him, especially if something should ever happen to her. Chad snatched the thought from his mind, extending his hand to greet his father-in-law. The grip was firm and short as usual, even at a time of crisis. Chad quickly searched for Sally.

"Oh, she's at home." He responded before Chad could get the words out. "Christine's mother is here, Valerie." For some reason, Sally was never around; Valerie seemed to be more involved.

"What happened? I received the phone call from Valerie and panicked. I stressed my worries of concern." Mr. Crawford didn't say much of anything; he always made it seem like there was nothing to worry about. Chad guessed that came with his ego and pride.

"She's been in a little fender-bender ... well, more like an accident."

"Is ... is she all right? My God, what happened?"

"I don't know, someone passing by saw her car in a ditch, the goddamn driver who hit her didn't even have enough nerve to stop!"

"You mean it was a hit and run? What the hell!" Chad stood shaking his head wondering who would be so cruel. "The baby, what about the baby? Is ... is it all right?" Mr. Crawford gave no response.

Valerie stood waving her hand on the other side of the nurse's station, motioning them into the waiting room. Mr. Crawford and Chad turned to notice two doctors standing beside her. Chad rushed by him, anxious to hear what the doctors had to say. Mr. Crawford wasn't too far on his heels.

❧

Paulette struts her stuff through a crowd of people waiting in line. She had the VIP to bypass what she called the non-important little people. Paulette's theory was that most of the men had barely, if any, money and no game. They just wanted to buy you a few glasses of cheap dark liquor and expected sex. How depressing, she thought, waving the pieces of her weave to the back. Big Huey stood outside guarding the VIP entrance like it was a bank full of money. The name fit well: he was 6' feet tall, 300 hundred something pounds, with a smile that could kill. He smiled once

Paulette got in view, placing one hand on the door handle letting her know she was all right to enter. Paulette ignored the dirty remarks and stares from the other girls.

The music was bumpin'. Once inside, Paulette felt at home. She made her way straight to the VIP area. It didn't take long before placing her eyes on her first catch: a tall, thin, caramel-colored man, standing alone by the bar.

He was too fine to be alone, there had to be a woman somewhere, or maybe a wife he left at home. Well, as long as she was at home, Paulette didn't care. She carefully sized him up. She could tell by his suit and wristwatch he was ballin' big time. He was smooth; they made eye contact several times before his woman stepped in. "What a disappointment," said some flaky hoe, wearing some cheap dress from the ten-dollar store. "He's gotta have something better on his hand then that slut." Paulette didn't pass up the fantasizing; she envisioned the two of them in the bed waiting for her at home. From the way he dressed, he had to have it go in on.

Paulette sat at the bar two chairs down from who she thought was Mr. Right. Regardless of his girlfriend or wife, she didn't care; he was dripping in money. Her eyes were set. Before she could order a drink, a bottle of wine chilled on ice sat in front of her. Just as she suspected, it was expensive. She eyed every man in the VIP area. No one caught her eye or even gave a clue from who it might be. Enviously, Paulette continued eyeing the couple down next to the bar. She yearned for the love he expressed for her, but couldn't stop focusing on his diamond gold-plated watch and huge earrings. She exhaled deeply, loud enough to disturb the two who were kissing and hugging. The woman stood up and rolled her eyes, turning her back on Paulette. She refused to turn away from the eye contact given between her and Mr. Right. Even though his woman was there, his eyes were talking sex. Paulette played the role, shyly smiling and winking. She crossed her legs showing off her light brown figure; the moment was enticing.

He was sucking on her neck while being turned on to me, she thought. He smiled back and nodded his head. Paulette's eyes focused on the bottle of wine. His smile grew and she knew it was from him. She noticed a paper attached to the back of the bottle. With no hesitation, she unfolded the short note. Paulette smiled, nodding her yes in response to his gaze.

Paulette's name was going around the VIP area. Most of the men knew her, had given her a few hundreds; the sex was on that night. Little did she know her name was quickly passed by Big Huey. On the down low, he was letting others know that she was an easy hit for a night.

Paulette could count several men walking around who she had already slept with or was sleeping with. Most of them were married or had a girlfriend. Once they got what they wanted, they barely made eye contact or said "hi" unless they wanted sex or a quick head job. They just wanted some good sex, or perhaps they didn't care if it was good, they just wanted something different, a female that would keep her mouth shut. Most of them knew they could count on Paulette as long as she got something in return.

Thirty minutes had gone by. Paulette sat waiting in her car in the spot Julian told her in his note to be, across the street from Gillian's restaurant. She couldn't wait; her insides throbbed with excitement. The time in her car read 2:00 a.m. She tapped her nail on the side panel. A BMW C230 was approaching and then stopped, switching off its headlights. It had to be him. The car he drove turned her on more. Her excitement was all over the leather seats. Paulette drove the corners of her skirt up higher revealing more of her thighs. She watched the tall figure approaching. Once he got close enough to her car, Paulette got out. She smiled from ear to ear; he was fine. He introduced himself with a firm grip.

"Noticed you the moment you walked in the club, you're so damn fine. What were you doing alone?" Paulette picked up on his corniness quickly.

"That's a long story, one you don't wanna hear. My name is Tracie, Tracie Pauley." Julian responded with a perplexed look; he remembered Big Huey telling him her name was Paulette. *It's all good*, he thought.

"Well, Tracie, I don't have long." She watched as he pulled back his suit coat revealing his watch. It had more diamonds up close. The thought of all those diamonds flashing made her hot.

"So, what do you have in mind?" Paulette asked, tugging at his suit coat, softly rubbing herself against him. His white teeth gleamed in the moonlight.

"Let's take my car." Paulette was delighted. She followed Julian by the hand like a little girl.

Paulette couldn't take her eyes off his pimped out BMW. It was breath-taking. She felt on top of the world again. All this money surrounding her was intoxicating. Paulette placed her hand on the console while Julian made his feel, exploring between her legs. Julian could barely keep focused, resulting in a few close calls. He quickly swerved back on the road. Julian's hand gripped the wheel tightly as Paulette's hand ran between his legs, gripping his manhood. She unzipped his pants. She insisted he hold on to the wheel; she had a surprise for him. Julian moaned in excitement. Paulette thought about the money, rendering oral pleasure.

Julian pulled over on the side of the road in the middle of nowhere. He couldn't wait, time was winding down. He let back the seat quickly placing on a condom. Paulette pulled aside her thong, straddling him slowly, engulfing his throbbing, hard flesh. The two of them moaned. Besides the money, Julian's forceful grip was the only thing that turned her on. His heavy breathing soon fogged up the windows. Paulette couldn't wait for the moment to be over, faking her disappointment in moans. Julian had no sexual technique. *I bet if he had to find where to put it, he couldn't. Lucky I was on top.* His penis was small, but worst of all, his grinding was off beat. He screwed like an offbeat prep trying to dance. To make matters worse, after a few minutes his body began to stiffen like a seizure victim, grunting aloud as if he'd done something. *I would have had more fun playing with myself.*

Paulette continued faking her moans, pretending to

have an orgasm. It hadn't been two minutes; she couldn't believe he was finished.

"That was good, baby," Julian replied, shoving her off of him. Paulette continued lying, like a criminal trying to defend his innocence.

This is what I waited for, this shit! Paulette observed him as he glanced at his watch. It was obvious he was hinting around. *His lame tail didn't have to tell me twice.* Julian, the bastard, barely had two words to say, zipping up his pants as if he had done something.

Paulette drew focus on the wallet in his hand. She got a good glimpse to see it was full of big bills. The sex wasn't good but seeing all that money put a smile on her face. Her smile grew grim once his pictures unfolded, which Julian quickly tried hard to hide. He fumbled about, stuffing them back in his wallet. It was obvious; you could see the muscles in his face went slack. Her heart skipped a beat. There was enough time to see a wife and three children, two boys and a girl.

He drew out a few hundreds *like I was some cheap whore, placing them in my hand, tightly sealed with a sloppy kiss I had no warning for.* Julian was so non-romantic, it was all a front at the club, and the girl at the club wasn't even his wife. His wife was a white woman. Julian must have been starving for some black ass. He was willing to pay; he even wanted to start setting up regular sex dates. She so wanted to pass, but the money, the hundreds, kept coming when she didn't answer him. Once he hit four hundred, she snatched the money quickly from his hand. She couldn't refuse. Even though he wasn't packin' the punch she needed and the sex was lame, his wallet was talkin.' She guessed she could put up with a few freaky nights and fake it. He apologized several times before leaving, promising to make it up. She could think of several ways for him to do that: a trip to Jamaica, Brazil or maybe somewhere extravagant. *That I can't wait for.*

Julian drove her back to her car. Paulette was left fumbling at her car door after practically being thrown out. She watched as he sped off, leaving a trail of debris from the side of the road behind.

As Julian drove away, he said to himself, *I can't believe this bitch is trying to play me. I know her name is Paulette Daniels from two of the guys at the club. Marcus told me if I wanted some quick sex, Paulette was willing. The light skinned, bleached-haired whore at the bar,* he thought, chuckling aloud. *That's okay, if she wants to play, we can do that. That ho doesn't know who she's messing with! All I know is the ass is free as long as I lavish that trick in something expensive.*

That wasn't hard for Julian; he was rolling in millions. It was definitely no shirt off his back, a multi-millionaire who had built his company from the ground up, with the help of his wife, Joyce.

⟵∾⟶

Paulette rushed through her apartment, stripping off her dress. The sweaty wetness she shared with Julian was driving her crazy. Her clock read four in the morning. Paulette stopped at the answering machine; it was blinking. Her first thought was Chad. She anxiously picked up the phone, searching through the LCD. Disappointment struck; there was no message left from him. Paulette stood half nude, outraged. Several messages from her mother were left. It had to be important. Paulette let the answering machine play while stripping off her shoes. She ran into the bedroom, pausing at her bed. *That bastard!* She thought, quickly turning away, with her back facing the bed.

Paulette glanced around the room. She focused on everything: the closet full of clothes, shoes, everything material was purchased by some man she slept with. Paulette drew focus away from everything, telling herself she deserved it all while fighting off her denial in the mirror, trying desperately to shake off her frustration.

Damn it, Paulette, why do you do this! Something was missing; the person who resided inside her was lost in worldly temptations, while a different personality reared its ugly head. Her anger was expressed at the mirror.

Paulette stood in the bathroom, waiting for the water to warm up. She watched the water from the shower head fall onto the tub floor. The messages from the other room were loud enough for her to hear. Frantic cries from her mother frightened her. Paulette stepped into the other room to hear the message ending. She stood frozen over the answering machine. Another side of her knew why her mother was calling but Paulette didn't care. She momentarily turned a deaf ear to the voices in her head.

That's what that bitch gets. Out of anger, Paulette picked up the phone, dialing the number she had intended to do before leaving for the club. The phone rang several times before the answering machine picked up. Paulette was aroused over the husky greeting, waiting for the beep to sound. It was the moment she had waited for, to fuck with his wife. *That will teach that bastard for standing me up again.* Deviousness spewed from her mouth; there was no remorse in her heart as Paulette disguised her voice. Chad was in for a rude awakening once Christine got the message. Paulette didn't give up; she dialed his cell phone, angry that it went straight to voicemail. She swore at the top of her lungs, yanking the phone cord out of the wall.

"Damn it, I hate her! She's always interfered! Ever since we were kids, her and that snooty father of hers! The hell with them!" She screamed in a sudden outburst.

❧

Chad focused more on the paintings hanging from the wall than what the doctor was saying. Every word that Doctor Spindel said overwhelmed his brain. Two police officers stood off to the side. *What were they doing here?* For some reason, the pounding in his heart wouldn't stop. Chad continued making suspicious eye contact with the two officers. His palms were sweaty and sweat beads dripped down his armpits.

What was going on? He wondered. Something definitely didn't feel right. Christine must be seriously injured. Luckily, they were able to save the baby. Doctor Spindel said that it would be a painful pregnancy; Christine needed a lot of bed rest and no stress. The disk in her back was driven out of place from the impact of the rollover; surgery was an option but Doctor Spindel needed to run more tests. There was some internal bleeding which brought concern so they were keeping her overnight. She suffered a concussion that needed supervision along with a large gash on her forehead above her hairline. Doctor Spindel patched Christine up with forty-eight stitches. *How could this have happened? I feel bad. We argued about the baby situation two days ago.*

Mr. Crawford was overheard yelling "I want the best doctors for my daughter" and he didn't care how much it cost. Chad made sure to remain out of his way.

Christine was four months' pregnant. It was our first child together, one that I really didn't want. Suddenly he felt bad for all the horrible things he said about the baby. *I didn't want any children, but I didn't want her to lose it. This was all unplanned.* Christine insisted on keeping it regardless of what he thought. *Our marriage was somewhat out of a fairy tale book. Her family came from a well-off generation of wealth, power and money. I had to dig my shoes in somewhere, but our agreement was no children. Christine wanted them. Every discussion leading to children resulted in a huge argument.* Mr. Crawford paid for the entire wedding, fifty thousand dollars, if not more. *We had a lavish wedding with a lot of important people.* Christine had the wealth, power, and money, plus a big-shot father who didn't take any crap. Needless to say, Chad had nothing without her. He needed something to blame for his infidelity. Five years into marriage and now this? There were a lot of wrongs and huge regrets that he knew were coming to bite him hard in the butt.

☙

Chad mind slipped back to how he had met Paulette Daniels. Two years ago, a good friend of his recommended Paulette to him. They had been keeping it strong ever since then. That night he needed to release some tension from an earlier argument with Christine. Word had got around that Paulette was good for sex, so he was in. Paulette was tall, slim and had a body to kill. Her breasts were perky and revealing in the skimpy outfit she wore that night. She had an ass you could bounce a ball off. She delighted in him; the lust he felt for her could be seen by the bulge in his pants. Once he gave Paulette his cell number she rang it off the hook, nonstop. Phone sex was getting old; he was ready to take action. All the hot, heavy breathing back and forth and masturbating wasn't enough. Paulette was talking some good stuff, and he wanted it.

The first night they hooked up, he couldn't wait. They stripped down to nothing in a matter of minutes at her apartment in upper New York. Paulette had some kind of control, something he couldn't say no to. She could see it in his eyes. She grabbed between his legs, engulfing him whole; his legs became weak. No matter how many times Christine gave head it was never like this. He could see the disappointment appearing in her eyes when Chad pulled out a condom. On the other hand, Paulette's body torpedoed downward. He quickly unwrapped the condom, slipping it on. Soon he was swallowed whole, watching in amazement in the mirror behind her as her body traveled up and down. Paulette was sure to please in whatever way possible. Chad offered stability and she lacked foundation. He knew he had her in the palm of his hand. Afterward, they lay wrapped in each other's arms embracing the moment. Christine never crossed his mind that night.

Chad was taken aback by Paulette's sudden outbursts. Oddly, she knew a lot about Christine, that's all she seemed to speak about. How beautiful and wealthy she and her family are. Paulette even knew a lot about Christine's childhood, things he never knew. That was strange; even when Chad became inquisitive, Paulette blew it off as if it were nothing. She always switched the subject. Her outlandish behavior struck a nerve. Paulette was a good actor because she pretended not to remember all the horrible things she said about Christine.

Chad remained transfixed on the paintings at the hospital. By now the two officers were speaking alone to Mr. Crawford and Valerie. Valerie was weeping; Mr. Crawford wiped the sweat from his forehead. Witnessing this made Chad even more inquisitive. *What could the police possibly have to say?* Chad eased his way over but before he could extend his hand, Mr. Crawford interrupted, introducing him. Chad was taken aback again; Detective Marsh was a very good friend of the Crawford's.

Marsh's theory was this was no accident. They all stood, perplexed. Everyone's eyes traveled the circle as if already pointing blame. For some reason, the circle ended with

Chad. His heart deflated like a punctured balloon. He was one blink away from an onslaught of tears. Mr. Crawford was outraged, coldness escaped from his mouth like an arctic freeze. He demanded that no matter how much money it took to find out the real truth if it was caused by someone's carelessness, they were going to pay. Chad unconsciously stepped back. No matter how many business deals he had seen go bad, he had never witnessed Mr. Crawford's anger.

Detectives Marsh and Alexander continued their theory. Their only witness, a young man, had just flown out of town for a funeral and wouldn't be back for weeks. He claimed to have seen what happened. He said it was no accident, it was deliberate. Chad felt his muscles tighten up. He swallowed back a thick buildup of saliva.

"We need him, goddamn it!" Mr. Crawford yelled.

"Right now, all we can do is wait. I know how eager you are. We all are."

"No, you don't, damn it!! This is my only child. She's only twenty-nine. If someone has a problem with her I wanna know now!" Valerie cracked a small smile through her tears. No matter how many times her ex-husband remarried women with other children, Christine would always be number one.

Valerie cooled her heels on a nearby chair, sobbing uncontrollably. The least Chad could do is offer his support. He sat next to her, softly rubbing her back. Chad struggled to get rid of the sudden lump in his throat. He cleared it numerous times but nothing seemed to work

The room was quiet when Doctor Spindel arrived again. He gave them the okay to see Christine. Chad glanced up, submerged in guilt, clearing his throat. He was incapable of shaking the accident. Valerie shot to her feet, demanding she be the first to go in. Christine was groggy and still in a lot of pain and barely conscious. Doctor Spindel stressed the importance of one person per visit and keeping them short. Christine and the baby needed their rest.

⌘

Dana sat around, longing for a good time. She picked up the phone and dialed some old friends she knew would bring an end to a good night. Whitney spoke about a couple of parties. Dana wanted in, begging to tag along. Being in the room with a bunch of millionaires was enticing. Tamara, Dana, and Whitney, along with a group of friends, headed to one of the premier parties: a hot spot for digging your heels into a rich, powerful man that is if he didn't have his wife or girlfriend on hand. There was a room full of NBA stars and millionaires.

Dana had felt appreciation seeing her friend's frequent parties and getting what they wanted. She sat back, blushing from all the sex talk. Tamara and Whitney continued rambling on about all the men, sex, and money. Dana was a rookie at the money game. This was her first night hanging out and she saw her friends being enticed by the money and power. Trading sex for money didn't seem like a bad idea. Whitney and Tamara were doing it and it seemed to pay off.

Tamara had several guys she sucked money from. She was in her late twenties and more into the older rich guys. Tamara's short-cut blonde hair lay smoothly, lining her round face. Her tanned skin shimmered in the moonlight along with her blue contacts. The short, backless dress she wore matched the color of her eyes. The first things you noticed when approaching Tamara were her big, beautiful eyes; with or without contacts, she was a white beauty.

Tamara learned to realize the power of what she had between her legs by age fourteen. Her busty bosom caught a lot of eye contact, mostly from older perverts. The younger boys dreamed of touching them but wouldn't dare. Tamara was too busy baiting married men. The first man was a neighbor, Mr. Vincent. He resembled an old pervert you were likely to see in the registered sex offenders' lists. His hair was thinning; the little he had was combed over the top, leaving bald gaps. His wife, Mrs. Vincent, was kind. She always seemed to come through and lift Tamara's spirits up when her mom and dad fought. Tamara had another plan. She used her breasts to her advantage, taunting and teasing Mr. Vincent. Once she knew he couldn't resist, Tamara went for the full course: twice a week blow jobs in the back yard or garage. Seeing that he was paying, she was willing to take it further. Having sex for the first time was rough. Mr. Vincent threw himself on her like he had never had it before. It was more painful than pleasing; he was tasteless. That night Tamara pocketed two hundred dollars. The pain was worth every bit.

At fifteen Tamara was known as the school slut. Most

every girl hated her. Tamara took it as them being jealous. She began using her wicked scheme on several teachers. After-school tutoring (indulging in sex #1) soon changed her Fs to As.

Dana couldn't stomach sleeping with an old man. The disapproving glances made her feel uncomfortable. Whitney's old man was old enough to be her father, in his late fifties, and now Tamara was working her moves on some other old guy in the Mercedes next to them who appeared to be the same age. She thought he had money. Dana frowned, rolling her eyes, looking the other way. She remained transfixed on the lighted billboards until she noticed the car pulling over. Tamara threw the car in park and hopped out of the driver's seat and began working her magic. Dana could tell the guy was married. He was old enough to be her grandfather.

He probably needed Viagra just to get an erection. Gross. Did I make the wrong choice hanging with them? She thought to herself. Tamara had pulled out all her tricks to make him feel like he was important. Two could play that game. Dana watched in disgust as he played the same game back.

Whitney was different, a twenty-four-year-old beauty. Her curly black hair hung down to her shoulder blades. She was a mixture of several nationalities, mostly from the West Indies. Whitney started securing her future at age nineteen. She was now on her third marriage to a wealthy man old enough to be her father. Bartley Stevens was fifty-nine, graying and out of shape. He was short and fat but all Whitney saw was security. She was already on her third child fathered by three different men. Dana knew for sure she didn't know who the fathers were except for her last one. She claimed it was Bartley's. Whitney spent more of her time in the streets. She was a horrible mother. Bartley wasn't any better as a parent. The live-in nanny did all the work raising her six-month-old, nine-year-old and two-year-old.

One thing Whitney did have was a lavish home with a lot of expensive material things; nothing but the finest, from clothing to jewelry and cars.

Bartley owned several restaurants on the strip. Whitney thought for sure he would be one of the guys who was not abusive. Her secrets remained hidden for a short time. Her bruises were revealed once Bartley's business took a fall. Tamara and Dana grew skeptical; the beatings were coming too often and becoming more intense.

Whitney had just received cosmetic surgery on her nose for the fifth time this year. She even had her chin reconstructed twice. Her excuses of "I fell and hit the coffee table" were running out. Tamara and Dana didn't care how ditsy she was, they knew Whitney wasn't that clumsy. Two of Bartley's restaurants had closed down due to the economy, but he refused to downsize. The financial loss made things hard with too many expenses to pay for. Whitney always claimed one of her other men hit her. Tamara knew it was a cover-up; Bartley was behind the abuse.

Whitney wasn't herself anymore. Over the years, she changed in several ways: the way she dressed, acting like she didn't care, almost like she was a walking zombie. Bartley manipulated her into doing horrible things. It was the opposite of what usually happened - most controlling men demanded you cover up. Bartley insisted she wear more provocative clothing. Tonight, the top Whitney wore was see-through, leaving nothing to the imagination. Her nipples screamed to get out of her Chanel top. Her skirt barely covered her butt.

Bartley got wind of all the happening parties, and likely to be friends of his. He demanded Whitney to be at all of them. He always gave Whitney a lineup of people he wanted them to meet. Tamara knew once the phone call from her hubby came, covered with phony I love you's, Whitney would find an excuse not to stay long. Dana watched as she threw her excitement around as if she had other plans. Leaving Tamara at the club was a ritual. Once she set her eyes on the right men she was gone. Tamara was sure the disappearing act would be played tonight. Whitney spent most of her time latching on the Mr. Rights in case Bartley didn't work out, checking in with him like some escort business he was now making money off of.

It was disgusting watching them speak on the phone. Their phony acts deserved an Academy Award as Whitney crooned into her cell phone. Her unhappiness showed on her face like a person being held captive awaiting death. Whitney wasn't happy; all she did was complain. She would forget everything once he gave her money and a little freedom.

Dana refused to end up like Whitney, a mechanical zombie. Deep inside she wondered if she was willing to take the risk of living their lifestyle if the tables were turned. Dana couldn't fathom the thought.

Tamara was worse, acting like some upscale hoochies, waiting to suck the blood from men like a leech. Tamara and Whitney swore it was no different than having sex with your boyfriend. You either had sex to get money or did it to get your heart broken. Either way, one of the two was going to happen. Both of them raised their palms in the air giving high fives. Dana ignored them; she just couldn't stomach the moment. They sounded like a bunch of women waiting to exhale once the right man came along. They were too blinded by money to see anything else.

Dana continued staring into space. The more she listened, the more their conversation turned her off. Tamara and Whitney advocated marriage at whatever the cost necessary. *What a drag, who the hell do these hoes think they are? Tamara invited me along to take notes. Shoot, forget that these hoes were nothing but leeches!* She thought. There was no way in hell she was taking lessons from them. She was feeling out of place and couldn't think of one man she had sucked money from. She had had more than a few one-night stands but that was it. *This is a total turn off!* Dana thought, concealing her dirty looks. Tamara's and Whitney's glasses clinked, and laughter filled the air as they continued telling their stories, swotting high fives in the air.

❧

Chad sat staring into space. His leg bounced nervously out of control. The racing in his heart wouldn't stop. Both

Christine's parents were in visiting with her, ignoring Dr. Spindel's request of only one visitor at a time. Chad couldn't wait to see her. Paulette crossed his mind and he thought about how upset she was going to be, but seconds later, the thought was gone. Chad hoped she would understand once he told her his wife was in the hospital. Chad rose up at once, seeing Mr. Crawford's light blue polo shirt poke out from the room. He watched him inch his way out slowly. Chad sucked in several deep breaths as he stood up. Before approaching, he ran his hands down the front of his dress pants, smoothing them out, wiping the sweat off. The look on Mr. Crawford's face was unquestionably intimidating; with a dispiriting sensation, Chad's heart beat faster. There was no way to read how good or bad Christine was; Mr. Crawford showed no emotion.

Valerie came out from their daughter Christine's room along with Donny; their conversations were muted. Judging by Crawford's hand gestures he hoped everything was alright. Chad crept toward them unannounced, giving them a silent, sad puppy dog look.

Mr. Crawford's blistering eyes left Chad's body in a slump. Anxiously he waited for the words he didn't want to hear to come out. "Christine's moving back in with us." Chad slumped over at Donny's unexpected comment. He didn't know whether to be happy or sad. He stuttered, trying to get out a response. The word "but" barely graced his tongue before being shot down by Mr. Crawford's dirty look, as if he was daring him to say something. *This is ridiculous!* He thought. "Can I see her now?" Chad backed away, uncertain. The Crawford's looked at him as if he was uninvited, but was even more dreadful; it was as if he wasn't their son-in-law. Deep inside, he wondered if Mr. Crawford was on to him. For God's sake, he hoped not. What a chaotic mess that would be. Relief came once his mother-in-law, Valerie, stepped aside. Chad took that as a go. His father-in-law never budged; he guarded the door like Fort Knox.

Chad hated hospitals. So did Christine. He remembered her telling him that two weeks ago when she came to visit her passing grandmother. Slowly, he approached her, his eyes quickly gazing over all the tubes running in and out of her face and arms. Chad swallowed back the heavy saliva build-up in his mouth. All her vital signs were stable. Doctors said the pain medication made her sleepy and groggy. "Christine," he mumbled in a low tone, standing over the top of her. A large bandage was wrapped tightly, covering her forehead. He knew there was no way she was going to answer with all the pain medications she was receiving. Chad just wanted to let her know he was there. Slowly he reached over to hold her hand, the other he placed on her stomach. Chad blinked away his tears, and pain flooded his face. He stood there, crying. "This is all my fault," he mumbled. "I shouldn't have, but I did, I can't control myself." Chad stood with his eyes closed, crying out his heart, revealing part of his dirty laundry.

Christine cracked her eyes open enough to see Chad. A smile graced her face, but only for a moment. Her heart suddenly beat faster while tuning into Chad's muffled cries. *He can't control himself, from what?* She wondered. Christine made sure to stay relaxed, not to make any sudden movements that would alarm Chad but she was listening. This was no time for confessing, but his confessions were getting interesting. Christine began to get angry after hearing him ramble on briefly about some girl. It was hard making out what he was saying with all the sobbing. Chad's head was down. Christine thought about the long nights, the dinner meetings Chad had lied about, the overload of women's perfume lingering between the two of them at night. *I just want him outta here now!* She thought. In a matter of minutes, Christine's vital signs shot up. She tried lying there, concealing her anger, but the buzzer and rush of doctors into her room showed differently.

"Sir, we need you to leave!" Doctor Spindel announced, standing behind him. Startled by the rush of doctors, Chad backed away slowly.

"What … what's … what's going on?" he questioned, getting no response. Several doctors rushed to Christine's bedside. Donny and Valerie rushed through the door with suspicion and concern written all over their faces.

"What the hell happened? What did you do to her?" Mr. Crawford screamed, pointing his finger. Chad momentarily lets go of her hand, confused, backing away, terrified.

"Sir, we need you to leave now!" one of the doctors shouted again. Chad's feet stuck to the floor. After witnessing Christine's body stiffening up he trembled from head to toe. Before the doctors could tell him again, Chad started to run out of the door. He stopped for a second in front of Donny and Valerie, unable to make eye contact.

"What the hell happened in there?" Mr. Crawford's voice was faint but the anger spewed from his mouth like hot breath. Chad was spaced out.

"She was fine when we went in there." Valerie wept uncontrollably. "Did you see her, honey, she's never ... she's never done that. What ... what's going on?" Chad wondered the same. Afraid to look up, he nonetheless watched the two of them embracing each other.

"Chad, what's going on?" He is heartfelt embarrassed to see his mother, Jackie, standing behind him. She reeked of cigarette smoke; she had probably dropped the butt at the entrance door before coming in. He had forgotten the frantic call he placed hours ago. Chad now regretted it. One person, he tried hiding from the Crawford's was his tasteless mother. She was like a rag doll in need of throwing away. Her blonde hair was burned four inches if not more at the edges from all the heavy dying. She looked like a crack head in need of a nutritionist. Jackie's style of dress was six years out of date.

She had the nerve showing up with one of her many boyfriends. Chad never knew his father, a onetime man his mother couldn't remember sleeping with, who had split once he found out she was pregnant.

"Mom, I don't need you here," he mumbled under his breath, pulling her to the side by her arm.

"Aren't those the Crawford's? I wanna find out how Chris ..."

"She's fine. I mean, no, she's not. Please, just leave!" he demanded.

Chad imagined the dirty looks the Crawford's would have by now plastered on their faces. They always thought they were better than everyone else. Chad's mother and her mutty-looking boyfriend were people they looked down on. Jackie stood withdrawn from everything, paranoid at whoever walked by. Chad wondered if she was high. This wasn't the time or place to be high. He thought of ways to get rid of his mother and the scum she was with before Christine's parents saw them. The upward movement of his mother's eyes startled him. As if the moment couldn't get any worse, Mr. Crawford approached, pointing at them, accompanied by several men. Chad was dumbfounded.

"I know they're not..." The words barely escaped his mouth. Three security guards made their way over to them. "What ... what's going on? Who are you?" Chad questioned, forcing his way over to the Crawford's. He felt restrained by a tight grip. Chad glanced down at the guard's hand, confused. "Donny, Valerie, you can't do this!" he sputtered. They both turned away, ignoring his protests. Donny gave Chad a last sneering evil glance. Chad felt his body being guided in the opposite direction.

"What the hell!!" Jackie screamed in the confusion. "My son is married to your daughter for God's sake. He has every right to be here. How dare you!"

"Mom, shut up! I've asked you to leave!" He yelled, fighting off the forceful grip. "I know how to walk, damn it!"

"This is bullshit! You bastards!" Jackie screamed, before being forced into the elevator.

How humiliating, Chad thought. His foul-mouthed mother and her erratic behavior didn't help matters any, either. Chad's eyes darted back to room 220 before the elevator doors closed. Somehow, Mr. Crawford managed to reach the elevator doors. Chad swallowed his heart, resting his back against the wall. It gave him some sense of security as Mr. Crawford stared through the crack, griming him. The lump in his throat seemed to get bigger by the second. Finally, the doors shut. Chad took several deep breaths. He felt awful; his wife's condition had worsened, and still as her husband, the Crawford's had the power to override his marital status to their daughter.

"They have no right to do this!" Jackie screamed.

"Yeah, you're married to her!"

"Who the hell are you, man?" Chad yelled.

"What's right is right and what's wrong is wrong!" Jackie burst in. "You two are married!"

"Donny will always control Christine and our marriage." Chad dejectedly hung his head, swimming in guilt.

After arriving home, Chad rushed through the door, dropping his keys on the living room table. Discouraged, he rushed over, pressing the blinking red light on the answering machine to retrieve the messages. Chad undid the top button of his shirt pacing the floor listening. Most of the messages were for Christine. Chad's heart stiffened when hearing the last message. He rushed overturning up the volume. He couldn't believe what he was hearing. Anger flooded his face. Chad punched a hole in the wall. Christine could have heard that! He scanned the LCD but it was anonymous. The voice was mechanically cloaked making it hard to even speculate. He had a sinking feeling he knew who it was. This was awful. *What the hell was she thinking?*

Chad watched the clock on the wall. Each minute went by slowly while waiting for the phone to ring. What was the use? Donny wasn't going to allow anybody to phone him about how his wife was doing! That man has too much power over everyone, even the doctors, and nurses.

❧

Tamara, Dana, and Whitney pulled into a classy limousine rental place. Bartley had already lined up a driver, Mario. A stretch Benz sat waiting for them to grace the seats. Dana couldn't believe her eyes; she wanted to cry. Tamara and Whitney were used to the expensive rides; it was usually no sweat off their backs. Tonight, their excitement revealed a different side. They all overreacted like a bunch of school girls.

"Oh, my gosh, just wait until they see us!" Tamara squealed, envisioning herself exiting out onto a red carpet.

"Dana, have you ever rode in style before?" said Whitney derisively.

"Yeah, once or twice," she responded nonchalantly. *Seriously,* she thought to herself angrily, *I'm the only one with a nine to five that I've been on for years, and these tramps, all they do is use men to pay for life.*

"Come on, Dana, the most excitement you've had was with that creepy ex of yours." Whitney and Tamara exploded into laughter.

"The one who always cheated ... what's his name ... Gary!" Whitney taunted, poking fun.

"Gary, yeah!" replied Tamara.

Dana was ready to explode. It was hard concealing the blistering anger she felt right now. *These hoes had a lot of nerve. At least I could keep a man. It wasn't until the fourth year that Gary began cheating. Sluts! Why the hell am I here? I have a feeling this is a big mistake. Whitney's got jokes and she's being hoed by her own husband, and Tamara, that's a laugh in itself!* Dana thought, watching them continue to make it look like her life was boring. She rolled her eyes in disgust.

Tamara flirted with the limo driver, Mario, flashing her C-cup breasts while he drove. The smile on his face showed he was enjoying the moment. *Tamara was like a cheap floozy in heat.* Dana though, if anyone was more anxious to reach the party, she was.

The car rolled to a stop in front of the nightclub. Mario ceremoniously opened the back door, helping the girls out. Tamara was the first to appear, flirting her way out the door. She had to be the one sucking up most of the attention first. The line behind the velvet rope was long, mostly women waiting to get in.

Whitney appeared second. If anyone needed teaching on class Whitney could use some brushing up on the proper way to exit a limo in front of people. The skirt barely covered her thighs; instead of pulling both legs together and placing her handbag over her lap, Whitney stepped out with her right leg first, leaving her personal ads wide open for the crowd. She didn't leave much to the imagination in her tawdry outfit. Her lucky charms were bared in front of the cameras. It was plain to see Whitney and several celebs had a lot in common.

Dana appeared last. Everyone watching would have assumed they were someone, but no one knew who. You could tell Dana was a first timer on the red carpet; her nervousness escaped like a preschool kid's first day. This was not her type of scene, yet it felt good having people think you were someone important. Whitney and Dana doubled up behind Tamara who sucked up all the attention. The men openly ogled; Tamara ate it up, while the women expressed their jealousy. This was a gold digger's utopia.

Tamara rudely brushed herself in past the others. Anyone who was someone was here at the club. She continued her master plan of seeking out the richest, most powerful man first. Tamara walked around in her tawdry outfit like a lion on the prowl. She stumbled into the crowd of people in VIP, through their toasted-up champagne glasses stood one of a kind. Tamara felt her heart jump out of her chest. She focused on his Italian tailored suit, undressing everything but his money. Even nude he was still dripping in money. Tamara slipped her way through the unknown, pretending to mix in. Her hoochie mama outfit was beyond trashy, giving her away. Tamara toasted a glass she managed to steal off a tray from a passing waitress. She slipped in closer, just enough to make eye contact with him, sticking out her assets so he would notice.

Everything went smoothly until she got stopped. Tamara paused, disappointed, her body slumped to the side.

"Who invited you?"

Tamara wondered who the girl was. She rolled her eyes to the question. Whoever she was, she was tall, slim, and with light brown hair. Her green eyes cut into Tamara like a blade; she stood, unexpectedly blocking her from moving any further.

"Who invited *you*?" Tamara replied sarcastically.

"Look, I know damn well you don't belong in this VIP area," the women replied, stepping back, checking Tamara up and down. Tamara knew she was a little under-dressed for their area. She knew there was no way she was going out looking stupid.

"Look, I don't know who you are."

"The name is Maddex, Maddex Chaplin." She replied with confidence, throwing her hair to one side. Tamara hated everything about her. Maddex sounded like some rich person's name. "I'm Jerick Russell's cousin, the one you're eyeing down and perhaps trying to make the moves on. I keep an eye out for bitches like you. I quash simple minded roaches like you. You know the ones who try and secure their future by fucking the first thing ballin'! I will do what it takes, even if it means whippin' yo' ass out of VIP!"

"How dare you, you don't!"

"Slow your role, honey." Several girls appeared on the side of Maddex.

Tamara backed away as Maddex's voice suddenly went faint. *Jerick Russell* is all she thought. He was a paid, full breed pedigree, but his friend and army were a pain in the butt, and her insults were getting old.

Tamara continued rolling her eyes, wishing she'd leave. "Honey, I know you're the type of female who walks around 24/7 with a mattress tied to your back. I bet you have some knee pads in that cheap ass purse of yours." Tamara couldn't believe she was talking out loud, degrading her. Each of the girls laughed.

"I need you to leave or my girls and I will make you!"

"All right, all right." Tamara tried not to embarrass herself anymore. Maddex wasn't taking no for an answer and people were starting to stare.

Whitney was lined up with the man her husband wanted her to hook up with while Dana stood looking like an obvious first timer. She sucked down the smoke of her cigarette, blowing the rest in the smoke-filled air. Whitney approached Dana with some white guy old enough to be her daddy. Dana looked into Whitney's eyes. She was a sad case. She couldn't help mentally stripping the makeup off her face. Two hours ago she and Tamara pilled goo, gobs of make-up, to cover her blackened eye and busted lip.

Thank God Tamara had returned. Dana relaxed, giving her a brief smile of relief. "Here comes that lame excuse to why Whitney has to leave. Get ready for it," Tamara said, gulping down the stolen wine.

Whitney was gone and Tamara was back on the prowl. The guys were eating up her skimpy outfit. A few them expressed aloud what they wanted to do to her. Tamara was eating it up. It wasn't long before Tamara set her eyes on someone else. She had her nails dug into him quicker than a werewolf. A longtime friend, Trevor, now single, had his hands all over Tamara. He spoke about all the money his self-employed business had generated in the last three months, which was probably a lie. He appeared to be the type to lie and put on a front just to get what he wanted. Tamara's dumb butt was falling for it.

Tamara faked her emotions, playing the game. The more money he talked about the more she wanted him. Trevor wasn't the finest, in fact, he was dirt-dog ugly, but his money was attractive. Dana overheard Tamara making plans to spend the night with him.

Dana's face had grown grim. She stood facing the bar to order a drink, trying to block out Tamara's phony lies. She pulled another cigarette out from her borrowed Gucci purse, placing it up to her mouth, unexpectedly getting a light from a tall dark shadow standing beside her. Dana felt her heart sink. Her heart was pumping as the tall dark shadow studied her movements. Dana tried to conceal her nervousness. She blew out the smoke and cleared her throat. "Th-thank you," she stammered over her words, sucking in his strong cologne lingering underneath her nose.

"You're welcome."

His deep voice was masculine, leaving Dana ready to melt. She watched him step out of the shadow.

Just my luck. Dana's mind flooded with thoughts. Tamara wasn't going to be too happy about this one. Dana stood strong. Deep inside she couldn't wait until Tamara saw, especially after the insulting comments she and Whitney had made in the limo. Tamara had probably followed his every moment around the room.

"So, what's a beautiful girl such as yourself doing alone?" Dana could feel her cheeks blushing. Either he had a way with words or she was just weak.

"That's a long story." She placed her hand over the plastered smile on her face, chuckling. "My so-called friends, well, they left me."

"Let me properly introduce myself. My name is Jerick Russell, and you are?" He extended his hand with a firm grip.

"Oh, my name is Dana, sorry, Dana Yardley."

"So those are your friends?" Dana wondered what he meant. "Yeah, I noticed you the moment you came in and those girls don't look like the kind of people you'd be involved with." Jerick watched as the smile grew more on her face. "You're much too classy and you sure don't dress like them. Take it from me, females like that can ruin your reputation around the club."

"Thanks. I'll take that advice to heart, seriously." Dana chuckled aloud. She wished Tamara and Whitney were around to hear this.

Tamara's eye darted around the room while practically undressing Trevor in the corner. Maddex was gone, so now was the time to make her move. She had positioned herself for easy sex on the down low at a corner table shared with Trevor. This suddenly turned chaotic and Tamara's face grew grim. She lifted herself upward, ignoring Trevor, taking what she had offered to give. He had already slipped on a condom, plunging inside her, discretely grinding himself to satisfaction.

Trevor marveled over the quick sex, nibbling down the side of her neck. He leaned back, caressing Tamara's back, handing her a pill. Trevor was too relieved to see her tenseness was slowly becoming a problem. "That bitch," she muttered, popping the pill in her mouth without looking to see what it was. She let the pill dangle on her tongue before swallowing. Trevor always had a drug of choice whether it was heroin, ecstasy, or just your average smoking a blunt in the corner. Tamara had managed to remain cool on the outside, but on the inside, she could hardly wait to intervene.

Tamara managed to get away from Trevor. She floated through the VIP, high on ecstasy. She strutted with renewed energy and aim.

There was no way this newbie tramp was taking my security away. I'd set eyes on him first! Tamara thought furiously, running both hands underneath her breasts, pushing them up. *My assets were going to win tonight; they did with Trevor. Back off Dana!* Tamara swooped in for the kill. She stepped between Dana as if she never existed. "I'm sorry, Dana," Tamara said, brushing Dana aside. "I haven't had the opportunity to meet you," she said to Jerick. Jerick stood smiling, upright, placing his eyes on her breasts. *Got 'im!* She thought.

Dana couldn't believe the desperate measures Tamara was using.

"Once a hoe, always a hoe, don't care how much lipstick you put on a pig, it will always rumble in the mud."

Hatred beamed from Dana's eyes as she heard the words coming out of Tamara's mouth. Dana envisioned ripping off Tamara's too-tight shirt. This overanxious, money-hungry whore! If Jerick had any chance of showing he's man, it was now. Males are attracted to hoes, but not real men. If so, they just want quick sex. Dana stood back watching.

Tamara couldn't have gotten two minutes into her conversation before Jerick placed his eyes back on Dana. Her heart leaped for joy. Tamara continued pulling every trick out of her breast to get his attention, but it didn't work. Jerick showed more interest in Dana. Tamara was furious; the evil looks she gave Dana could kill. Dana didn't give a damn. Jerick had already left her standing alone at the bar. "He had a girlfriend!" Tamara yelled out loud. Jerick and Dana ignored her. Whether there was some truth or not, he was showing Dana the attention and Tamara was jealous.

Jerick and Dana sat alone at one of the tables. He ordered the finest champagne chilled on ice. Tamara and Whitney were right - it was her first time and she loved it. Jerick softly kissed each part of her neck. Dana felt a bit embarrassed; people were staring. Dana was ready to give him everything, but she had to keep her womanhood classy. What if Tamara was right, what if he did have a girlfriend?

"So, is that your girlfriend?"

"No." Jerick looked Dana right in the eyes. "Maddex is my cousin. She keeps the rats away if you know what I mean. Jerick and Dana laughed. Once they see a piece of cheese that's well-off, they come a runnin. I'm pretty hip to all the games and different types of females. I know a woman when I see one. Dana blushed. That girl is trouble, she's known around here. Well known. You don't want your name associated with that."

"No, no I don't." Dana lowered her head. Jerick placed his hand underneath her chin lifting her head back up.

"We all make mistakes."

Before too long, Tamara popped up with another excuse to pull Dana away. The nerve of her demanding that we leave! Jerick and Dana laughed it off. Tamara felt foolish hearing him offer to take Dana home. She turned away spewing a few cuss words.

Thirty minutes later, Tamara was leaving with Trevor. She was still angry.

❦

The knock came suddenly, as Whitney sat on the bed. Her husband, Bartley, opened the door. She peered around the side of him to find an unfamiliar guy standing outside. They exchanged very few words, none which she could make out beside the laughter bellowing out. Bartley invited him in. He was white and tall; he wore a pair of jeans and a white shirt. He must have been in his early fifties. Brown hair and green eyes, he didn't look too bad apart from his horrible skin complexion. His lecherous smile revealed a gold tooth in front. He was anxious after eyeing Whitney up and down, demanding that she get started. His introduction was short as usual. She knew just what he had come for and what he insisted.

Whitney found herself nude, standing over the white guy, placing one leg over him as he waited. Her husband moved against her backside, thrusting himself against her. Whitney's hips were being controlled by two different men. Despite it all and feeling dirty inside, she pushed harder, grinding at the beat of each movement. It didn't take long before Bartley and the white guy reached climax, but they still wanted more. She found herself sinfully doing the unthinkable. As Bartley watched, he filmed their every move with his phone. The thrust came fast and hard as he firmly rode her from behind. Whitney felt the shame. Moans echoed the room. She felt ashamed but her body couldn't fight the pleasure arising. Bartley lifted her head, laughing again, making her feel like a cheap whore.

Out of all the nasty disrespectful names used, her husband was ahead of them all. Whitney was used to nasty names, her system had become immune. Bartley seemed to be using them all the time, even when they weren't having sex. She had been used like a sandwich, three men as the bread and her, a piece of meat. She watched weakly and out of breath, hiding her shame with the bedspread as the men got dressed. An exchange of cash was given, but she didn't know exactly how much. That was something she'd never know; Bartley would never tell her. *I can't do this anymore,* she thought. An unexpected slap stung her cheek.

"You do as I say or else, girl!" Bartley pointed his finger at the tip of her nose, pushing harder, knocking her off balance. "Do you understand me?" He grabbed her throat, demanding an answer.

"Yes, *OKAY*, I hear you!"

"It will be the last time you leave anyone, if you leave me, bitch!" She nodded, backing away as he held his hand in slap position over her head.

Afterward, her husband made his demands, as usual, to clean up and get home to the kids. She stood in the shower, crying, soaking herself with soap, repeatedly rubbing her private parts until the pain struck. She hated herself more and more for what she was allowing her husband to do to her. Where was her self-worth? Facing it, she had none. She had gone from a straight A student, with a promising future, with once a good job, to a slut sleeping with numerous men daily, and sometimes women, all for her husband's satisfaction, who claimed to love her. It was fun and exciting in the beginning, but now it was dreadfully humiliating as each demand became more bizarre. Each fantasy role-playing became a lascivious sexual cycle of pain.

She ran her fingers across the scars of a past burn when a guy had demanded sex. Water mixed with the tears that ran down her face. She wondered how she could face her children without revealing the pain and shame. Bartley didn't even know of the times she was being raped and beaten. What did he care? He was doing it as well. Everything came so fast and shockingly without warning, she didn't dare refuse. Turning him down was out of the question and so was telling her husband about her doctor's appointment last week and what she found. In a way, she didn't want him to know. She wanted that bastard to suffer the same pain she felt. At least that was the way she felt now until Bartley made up to her. She was always a sucker, believing him when he told her this was the last time. She couldn't stop crying; an open marriage was nothing but lies and corruption.

Suddenly the water shut off. She opened her eyes and met her husband's steady gaze, which kept her frozen with fear, wondering what he was planning next. Bartley's stare was always that "bitch, it's too late to feel sorry for yourself" look. He never had to say a word. His silence spoke a million words and so was the money he was making off her. Her body was being maxed, weakening and numbing her entire existence. She couldn't go on sleeping with several men three to four times daily. She was too ashamed to count the total amount by the end of the week.

⤳

At six o'clock Friday morning, Chad sat fishing through the computer desk for some important documents. This would make the second day he was unwillingly working from home. Mr. Crawford's assignments were short and brief, with Secretary Olivia delegating the messages. There was never any mention about the other day. It was forgotten like all the rest of the powerful schemes Mr. Crawford got away with.

On the days Mr. Crawford had his big meetings; Chad managed to sneak in to see Christine at the hospital without him knowing. She was always sleeping or didn't feel like talking. Chad thought she seemed a bit agitated or maybe it was the medicine. The house was empty without Christine.

Several plans to see her were shattered with her family hanging around the waiting room. Chad had nothing but determination on his mind that day. He stood back, watching, waiting for a spot to clear. Once the waiting room began to thin out, Chad snuck his way through two women were too engaged in their conversation about their husbands to see him slip by. It was nice hearing the two women say Christine was doing better. They spoke about how she laughed and smiled. It had been two days and Chad has never seen her crack a smile.

Once in the room, Chad reflected back on her spasmodic episode, staring about in a daze. Quickly he withdrew the horrible thought from his mind. Her condition was still the same. He felt sorry seeing her lying there in pain. Her room was filled with an array of cards, balloons, and flowers, too many to count. Chad drew his attention to the big, pretty bouquet of flowers he sent rush delivery yesterday. Either Mr. Crawford suddenly grew a heart or he wasn't too interested in reading who the cards came from. The last memory Christine had was the two of them arguing, thought Chad. He was careful not to wake her. He sneaked around like a creeping late-night prowler. His body slumped once, noticing Christine's eyes had opened. She softly called his name. Chad tiptoed over to the side of the bed, planting a soft kiss on her lips, holding her hand tightly. The two smiled at each other. Christine's tears flooded her face. Chad insisted she remain calm while she apologized remorsefully for the other day. He wondered if she remembered the horrible incident involving her father.

The visit hadn't lasted very long before her Aunt Vivien barged into the room. She expressed her fake hellos and how much she missed seeing Chad. Deep inside, she didn't give a damn. Once Vivien secretly placed the call to Donny, things worsened. Mr. Crawford now knew Chad was there. He had sent an urgent message for him to get to the office right away. Aunt Vivien stood guarding Christine's room like a watchdog, waiting for Chad to leave. Chad knew he had set the whole thing up. Mr. Crawford's timing was just right; it was as if someone was watching from afar, or worse, close up. The meeting at the office was called off when Chad left the hospital parking lot. Just when Chad thought he could apologize face-to-face for the other day, the idea had fallen apart. Mr. Crawford's overbearing, calculating personality was no match for a rookie in training. Chad never gave a second thought to someone watching him.

⸻

The doorbell rang. Chad's head hit the top of the desk. *Who the hell?* He wondered, hoping to God it wasn't Mr. Crawford. Maybe it was his good friend, Quincy. Chad scrambled through all of his friends and some of Christine's. It could be anyone.

The thoughts left his mind at ease while opening the door. Chad's mouth hit the floor. He could not believe she was standing at his doorstep. Worst of all, Paulette was dressed like some street hooker. A short skirt and tight-fitting shirt that barely covered her squeezed breasts.

"What the hell are you doing here?" Chad hissed, trying to keep a low tone. His eyes darted around suspiciously. He grabbed her arm to try and pull her in.

Paulette yanked down his hand, inviting herself in.

"You need to leave, Paulette!"

She ignored him, placing her purse on the hat rack. Paulette smiled scornfully, rolling her eyes at the lavishly decked out expensive material things. It made her hate Christine even more.

"I heard about your wife." She turned toward Chad. "I'm sorry, how is she?" Paulette rubbed the lower part of his back, staring seductively into his brown eyes. She expressed her phony concerns while analyzing him. He was weak and in need of some attention plus she knew about Donny C. throwing him and his mother out. A devious smile graced her face.

Chad stared at her perky breasts. Paulette had a hold on him that he couldn't resist; yet, there was something about her that flashed warning flags.

"Paulette, please."

"Come on, she won't know," she begged, pulling him to another room. Paulette knew she had Chad right where she wanted him.

Christine is in the hospital, he thought, staring between Paulette's legs at her brown tights, drooling. Chad gave no second thought to Paulette's knowing where he lived; his manhood was standing at attention and he was ready to take action.

Chad watched Paulette striptease down to nothing. Suddenly he felt exposed. She leaned herself against him grinding slowly. Chad closed his eyes embracing the moment of pleasure with her breasts staring him in the face. With one hand he quickly removed his clothes while Paulette seduced him slowly. She focused on the wealth around. It was millions and Paulette wasn't leaving without a piece. She pulled Chad from the couch, leading him to the table where he watched as she climbed on top, opening up to him.

I got him right where I want him. She smiled. With Christine in the hospital, there was enough distracting his mind to fall into her trap.

Paulette's nails ran across his backside, softly kissing Chad's shoulder as he plunged himself into her. She stared at the ceiling smiling each second while she grew angry thinking about Christine. Chad was breathing rapidly which meant he was about ready to do his thing.

Chad felt awful; he thought about Christine. He ignored Paulette gently kissing his chest. Chad placed his hands over his eyes. He felt that, for some reason, Paulette was too content.

"This can't happen anymore!" he spoke aloud. Paulette lifted her head, confused, before being shoved off onto the floor.

"Chad, what...?"

"You have to leave now! You got what you wanted."

"And so did you."

"You shouldn't have come here, Paulette!" Chad reached down, grabbing her clothes and tossing them at her. Paulette's heart sank. "Please leave now!"

"Okay, okay!" She shouted, throwing on her clothes. "You don't have to be so mean about it. I love you. Why can't you see that?"

"Love? What the hell are you talking about?"

"You said you loved me! Oh, now you don't remember?"

"I never told you that. I'm married, Paulette, get real! What are you playing, mind games?"

"Damn it, you did say it!" Paulette screamed, shoving her arm through her shirt. "Christine will never give you what I can."

Chad stood, confused. *Paulette knew the deal. It was just sex, that's it. What the hell was wrong with her? We agreed upon this. Now's she trippin' on this love shit!* Chad had grown to trust Paulette over the two years, but this time, his trust had run out.

"You remember one thing." Chad approached, staring her face-to-face. Paulette squirmed in fear. "I love Christine. Get out and don't come back again or else!"

"Some love, that you'd bang some woman in her house! You're not in love … you're in comfort! Her damn family pays for everything!"

"Shut up, Paulette!"

"What … what are you going to do?"

"You don't wanna know what I can do. I'd rather not go there, Paulette. I do care about you, but I'm married for God's sake. Maybe we should…"

"Don't tell me." Paulette interrupted, cutting him off. Chad ducked from the swing of her purse as she grabbed it off the hat rack. The door slammed; there was no goodbye. *What have I done?* Chad thought. *What is wrong with me? Paulette's been trippin' like some crazy person. This can't happen anymore!*

✧

Chad offered stability and security that had been missing throughout Paulette's life. Raymond was all about getting all the material things she needed. The others were sex and money. She couldn't lose Chad or Raymond; they were her foundation and without them, she'd crumble. She didn't have time to get to know another fool; it took time to train them. The others were like loose change in the bottom of her purse. Paulette drove her Honda Civic slowly down the long curved driveway. Her mission was accomplished. *Forget Christine, he's mine! All mine! He doesn't love her, that's why he's screwing me!! Pretty soon, Chad will be all mine! I won't stop until he is. No one will ever get in the way of the love I have for Chad! I know it's not right but ... shut up, Danielle! I won't let you interfere!* Another personality spewed out of rage. *I'll just keep sexing Chad, I know his weakness!*

Paulette gripped the pair of platinum gold earrings she had stolen off the end table. She balled up her fist, squeezing them tightly in her hand until they broke, leaving the stem poking out of the palm of her hand. Paulette ignored the blood spewing from her hand as if nothing happened.

Blood ran down the wheel landing in her lap. Chad's words floated across her mind, driving her madly insane.

❧

No sooner had Paulette left then another car pulled into the driveway. An older women in her fifties stepped out. She was concerned about why Paulette was there without Christine in the home. Discretely, she'd been waiting outside, noting the time spent in the home. She wondered what the hell Chad was doing with her.

The knock at the door came suddenly. Chad stared at the door, baffled. He knew it was Paulette again. He took in a deep breath, wiping the sweat from his face with his shirt opening the door. "Haven't you had enough?"

Chad's heart deflated. He cleared his throat at the moment of embarrassment, quickly throwing back on his shirt. The woman stood at a loss for words, more so afraid for Chad's life. Everything she wanted to say rested on the tip of her tongue but wouldn't come out. She stammered over her hello. Chad took a deep swallow of his saliva. He stared into the women's eyes. The resemblance was obvious. She had the same facial structure and feminine build.

It couldn't be. Chad quickly buttoned his shirt.

"May I come in?"

"I … I don't … it's, not a good time. Besides, who are you?" He questioned, already knowing the answer.

"You know damn well who I am! You haven't been standing here with your balls on the ground staring me down for nothing. I'm Sally Crawford."

"Crawford!!" *Please don't tell me she's married to ... She's the one that no one ever sees. What the hell is she doing here?* He questioned himself.

Chad could feel his body slumping over. The hairs on his neck stood straight up and he broke out into a cold sweat. He stood shaking his head in disbelief, numbed, in a daze.

"You've made a big mistake, mister." Chad wondered what the hell she was talking about.

"I'm Sally ... Paulette's ... Danielle River's mother." Sally stood with a smirk on her face. Chad exploded into laughter, not realizing the severity of what was going on.

"No, Mr. Crawford's stepdaughter's name is Danielle, not Paulette, and she told me her mother's name was Melissa. You're the one Donny keeps secret and away from all family functions?"

"Yes, that's one of the many names she gave herself and me. Can I come in now?" Chad stood flabbergasted. The more she was talking, the more confused he got. *Donny has Valerie at everything!*

"Ummm, really, it's ..."

"I'm not stupid, Chad. I know you're screwing her and I also know my step-daughter is in the hospital."

"Step-daughter. He mumbled. Oh shit! This can't be! No way."

"Don't try and cover your crime scene now, it's too late. I need to talk to you and it's important." Chad felt like he had been shit on several times. Sally must have gone into her life history and then some. Chad's blank stare remained plastered on his face. It was hard to fathom the thought of Sally being married to Mr. Crawford, Christine's father.

Chad had heard enough. "Paulette knew this! That's why she knew so much about Christine. There's no way she can find this out...there is no way Mr. Crawford. . . . My gosh, my ass is on the line!" He blocked out Sally's faint voice sitting across from him by burying his face into the nearest pillow. He took in several deep breaths, trying to calm his nerves, and removed his face from the pillow. "Mrs. Crawford. Sally. There is no way Mr. Crawford or Christine can find out about this." He leaned forward staring into her eyes grievously.

"I'm telling."

"No, please!"

"What the hell do you want me to do?" She questioned, curious. *There was no way I was taking this to Donny. Donny dislikes Danielle. If he finds out my child is involved with Chad, I'm in a world of trouble* Sally thought.

"Please, just give me time to think about this!"

"Give you time? You had plenty of time, Chad. You knew who you were dealing with. Besides, I'm not risking my fortune on your ass. You ain't worth that shit."

"Please, Sally. How come you never mentioned your daughter before?"

"Maybe I have, you just got all the names she uses mixed up."

Chad thought hard. He needed a quick excuse to shut her up. One thing that sat heavily on his mind was Mr. Crawford's ex-wife, Valerie, who seemed to be in the picture more than Sally was. Mr. Crawford always spoke highly of Valerie, not Sally. At the office meetings, traveling out of town and family functions, Valerie was there, even at Christine's wedding. Not to mention the overheard conversation at the hospital from Christine's Aunt Vivien. A devious smile suddenly grew on his face. This was one time he needed to play his cards right; his entire life and career were at stake.

"You know, Sally, I don't see much of you around. That's strange when you're married to my wife's father." Sally uncrossed her legs, sitting up. Chad watched as her eyes ventured around the room. He knew he had struck a nerve.

"What's that got to do with you screwing Christine's step-sister?"

"A lot. I overheard someone speaking about Mr. Crawford and his ex-wife and how she spends more time with him than you do." Judging from the up and down movement of her chest, she was pretty pissed off. Out of the twenty minutes that Sally had been there, she was suddenly without words. Sally knew just what Chad was getting at.

"Look, your ass is the one on the line. Once he finds out…"

"You wouldn't dare…"

"Don't doubt me, you bastard!"

"You know Mr. Crawford's still screwing his ex-wife?"

Sally could feel her heart drop. Out of all the times, she thought of it, it was worse hearing it coming from someone's mouth.

"They are together now. Donny always had an excuse to keep me at home, even when it came to Christine being in the hospital. He insisted I stay at home, that Valerie needed to be alone with their daughter." Sally could feel her body slumping over. She quickly straightened her posture, hiding her shame from Chad.

"You don't know what the hell you're talking about! Sally continued. You're just a poor bastard child, whose mother sleeps around and drinks herself to death! You only married Christine for the money! That's why you're sleeping with my daughter!"

"The nerve of you! Bitch, you came from nothing like I did! You can't even face the fact that Valerie's screwing your husband more than you ever have! He's still in love with her. I heard it personally from her sisters!" Chad stood behind a smirk of deceit. Sally felt defeated, ashamed as his words pierced her heart. "It's amazing what money will make you do, huh? Besides, that makes your daughter look like a whore. Like mother, like daughter."

The slap Sally gave him caught him off guard. Chad grabbed the side of his face.

"Slap on, Sally Crawford, because you're in this just as well as I am!"

Chad stood, furious, watching as she grabbed her purse, storming out the door. Another part of him couldn't wait to give Paulette, Danielle, whoever the hell she was, a piece of his mind. Sally's threats were troubling. She had insisted on telling Mr. Crawford. *Maybe fighting fire with fire wasn't the best idea*, Chad thought. He knew Sally wouldn't be that stupid to tell, not with her child involved.

Chad stormed angrily through the house and into the

kitchen. He grabbed his cell phone from off the counter. His mind flashed back to the night he and Christine married. Danielle was nowhere in sight. Christine did mention something about a step-sister, Danielle … he remembered that much. *William, that so-called good friend of mine, he hooked me up with this psycho* Chad thought, dialing William's number.

⌾

Thirty minutes away from her apartment, Paulette sped down the freeway, steaming hot. She couldn't get over the way Chad acted. Anxiously, Paulette awaited his phone call, fighting off every urge to dial his number first. Fifteen minutes later her cell phone rang. A smile graced her face after seeing the number appear.

"I thought you'd change your mind."

"Trick, I know who you really are!" Paulette was shocked. It was Chad, sounding worse off than before. Her hopes were shattered, but this time, she wondered why.

"Don't talk to...."

"Shut up, you hoe! I'm so sick and tired of your lies! It's over, Danielle!" The name she didn't want to hear echoed over and over. "Bitch, don't bring your lying ass around me and my family again!" Her heart sank into her chest.

How … how did he know? Ran through her mind. She sat speechless, holding the phone. Chad continued tearing into her like a double-edged sword, the threats made came as a shock. Paulette didn't have enough time to think, much less time to cover her lies. The only thing that remained on her mind was how he found out. *Momma!* She had to have told him, but why, what would be her reasoning? She couldn't possibly know about them. And for her to mention Paulette, that was odd. Mostly everyone in this state knew her as Paulette, except a few losers. She wondered what else her momma knew ... or how? A quick sequence of horrible events flashed through her head. Seeing and hearing Chad's threats made her angry.

"She'll never have you to herself, damn it, you don't wanna mess with me! Chad, don't you know what I'm capable of doing to you? Chad was silent. You can't just quit me, who the hell do you think you are?"

He pushed the phone closer to his ear, making sure it was the same person. The voice sounded different, more like a threat, Paulette would make. He wondered what she meant by "you don't know what I'm capable of." The thought crossed his mind, but he quickly shook it off. *No, they're sisters for God's sake,* he told himself.

"Whoever told you that is lying! I know who the hell I am! Paulette lied, trying to convince herself. My name is Paulette. Call me Paulette, damn it!" She yelled continuously in the phone.

What kind of psycho have I gotten involved with? Danielle's crazy ass swore up and down she was Paulette, and her psycho mother said her name was Danielle. It was all confusing, but it was more frustrating. Danielle had close ties with Christine, which was scary. Who knew what she was capable of doing or saying. That explained why she knew so much about Chris's past. There was no way Mr. C.

or anyone could find this out. Chad never thought the words would grace his tongue after hearing Danielle threatening to tell. "Bitch, I'll kill you if you open your mouth!"

Paulette stammered over her words. She swooned over Chad's masculine voice making threats. She wanted him pissed off. *The sex would be better with a little pain mixed with pleasure,* she thought.

"Why don't you meet me and release all that anger?"

"You're sick! The only one releasing anything would be my hands from around your neck when you're dead!" Chad hung up after realizing he was getting nowhere fast. He paced the floor, plotting ways to get back at her, desperately needed a way to keep her mouth shut.

Paulette's phone projected through the air, shattering it into several pieces. She stared at the small visible crack in the windshield, sighing.

"He's not going to get away with this! I will, I swear I will, I'll do it!! No, I can't, I won't let you!" Danielle fought with the multiple voices in her head.

⸻

There was no reason to wonder why Danielle never showed her face at the family functions. She didn't want anyone to know the truth. It explained why she knew so much about Christine's family. What was startling was Danielle seemed to harbor a tremendous amount of anger against Christine. Would Danielle be that stupid to..? No. Chad buried the thought deep in his head, but the witness said it was deliberate, it was no accident. *It can't be or my marriage and life is over.*

⌘

Paulette raced into her apartment. She slammed the door shut, threw down her purse violently, grabbed the phone and dialed. She paced the floor waiting for an answer. Paulette couldn't wait to spew the words out of her mouth.

"Yes, Danielle." The voice replied.

"Damn it, you just had to! You couldn't just let me have my fun!"

"Don't you call here yelling at me. What the hell are you talking about?" Sally rushed into another room shutting the door behind her.

"You know what you did. You told Chad!"

"Told Chad what?"

"You told Chad that name." Sally listened, waiting for her to spill over, pretending.

"What does your real name have to do with Chad? Why the hell are we even speaking about Christine's husband? Do you know she's in the hospital, Danielle?" She sat, silent, unsure how to respond. Someone was playing the game better than she was. "Do you?"

Chad said it was momma who told, but Momma is acting like she didn't have a clue. She thought. *Maybe she opened her mouth too soon; if he lied, what was his motive?*

"Danielle, I'm speaking to you, damn it, and I expect an answer or I'm coming over there! I've been trying to reach you all day!" Momma always made good on her threats. The last thing Danielle wanted was to see her in the state of mind she was in. She blocked out the part about Christine being in the hospital, thinking of ways to cover her butt quickly. Her mother waited for a response; she knew Danielle was up to her old schemes and lies.

"I haven't listened to my messages, Momma. What do you mean Christine's in the hospital?" She replied in a lower tone of voice. Deep inside, she didn't care.

"She's been in an accident."

"Is the baby okay?" Danielle asked, crossing her fingers, hoping she had lost it.

"Yes, the baby is okay" Her heart sank. Danielle released her anger silently.

"You're not getting off the subject that quick. What's this about Chad and your real name?"

"Nothing."

"You're a damn liar! You are up to your old tricks again, lying and sleeping around with everyone!"

You've got nerve she thought to herself.

"It better not be with Christine's husband! I'll be damned if I'll let you ruin my marriage to Donny, Danielle! Not this time! You will not come to me with your twisted lies of betrayal because you're unhappy with yourself! You should have stayed in counseling like I said! You stay the hell away from Chad!"

"But, Mom ..."

"Don't "but mom" me! I mean just what I say! Donny has paved a way for me and I have it made!"

"It's always about you, Mom" She spoke, disappointment in her voice.

"Yeah, and don't you forget it. Keep your damn legs closed before you catch something you can't get rid of and I'm not paying for your damn doctor bills! You have no insurance, you can't keep a job! Every marriage I've been in you found a way to destroy it, but not this time! If I find out it's Chad, that will be the last person you sleep with! But you wouldn't be that stupid, would you Danielle?"

"No. She stammered, this time feeling the heat from her mother's threats. I have to go, Mom."

Danielle plopped down on the couch after hanging up the phone. Anger seemed to ride her shoulders from every end. Everyone cared about Christine, even Danielle's own mother.

"That wench didn't lose the baby!" She screamed out of the blue. I hate her!" At least she didn't know about the other thing, no one could. Paulette knew her mother would be too stupid to figure that one out. She reflected back to seeing another car's headlights shining. It came out of nowhere, Paulette remembered. *I hope no one saw. I made sure the coast was clear.*

Sally knew she had to cover her butt by pretending not to know anything in order to keep her marriage. If Donny found out Danielle possibly hurt Christine it would be over. She wanted to question why Danielle was in another vehicle, and why she was at Christine's home without her being there, just to see what she would say. Danielle could never lie without her body language giving her away. *I don't want to know,* Sally said to herself, unwilling to take that risk, quickly blocking it out. The only suspicious thing was the car Danielle was driving; a large dent was visible on the passenger side. She claimed her ex-boyfriend hit a deer a week ago. Danielle willingly gave out information before anyone asked. Danielle was being very suspicious. It was all a mess. The last thing she expected was Chad opening his mouth.

⊂⊃

On day three, Christine was finally released from the hospital. The drive to her parent's house was quiet. Donny assisted Christine into the wheelchair slowly pushing her out of the garage into the house. Valerie stood waiting at the door wearing a smile. Chris smiled back as Sally stood with an angry look on her face. Valerie sat by her bedside, waiting on her hand and foot. Her dad popped in periodically expressing his love. It was nice seeing her parents together. Valerie was always around even though her dad remarried. Sally had no say-so in her mom's coming and going; Donny had made it clear either it was his way or the highway. Christine was just thankful God spared her life. She only suffered one broken leg and a broken collar bone. The car was repairable but her loss of life wasn't.

Christine scanned the room; Chad was nowhere in sight. Right now, he was the last person she wanted to see. The only thing lifting her spirits were the love and support of family and friends. Trisha, a longtime friend, had practically moved in to help out. She really could use the break, after her messy divorce. It had just been finalized a week ago. Trisha hadn't found a stable place to call home yet. She and her ex had separated six months ago. Christine felt obligated since Trish was a good friend and always there when problems occurred; the least she could do was help Trisha get on her feet and offer her a place to stay. Christine had always been there to comfort her and now Trisha was paying her back the favor.

Everything in her former bedroom was the way she left it. Not a single speck of dust could be seen anywhere. It had been years since she had been there. The computer on her desk was spick and span. Her collection of many dolls was stacked neatly on a shelf her dad built when she was seven. Christine smiled at a pair of blue and white pom poms hanging above her dresser. It brought back good memories of college.

Her mom and dad made a point to keep everything the same just in case she came back home. She had sworn up and down she would never return home. They proved her wrong; here she was.

Valerie insisted on her getting some rest. She couldn't shake that horrible night from her mind. Her nightmares frightened her; sometimes she found herself waking in the middle of the night, screaming. The headlights just kept coming straight for her. She had no room to swerve around. The only thing was to pray for the baby and her. The flash of lights was the only thing she remembered, and the horrible sound of the crash. Everything went silent, then dark.

Valerie paraded throughout the house as if she still lived

here. The house was too big to know if Valerie was staying the night. Sally didn't feel up to following her around to find out. Valerie passed by Sally several times throughout the day; there were few words shared between them, just dirty looks. Most of the time, Valerie flung her nose up in the air, rendering a fake hello.

Sally went into another room to suppress her anger. The thought of Valerie being there made her explode. *Maybe Chad was right.* She thought. Valerie had too much freedom to roam about around here and Donny didn't seem to mind. This needed to stop. She paced the floor, thinking of ways to get rid of Valerie. Each vile thought was tempting, but nothing good enough to fool or get past Donny and Christine. This was Christine's mother, and besides, Danielle's ass was causing enough problems, ones that could never be found out. Chad never admitted to sleeping with Danielle, but actions spoke louder than words. Besides, his blackmailing her was a dead giveaway, and let's not forget Danielle calling with her accusations.

⊂∾∾

Sally rolled over in bed to find Donny's side next to her empty. She ran her hand across the spot; it was cold and the covers were still rolled back. Her heart sank. The alarm clock read two in the morning. *Where could he be? There's no telling what time he left, probably when I drifted into a deep sleep. Maybe he's next to Christine* she told herself. Sally got up slowly, grabbing her nightgown off the bathroom door, placing it on.

Sally crept around the house, tip-toeing through every room in the dark. It was quiet, everyone seemed to be asleep. Christine's bedroom door was shut. Sally stood momentarily, hesitant in front of it. *Please let my husband be in here.* The silent words floated out of her mouth. She searched over each shoulder before cracking open the door. Sally scanned the room. Christine lay snuggled in several blankets. Sally closed her eyes shut, sighing several times, sucking back her tears. *Where is he? Maybe in the study?* There were too many rooms in the home to search everyone, but if she had to, she would.

∽∾

"I really love having you here." He spoke softly, kissing her ear. "I don't know why we got divorced in the first place. I told you it was too soon," Mr. Crawford whispered into his ex-wife's ear. Valerie sucked up the moment, enjoying every bit of the attention. The moment had been long overdue for the two of them to intertwine in full bliss. Three weeks ago in the office wasn't enough. A hot moment of sex over the desk was just a quick fix, not full satisfaction. With all the new business on the rise, lately that's all there had been time for.

"Donny, I think maybe we should wait." Valerie had little time to speak. She felt his hardened flesh entering. The moment was enticing, it felt good. Donny was the best at lovemaking; she could barely restrain her screams of passion. Valerie stuffed her mouth into the nearest pillow releasing her muffled moans until reaching satisfaction. "I love you, Donny C," she spoke softly, caressing his back.

"I love you, too, Muffin, always, I don't care who I'm with."

Valerie watched Donny place on his robe. She stood up, searching the couch for her undergarments. She dug deep into the pillows but found nothing. Valerie tried remembering where Donny placed them. She continued searching around the couch. "Donny," Valerie called. A startled look came across her face. A loud creak in the hallway caught both of their attentions. Donny turned silently, listening to the familiar sound. He hopped up from the desk. The two of them raced around the room in a panic as each step got closer. Donny quickly grabbed Valerie, shoving her toward another door adjoining the office leading into one of the extra rooms. Valerie stood on the other side of the door listening.

Donny braced himself as the door opened. Slowly he rubbed his sweaty palms onto his robe. He turned toward the bookshelf pulling down a book, collapsing on the couch.

Sally emerged from behind the door. She scanned the room in search of Donny and Valerie, disappointed to find her husband soaking his face into a book. Sally felt bad. She hated herself for thinking all those horrible thoughts.

Chad was wrong. Not Donny. She convinced herself. "Honey," Sally spoke softly. Donny turned as if stunned.

"Sally, what … what are you doing out of bed?" Whatever excuse she gave, he knew Sally was snooping. He waited as she stammered over her words. She made it obvious, scanning the room as if looking for something, or someone while pulling excuses out of a hat, none of which flew by Donny.

Sally vaguely focused on Donny slamming the book closed. The echo was startling. At first, Sally watched as he placed the book back, obviously trying to distract her attention. Sally couldn't get over the awful feeling she had inside. Donny seemed distant almost like he was hiding something. She expected a hug and kiss, but all she got was the cold shoulder. Donny stayed his distance, and then brushed by in a hurry, to stand to wait at the door. Sally took one last look at the room. The scent of a woman brushed against her nose when passing the couch. Donny continued waiting like a watchdog, waiting for Sally to follow him.

Sally listened to the door being locked. It was odd. *Was Valerie still in there?* Sally wondered. Donny kept the key with him. Rushing by, he closed his robe. She didn't have enough nerve to question him. Sally couldn't get over the smell of perfume; it was Valerie's perfume lingering all over Donny's robe.

Donny continued giving the cold shoulder once out of the room. Communications between them were non- existent. She followed far behind, looking back at the door as she moved further away. Her gut instinct was Valerie could not have been too far behind. Donny's shadow disappeared around the corner. He was almost to the bedroom. Before she could even pick up the pace, she overheard Donny scrambling around. He was already in bed with his back turned facing the other way. Giving a quick scan around the room, his robe was nowhere in sight. Sally slowly removed her robe and stepped into bed. An hour went by. She continued staring at the ceiling. *That bitch was in there I am sure of it!* Sally thought angered. *I can smell her damn perfume all over him. He could have taken a damn shower. He's mine damn it! Who invited her anyway? She's invading my space. There's only enough room for one woman in this house and Donny better realize it."*

⸎

The weather outside was awful, about as cold and dreary as Chad felt inside. All day, the rain had darkened the skies. He must have circled the block a hundred times in his car. A lady walking her dog had started to become suspicious at his passing by several times. He couldn't bring himself up to pulling into the driveway. Everything was a mess. He wanted to see his wife, just to hold her hand and tell her how much he loved her. It was going to be hard looking into her eyes without feeling guilty. He wished Sally and her daughter could fall off the face of the earth. His actions didn't make things any better, especially trying to have his cake and eat it, too.

⸎

Chad stood outside the front doors, anticipating every word as if it were the first day they met. His nose brushed against the top of the roses held in his hand for the fifteenth time. Chad stared at the large set of double doors, trying to calm down the fast beating of his heart. It was no use. Sally was in there and she knew the truth. *What if..? I don't wanna think about it … what if Paul...Danielle's in there … my gosh! Christine!* He thought.

Chad stood with his back turned toward the door. His second thought was to leave, especially after Mr. C. had thrown him and his mother out of the hospital. There had barely been two words spoken between the two of them since then. Chad felt horrible inside. One bad mistake had his life in turmoil and there was no turning back the time. His mind reflected back to the first time seeing Christine, a smile spread across his face staring into space.

Chad, now a successful businessman, had married into a wealthy family. His wife, Christine Crawford, was a snooty rich bitch who always had everything served on a platter. Christine and Chad met in the church parking lot. Sinful play began inside every Sunday morning as Pastor preached his sermon. Christine flirted on the down low; their eyes met for silent conversation. Chad's ego grew in response to someone like Christine, a woman of wealth, admiring him. Absently flipping through the Bible pages, he fantasized about Christine. Chad continued glutting, captivated by the moment, straightening his posture, revealing his broad shoulders to impress her more.

The day had finally come: Chad's chance to say something to Christine. He was once again captured by her beauty, but her wealth had him spellbound. Chad absently paced the parking lot, practicing putting his words together, wondering what to say. He paused for a moment, fishing for the right words to say. It was as if Christine had waited intentionally by her BMW for his approach. Chad watched as she fumbled around in the backseat; it was obvious she was waiting. He sucked up his nerve, approaching her slowly. He watched as a smile grew on her face, smiling back in return. Chad blew out a breath of fresh air, feeling a relief. *The invitation was open, wide open* he thought.

Christine and Chad secretly dated for months, creeping around town for midnight rendezvous. Their hearts danced in silence, thinking about one another every Sunday in the church. Christine couldn't wait another moment to be alone with Chad. Sinfully, she fantasized about the way he made love to her, blocking out the loud choir music playing. Christine thought of several ways to introduce Chad to her parents but it wasn't going to be easy. The thought was frightening. She was daddy's little girl and no man would ever be good enough to suit daddy. Especially Chad: he worked forty hours a week at a simple Federal Express job that he hadn't been on for six months. Chad had been in prison once before; the personal search revealed very little about his involvement with narcotics. He didn't willingly tell. The information was stumbled upon on the Internet. Christine loved the fact that he had no children, which meant no baby's momma drama. Who could be worse than the last boyfriend, Cliff Harrison? A rich asshole her father thought would be great to date, and perhaps to marry. Cliff was a CEO of his own company, successful, but one of the biggest arrogant jerks you would ever meet. It was his way or the highway. A woman had no say-so in his world. That relationship ended after a year of pain. Christine tried holding on to her dad's expectations after being humiliated for the last time.

Chad knew he would be nothing without Christine; she paved the way for him into her dad's multi-million dollar company. A month later, Chad moved his way from simple errand boy and on to the top in a matter of no time. He was still in school and two years away from finishing his business management degree. There was a lot to learn in a short period of time, but with Christine's round-the-clock help he was becoming a success.

Chad had made up his mind, feeling helpless, before taking a final step off the porch. Surprisingly, the door opened. He stood, hesitant, afraid to turn around. His heart dropped, envisioning Mr. Crawford standing there.

"Chad, is that you?" It was a relief as he turned around. Trisha stood, holding the door open. Chad forced a half smile across his face. "Forgive me if I'm wrong, but it appeared to me that you were leaving."

Chad shrugged his shoulders, his thoughts a million miles away, listening to Trisha comment how beautiful the flowers were. He recalled her ex-husband's infidelity and the messy divorce. His thoughts collided with Danielle. Chad wanted to ask if she had been there, but couldn't muster up the words.

"Hey, Trish," Chad spoke, melancholy, slowly entering Trisha's welcome. He wondered if the others would be so inviting. Trisha had no idea what would transpire today, and neither did he. He made sure his timing was right. Mr. Crawford was more than likely at the office by 11:00 a.m., and it was a little after. As for Sally, who knew where the hell she was. Trisha continued rambling on at the mouth, something about her ex-husband; Chad couldn't absorb all of her garrulous talks. It was troubling enough with his heart seeming to want to jump out of his chest. Each moment they drew closer to Christine's room. Chad was taken aback when Trisha took the roses. The last clear words he could make out were "Put them in water, please."

"Are you all right, Chad?" He wondered why she would ask that.

"Yeah, yeah, I'm all right." This was the time to assuage his guilty conscience, trying to put his mind at ease. For some reason, Trisha seemed a little more protective. *Having a guilty conscience is a bitch!* He knew one slip of the wrong thing and Trisha would spill the rest.

"Mr. Crawford?" Chad carefully asked.

"Oh, he's gone. Sally's somewhere around here." Trisha moved in closer to Chad's ear. "I think she's competing with Valerie, you know, Mr. Crawford's ex-wife."

"Why would you say that?" Chad's smile grew devious.

"Well, Mr. Crawford and Valerie were together, you know, *together*. I can't believe he's doing this to his wife." You could see the pain on Trisha's face as she expressed how wrong this was.

Chad's mind was filled with malice. Prying to get all the information he needed to strike back, he grabbed Trisha, pulling her aside, whispering, "What makes you think this?"

"I heard them, last night, just before Sally started snooping around the house. They almost got caught. I kinda wish they would have. You're so good to Christine." Chad's body slumped over. With all the cheating, he was smacked back into reality. "Valerie had sneaked through another door. We bumped into each other. She was surprised. I'm guessing she didn't expect to see me. A glimpse of her half-opened robe revealed her nudity. Judging from the up and down movement of her chest, they had almost gotten caught. What should I do? I'm …"

"This isn't your problem or business. It's probably what Christine wants anyway. You don't wanna piss her off and you damn sure don't wanna upset Mr. C. It sounds misleading but you gotta pretend it never happened." He explained unsympathetically. This has been going on long before you even suspected. By the way? He paused running his fingers across his mouth.

Has Sally's daughter been here?"

"That slut who calls herself Paulette!" Trisha blurted out. Chad could tell she obviously knew about as much as he did, at least. She knew that wasn't her real name. Not that I know of, but you know she's not welcome in this damn house. No one wants her here, not even her mother!" That was a relief and news to Chad's ears, one that Sally failed to mention. Trisha gave no second thought to asking his concern. She noticed the time on her watch. "Well, Chad, it was nice seeing you but I have to go." Trisha disappeared with a hurried goodbye as she went down the long hallway.

Trisha knew Chad was right, but she felt awful knowing the truth. She yearned to tell someone, especially when it was right in front of her face, and Sally was so close by.

Chad didn't care how big Trisha's mouth was, this was something he hoped she would keep to herself.

Chad smiled all the way upstairs. He hoped to run into Sally before reaching Christine's room. He stood outside the door, exhaling, recalling the sequence of events involving Danielle. The last one sped up his beating heart. He quickly threw it out of his mind. Chad took in several deep breaths before knocking. Her voice was music to his ears. A soft-spoken voice welcomed him in. Slowly he pushed open the door. To his surprise, Christine was out of bed and wasn't alone. Chad paused at the door. The anguish in his heart kept him from making eye contact. Christine sat in front of the mirror dressed in a robe. Chad braced himself for her penetrating gaze. There was an obvious smirk on her face. Valerie stood behind her, smiling. He could see where Christine got her good looks from. Valerie stood 5'9", with thickness in all the right places. Her black silky hair hung to her shoulders like Christine's. She was high maintenance and well taken care of, he was sure, by Mr. Crawford. Valerie could pass for a forty-year-old woman even though she was over sixty. There were very little flaws and visible wrinkles. It was obvious that black didn't crack on her or beauty and blessing went deep into the family.

Chad slowly approached, placing the roses on the dresser in front of Christine. The innocence in her eyes was tearing him apart, making him think about all the wrong he had done. She didn't deserve this. *If I could only take it all back*, he thought, dropping his head. The blow dryer blared, drowning out Christine's "Thank you." Valerie brushed Christine's wet hair until it was dry. Chad pulled up a chair next to her.

Christine was happy to see Chad, but another side of her wanted to kick him in the balls. Still curious to hear the rest of his confession; waking up in the middle of things made it hard to put together. She couldn't risk putting herself in any more pain. She didn't want to tell him about the baby, not just yet. Besides, she had overheard that her dad had thrown Chad and his mother out. Chad had this awful depressed look on his face, begging for forgiveness of something she had bits and pieces on. *Chad would be stupid to cheat, or fix his lip to lie to me,* Christine thought, smiling inside. Deep inside, she missed Chad. It was horrible remembering the argument shared between the two of them that were their last words. She missed him snuggled against her at night.

Finally, they were alone. Chad rushed over to help Christine get out of the chair by grabbing her arm and placing her body weight onto his. She was still weak; some of the bandages could be seen through her robe. Christine's tight grip on his arm felt good. She was soft, lingering with that same beautiful vanilla scent she frequently wore.

"I'm sorry."

"You don't have to ap..."

Their words seemed to come out at the same time. They both laughed in response.

"I'm sorry," Chad found himself apologizing again, attempting to assuage his guilty conscience.

"You don't have to apologize, honey," Christine said.

Chad stared into Christine's eyes. She couldn't wait for the long awaited kiss, his lips pressed against hers. She opened up to greet his tongue. Chad exhaled several times before letting go.

"Are you okay? Do they know what happened, how long you are going to stay here? I miss you at home!"

"I miss you, too, Chad." Now was the time to tell him; she couldn't wait any longer. "I don't know if my parents told you?" Chad could tell it wasn't good news judging from Christine's somber expression. "Why don't you sit down?" He took a deep breath collapsing onto the bed in front of her. He waited. Christine sat beside him embracing his hand.

"What ... what's going on, Christine?" Chad witnessed the turmoil growing on her face, her body slumped over. He gripped her trembling hands tightly together. A stream of tears fell rapidly from her eyes. Chad took in several deep breaths pulling her close embracing her. "Christine, no! Please don't tell me, they said everything was fine!"

Christine shook her head from side to side. "No Chad, everything was all right, at first. I lost the baby a day later. There was too much trauma, they couldn't stop the bleeding!" Christine yelled hysterically. Anger filled Chad's heart, leaving him numb. He leaped from the bed, expressing his rage by pacing back and forth.

Who would be so ruthless? Chad wanted to kill them, for hurting his wife and taking his only child away. *The bastard didn't even have enough nerve to stop! Jackass!*

Christine's weeping continued to get louder. Chad fell

to his knees in front of her, laying his head on her lap, crying. "They're going to pay for this, Christine, I promise."

It wasn't long before Christine fell asleep. Chad kissed her goodbye. He glanced at his watch. There was still time to rub some dirt in Sally's face before Mr. C. came home. Chad's heart wouldn't rest from hearing the bad news. He needed someone to let it out on.

❧

Valerie had finally gotten dressed and left.

I'm so tired of that bitch running my home, and Donny lets her, the nerve of her and him! Sally could be heard throughout the house, clacking dishes around in the kitchen. This was the second day she had cleaned up Valerie's mess left behind from cooking. It didn't take this many dishes to cook. Sally knew she was dirtying tons of dishes to keep her busy like some type of maid. *Donny would have a conniption if this kitchen was left a mess when he came home. There were over forty plates, ten glasses and a variety of pots and pans. This was in just one night. Who the hell is that messy?* She asked herself. *This would make the second night that bitch came in dirtying up the kitchen while I cleaned up after her.*

An unexpected laugh caught Sally off guard. She knew who it was before turning around. *How the hell did his ass get in?* She asked herself. Sally refused to turn around; she continued tossing dishes into the dishwasher. She tried drowning out Chad's footsteps getting closer. It was too late - by now he was practically breathing down her neck. Sally could see right into his devious chuckle; he was the last person she wanted to see.

"Sally, Sally C."

"I don't have time for this; besides the trash belongs outside. How did you get in?"

"That's none of your damn business!"

"Everything's my damn business in here!" She abruptly turned around placing one hand on her hip. Chad laughed.

"Everything is your business, huh?" Sally wondered what he meant by that. "Your stupid ass doesn't know what's going on in here."

"Christine doesn't know what you're doing! Get the hell out before I march up and spill it all!"

"Go right ahead, you unhappy witch! And risk your marriage to Mr. C." He laughed aloud. Sally gave a perplexed look. "I don't think so. Besides, you're too busy wondering where your husband was last night and whether he was diggin' out Valerie right under your nose."

"Go to hell, Chad!"

Sally took in a deep breath, releasing it slowly turning toward the dishwasher.

"It seems to me you're just the maid around here, cleaning up after Mr. C. and his wife … oops, ex-wife." Chad burst into laughter. Sally let it go in one ear and out the other. She wondered how he knew, worst of all what he knew. The last thing Sally wanted to do is show her weakness.

"You don't know what the hell you're talkin' 'bout! When's the last time you screwed Danielle?"

"Don't try and switch this around, Sally. If I lose everything, so do you! So I suggest you keep your damn mouth glued shut or you'll be lookin' for another husband to latch on like your daughter. You don't love her enough to let her destroy your marriage to Mr. C. You love the money."

Sally was fuming; the words crudely curled on her tongue but would not come out. Deep inside, she knew Chad was absolutely right. Sally was so damn upset with Danielle, she wanted to kill her. What came out of Sally's mouth shocked Chad. It was the opposite of what he expected. The muscles in his face went slack.

∽

It was late. Paulette waited outside Chad's and Christine's home, hidden behind a large hedge of bushes. She left her friend's truck parked up the street in a vacant spot at an apartment building. It was past ten p.m. Paulette scanned the yard carefully, sneaking up the pathway before reaching the back door. She pulled out a spare key and unlocked the door. Once the door opened she sucked in a deep breath and then exhaled. To her surprise, Chad hadn't set the alarm. It was a risk Paulette was willing to take; time was crucial. She closed the door behind her. She kicked off both shoes, dropping her black jacket on the floor, inviting herself in. She paraded through their home as if it was hers, marveling, clinging to her far-fetched fairy-tale, fantasizing the house belonged to her and Chad.

Paulette un-balled her hand looking down at the key, smiling. She managed to steal it one night while Chad fell asleep at her apartment. Paulette knew there would be a time she would need to use it. She waited anxiously for the right time and it was now. After she got in the house, Paulette started for the kitchen to make dinner, but mostly everything was frozen. She slammed the refrigerator door angrily. There was one good thing in the refrigerator. Paulette opened it again. She helped herself, pulling out a bottle of opened Dom Perignon, searching each cabinet for some wine glasses. Paulette filled three glasses and then gulped down the entire bottle. It didn't take long for the alcohol to set in. Paulette stumbled around, angry, taking in the view. She pushed over several pictures; while others she turned over, facing them down. *I'll show her! That ... that bitch will not steal him away from m-mme*, she muttered to herself, staggering upstairs. Headlights beamed throughout the house. Paulette rushed to the bedroom.

⌒⌐⌐⌐

It was mid-November, the full moon slightly hidden behind the clouds. Chad pulled into the driveway, still puzzled at Sally response. *She had to be crazy, just like her daughter,* he thought, walking up the steps. He twisted the lock and opened the door, where he stood momentarily. The thought of setting the alarm had crossed his mind before leaving. Chad glanced at the alarm system. The alarm was unarmed; it automatically read who entered from the wiring under the flooring. The red light flashed number two. He shrugged his shoulders, inattentive, dropping the keys by the door. The house was empty without Christine. Chad's mind floated back to the conversation between them. His heart deflated. *The baby*, he mumbled under his breath, dropping his shoulders.

Paulette remained hidden in the bedroom. Each chance she got, she peered down the dark hallway, waiting for the sound of Chad's footsteps. Her heart was beating rapidly with anticipation.

Chad arrived earlier than she thought, leaving no time. Paulette had planned to make dinner and have the table set before he came home. She was determined to prove how much of a woman she was to him. Paulette pulled out plan B. She got undressed, draping herself in one of Christine's silk robes, laying her clothes in a nearby chair. She made sure to rub Christine's robe all over her body, saturating perfume all over it.

❦

This is the last time I am going to let Valerie rule my house! Sally thought, humiliated, ready to burst into anger as they sat at the dinner table. Donny, Christine, Trisha and Valerie were laughing. The large table was covered in decorations his ex-wife changed from the ones Sally had set out. Valerie had even gone out of her way, making Donny's favorite, lasagna, with a large Caesar salad. The conversation wasn't going exactly the way she had hoped. She felt extremely out of place; she exhaled, sucking down gulps of red wine. Christine even commented about their past relationship.

This was going way too far. The dishes in the kitchen were piled up again. Valerie wasn't going to be lifting a finger to help do shit!

Sally slumped over, listening to her brag about his past-time favorites - travel, money and how she used to cook lasagna and several other special dinners especially for him.

The nerve of her. Am I not here? Do they not see me? I'm Donny's goddamn wife, not her! This was morbidly unfair. Was I invisible?

Donny was now on his second piece of lasagna. Sally watched as Valerie continued shoving it down his face. He marveled over the cheese dripping. Sally helped herself to a few vegetables being passed her way. She scooped out two spoonfuls, dropping them on her plate along with a small slice of Valerie's tempting dish. *Enough was enough,* she thought.

Sally's temples ached, her thoughts were whirling, from Chad to Danielle and this. She jumped up fuming; the table shook. Everyone stopped. They stared at her knocked-over wine glass. The dinner table grew quiet. Valerie had a devious smile lurking between the corners of her mouth, seen through the wine glass in front of her face. Donny had a disturbed look on his face as if he didn't know what was going on. Christine's mouth hung open, while Trisha held her head down. They waited for a response. Sally stood frozen, unable to speak the words on the tip of her tongue. Instead, she turned from the table in a hurry, knocking over the hard chair with a clatter.

Donny took in a deep breath; everyone's critical eyes darted around the table. Donny shrugged his shoulders, unconcerned about Sally's hasty exit. He continued stuffing his mouth with more lasagna.

Sally waited angrily in the bedroom, pacing the floor, waiting for the chance to express her feelings about everything. She was discomfited by Donny's response. Ten minutes had gone by. Her eyes darted back and forth from the door to the telephone. There was still no sign of Donny, not even a footstep in the distance. Laughter could still be heard. *Donny knows I'm mad, he still hasn't come up to see what's wrong! How could he?* Sally refused to harbor the thought of her marriage ending, because of Valerie, or anyone else's involvement. She raced over to the phone, sitting in front of it. Sally paused; she didn't know the number she wanted to call by heart. There were two messages left on her voice mail. She wondered who they were from. For now, they would have to wait. She searched the memory on her cell phone. Sally waited patiently, anticipating the placement of the call. Her first mind was to hang up, but something inside wouldn't give in. Disappointed after several tries and it going to voice mail, Sally hung up. There was no use leaving a message. She took a deep breath. Donny still hadn't acknowledged her absence.

My marriage to Donny wasn't so great after all, she thought. *Up until now, I had him on lock, at least I thought so until Valerie arrived out of the blue.*

❧

Valerie put the dishes in the dishwasher, while Christine gathered the rest from the dining room table. Trisha helped

Valerie wipe down the counter tops and stove, using a soapy wet dish towel. There was some talk about Sally and her hasty exit that brought a few minutes of laughter.

Donny marched up the steps. He stopped halfway to gulp down a second glass of wine, staggering the rest of the way upstairs. The hallway was dark. It was quiet. *If Sally was up here, she must be sleeping,* he thought. Donny wanted to know what Sally's problem was. Her being rude at the dinner table was inexcusable.

A few seconds of lights flashing by the window upstairs caught his eye. In a short glimpse, he couldn't make out where they had come from. Donny continued through the hall. He paused in front of the door taking a deep breath, slowly pushing open the door. Sally was nowhere in sight. He called her name twice, searching through their large bedroom. Donny glanced at his watch. It was 11:30 p.m. Maybe that flash of lights was her leaving. But where the hell could she have gone this late?

Donny rushed out of the room into the hallway. He called for her several times, still getting no response. Valerie overheard Donny yelling. Curious, she placed the dish towel down, heading in the direction of his voice. Christine and Trisha continued cleaning up the dishes.

Valerie followed the voice. He was calling for Sally as if she were gone. Deep inside she hoped she was. Valerie crossed her fingers for luck, slowly trailing behind, just enough so Donny wouldn't notice her. She watched amused, smiling as he shoved open every door. Valerie rushed to the spare room, quickly removing her clothes, layering her body in one of the scents Donny couldn't resist. Hurriedly she placed a robe over her body, running out the door back into the hallway. By now Donny was on the east side of the house. Valerie trailed his voice like a lion in heat.

It didn't take long before the scent graced his nose. Donny stopped to suck in a few whiffs. "Valerie!" he mumbled under his breath, turning around slowly. Valerie stood with her robe half open, caressing her chest. Donny smiled, placing his wine glass on the table nearby, forgetting his search for Sally. He watched as Valerie invited him into another night of seduction as her robe hit the floor. They embraced for a long kiss, Donny's lips still fresh with white wine. Valerie ran her tongue across his lips, sucking off the residue and slumping into Donny's arms as he lifted her into another room. Valerie's leg hit the nearby table, knocking over the wine glass, shattering it onto the floor. The two of them ignored it, rushing into the closest room. Donny threw Valerie's nude body onto the chaise lounge. Donny ripped open his shirt with the help of Valerie, tearing open his pants and removing them. She lay back waiting for his entrance.

❧

Chad threw his jacket over the chair. He waited momentarily for Christine's voice. After realizing the house was empty, Chad took a deep breath. Usually, by now Christine would have been screaming at the top of her lungs about the jacket lying over the chair. *Gosh, I miss her.* He reached into his pocket, pulling out his cell phone. Chad spotted

Christine's blouse tucked part of the way under one of the pillows on the couch. He didn't hesitate, lifting it toward his nose, sucking in the sweet smell. The scent always turned him on. He wished that at any moment, Christine would walk through the door. Using the opposite hand, he dialed her number. Chad let out a deep sigh, hoping Mr. C. didn't answer; Sally or Valerie would be easier to speak with.

"Hello," Trisha answered.

"Hel...hey...Trisha," He stammered.

"Oh. Hi Chad." The sounds of a woman screaming from the TV blared through the phone. Trisha muffled the phone, making sure Christine wasn't around. "Something happened, Chad."

"What do you mean?"

"It's Sally, she left in a hurry."

"Again."

"What do you mean again?" Trisha questioned, confused. Chad stammered over his words, trying to make up the quickest lie. He couldn't tell Trisha that he had spoken to Sally not too long ago. She was ringing his cell phone off the hook more than her daughter was. "I mean this probably isn't the first time Sally's left in a hurry, right?"

"Yeah, she got pissed and almost knocked the dinner table over when she left." Chad knew that was the time Sally had phoned. She had claimed she was on her way and needed to talk right now, but never showed up.

"So where is Mr. C?"

"Don't know, haven't seen him or Christine's mom, ever

since she snuck out of the kitchen," Chad smiled amusedly. "Do ... do ... you think he's sleeping with Valerie?"

"Whatever happened, don't worry about it, it's not your place" Chad spoke.

"Christine's worried enough."

Chad wondered what Trisha meant by that. The other line to his phone beeped. Just as he suspected, it was Sally calling. Chad refused her calls.

Trisha wanted to warn Chad about Christine's coming home tomorrow, but the words wouldn't come out. Maybe it was because she had offered to come along, and Chad probably wouldn't want it.

Christine wandered over to the front door. Trisha flagged Christine to come back into the living room to relax. Sally's hasty exit made Christine curious.

⟨⟨⟩⟩

Chad took two steps into the family room, pausing. His heart raced as he scanned the room, worried. A fit of paranoia kept his feet frozen to the floor. Almost all of the picture frames had been shockingly turned over. *What the hell?* Chad mumbled in fear. He slowly walked in front of the table, quickly turning each picture back to their normal position. He noticed their wedding photo had been removed from the wall and placed backward on the floor. *Who the hell would do something like this?* The muscles in his face went slack; he straightened his back, furiously clenching his fist together tightly. Chad rushed over, placing the picture back on the wall. Lightly, he tiptoed to the kitchen. His eyes zoomed in on a pair of shoes resting at the front door. *What? Oh, hell no!!* He thought, grabbing open the door and tossing them out.

The door slamming startled Paulette as she remained out of sight, hidden until the right time. She was excited, anxious to give Chad what he had been missing.

Chad stormed through the dark house. He flicked on a few far-off lights, creeping throughout the house. Calling the police was the farthest thing from his mind. The anger Chad felt made him want to handle the problem himself.

He stepped into the bedroom. Paulette could be smelled everywhere. *What if Christine came home?* He thought, taking a tentative step forward. He felt a faint breeze against his backside. A face floated in the darkness. Chad's thoughts were whirling with anger. He reached out, grabbing Paulette, pulling her forward by her neck. The force of his grip made her stumble to the floor. Chad's hand remained locked on her neck, tightening each second. Paulette fought to catch her breath. *The bitch had the nerve to be wearing my wife's gown.* He thought. Paulette scratched her way loose, leaving her nail marks embedded on his chest, stumbling out of the room. Chad tore off the nightgown, wrapping it around her neck. The force of his grip knocked Paulette hard to the floor.

"Bitch, you're wearing my wife's gown!" He swung, punching her in the face. Paulette threw up her arm, trying to block his swings, screaming. Her plan wasn't going the way she wanted. Chad continued kicking and beating her naked body on the floor. Paulette didn't have a fighting chance. Chad staggered into the room, grabbing her things off the chair. He searched each pocket pulling out a key. "Dirty whore!" He placed the key in his front pocket, staggering, out of breath, back to Paulette's limp body struggling to get away. "Get the hell out of my house, you useless no-good tramp!" Paulette squirmed to break from Chad's tightening grip around her arm. Blood ran down her mouth and nose. "I'll kill you, bitch! I swear I'll kill you!" The sound of his voice made her shiver; it was a side of Chad she had never seen before

"You can't do this to me! Damn it, you can't do this to me!"

"Shut up, hoe!" Chad struggled in outrage, dragging Paulette down the steps. The carpet on the stairs made it less painful as her hip hit each step. Chad thought of a way to get rid of her so no one would see. There was no car out front, plus she wasn't dressed. It was the last thing the neighbors needed to witness. Paulette's head flung back. Chad's grabbed a hold of her wig, yanking it off. She fought to undue his tightening grip but his strength was too much.

The floor was cold and dark. Chad didn't bother turning on the lights to the garage. Paulette sobbed, wiping blood drops from her face, too weak to fight back, unable to keep her balance. Chad continued his threats. She felt herself being lifted off the ground and slammed into the backseat of his car. Part of her body landed in-between the floor and the seat.

Less than ten minutes later, Sally arrived in front of Christine's and Chad's home. She noticed the majority of the lights off. Wondering if he was asleep, she sat, hesitant, unable to move. She dialed his cell phone number again, just to be sure. It rang forever.

Chad glanced down at his phone. It was Sally again. His first mind was to answer it and tell her about her stupid psycho daughter. *Sally would be thrilled to know how much of a problem she's being,* Chad thought sarcastically. It was past twelve o'clock right now; getting rid of her was the only thing on his mind. He glanced back through the rearview mirror. She lay crying in the seat.

"Get dressed, damn it!" He yelled veering off to the side of the road slamming on the brakes. Paulette managed to regain a little strength. She stepped out of the car to zip up her pants. Chad waited. Once she was finished, he slammed her body against the car.

Paulette grew angry. A rage out of nowhere attacked Chad as she swung over and over, hitting him in the face. Chad angrily punched Paulette; the force of his punch made her tumble down into the woods. Chad didn't hesitate and followed her body, kicking her the rest of the way down.

"I'm pre...pregnant, damn it!!" She screamed. The light shining on Paulette managed to show a very weak, devious smile across her face. Chad held back his kick. She hawked up a gob of spit, chucking it at him, just missing. Chad listened to the laughter echoing around as she laughed in his face. He couldn't believe she was saying this, not after Christine had just lost the baby. The anger shot through his veins. Several ways to murder her shot across his mind. "Go to hell, you! That damn baby and you can both go to hell!"

"It's yours!"

"There's no way, trick! With all the men you have screwed, get real, you ain't nothing but a hoe!" Chad thought about all the chances taken having unprotected sex. Lately, he had used a condom and there was no way. She was just trying to throw up another smokescreen, something to keep him near, even lying.

"Remember throwing away your condom full of semen? I was pissed 'cause you started using them. Christine and that damn baby! You asshole! After leaving, I grabbed it out of the trash can. Never leave your condoms in a place someone can get them, you shit face. I used a medicine syringe, removed your semen and injected it into me!"

Paulette's laughter irritated him, almost to the point of humiliation. Chad gave her two last kicks, aiming toward her stomach. Paulette tried blocking him, using her arm as a shield. Out of breath, she lay vomiting, spewing out her anger. Chad's focus was on Christine. He wished he had never met Paulette. He was going to make sure whoever's baby it was, it wouldn't be born.

✺

Sally drove halfway down the street, wailing in tears, stopping four blocks down. *What am I doing?" I can't let Valerie take over and run my house!* A bit of rage shot through, making her blood boil. Sally gripped the steering wheel, doing a U-turn in the middle of the street, accelerating over the speed limit back the other way.

Valerie's Benz was still parked in the same spot. Sally's

first mind was to ram it. She passed by it, angrily pulling into the garage, clicking off her headlights and taking in a deep breath. *Why am I so nervous?* For some reason, sweat beads poured like water from her armpits. She wanted to put the keys back in the ignition and leave, but something inside wouldn't let her.

Christine and Trisha were in the family room watching T.V. Sally felt her heart drop as she ran into the kitchen. At least they cleaned up this time. She scanned the area. Valerie was nowhere in sight. Sally passed by the family room. Her eyes meet Christine's. She wanted to ask where her mother was. Sally sucked back the words, pasting on a fake smile, turning away, with her back up against the wall, exhaling.

Their bedroom was empty. Sally dropped her purse on the bed, walking back into the hallway. She rushed into every room, nervously. Sally tiptoed to the east wing of the house. Her heart dropped, hearing a woman's light screams of passion. Sally followed the moans, stumbling upon a nightgown lying in the middle of the floor. She bent over, picking it up, placing her nose up to it and taking a whiff. *Valerie!* Raced madly through her mind. She turned toward their voices, gripping the nightgown tightly. Sally wore a sad expression of deep regret, thinking back to allowing Valerie around. Savagely, she tore Valerie's nightgown into shreds.

Sally didn't want to believe it, unable to force his infidelity out of her head, dropping behind pieces of Valerie's nightgown on the floor. Sally headed for the room, crunching through shattered pieces of glass. She lifted her foot off, noticing it was the same gold-rimmed glass Donny had drank from at the dinner table. The moans became louder; she moved closer. Her body nearly trembled from the pain of knowing the truth; the dryness in her mouth made it hard to swallow. Sally pushed open the door just enough to see. Her heart dropped. Her body weakening, she tried catching her breath.

Christine and Trisha caught a glimpse of Sally running past the family room. The sound of the door slamming echoed throughout the house. Sally's squealing tires could be heard backing out of the driveway. Trisha's head hung low, ashamed.

"Christine, was that Sally?"

"I don't know, but that makes the second time today," Christine chuckled sarcastically. Trisha didn't have the slightest doubt what was making Sally tick again.

"I wonder how Chad's doing." Christine twirled her fingers, blowing it off as if nothing happened. "I think I'm going to try and get pregnant again." Trisha lifted her head shocked. "I'm going home tomorrow."

"Christine, I don't think that's a good idea just yet."

"What - getting pregnant or going home? Why not?"

"Well ... well. I ... I don't know. You just lost a child from the accident. Don't cha think you oughta wait?" Trisha sounded confused and barely able to get the words out right. She wondered what Christine was trying to prove; besides, something didn't sit right with Chad, but she couldn't tell her; Chris would never believe it.

"What do you know?" Christine blurted out on the defense.

"Do your parents know you're going home, does Chad even know?" Christine turned toward Trisha, looking her eye to eye.

"No, I'm telling my parents tomorrow. And as for Chad, I pay most of the bills around there, I go home when I damn well please to!" Trisha let out a deep sigh. "You're more than welcome to stay here, or you can come to the house with me if that's what you're worried about."

Trisha smiled at Christine's warm welcome. It was something to consider. Her ex had spent most of the money and there was no way she could keep up with the mortgage payments alone. Their dream home had gone into foreclosure last week. Trisha had nowhere to go at the moment. It was going to take some saving to place a down payment on an apartment.

"I'm sorry, I didn't mean anything by."

"I know. I'm sorry for yelling at you. I'm still just a little upset about losing the baby. I really wanted this, Trisha, I'm thirty-two and still without a child and now this happens. I'm so upset inside." Trisha rubbed Christine's back. It was all horrible, but rushing into another child when Chad didn't want one wasn't solving much either.

Christine thought about a lot of things that made her angry, especially the night at the hospital, for one. It was a loss Christine could not escape. She was anxious to get home "I just need to get home," she muttered to herself, making it seem urgent.

"I understand, Chris."

❧

Tamara sat up half the night getting high and plotting ways to destroy Dana's and Jerick's relationship. In her mind, she was going to steal him away if it was the last thing she did. Her cell phone rang unexpectedly. *Dana?* Glancing at the screen, Tamara uttered a short laugh. The timing was just right. Dana's ears must be ringing! *Besides, what the hell does miss all that want?* Tamara concealed her attitude, pretending to be nice; the voice caught her off guard. It was a male's voice.

She tried slowing down the fast beating pace of her heart, torpedoing out of her relaxed position. Her mind instantly raced with sexual thoughts of the two of them engaging in sex. Reality struck within minutes of the conversation. Jerick was straight to the point. Tamara's heart grew angry, listening. Outraged, she kicked over the small table, pacing back and forth. She couldn't believe he was calling her to invite and help out with a surprise birthday party Dana obviously had no idea about. Tamara tried remaining calm; her attempts to keep him on the phone long enough to pry were unsuccessful. Jerick wasn't willing to share much information. Tamara knew if he was throwing Dana a surprise birthday party they had to be serious. Jerick must not have known they weren't the best of friends. She hadn't spoken to Dana in three months, but he didn't need to know that. Jerick was helping her get closer to him and she knew her seduction skills would pay off. She couldn't wait. He said it was three weeks away. Like a child, she wished for these days to pass, envisioning every moment.

After hanging up with Jerick, she skipped around the house like a child in a candy store. Several outfits flashed through her mind, but which one? Unconsciously her mind floated adrift: Jerick standing in a pair of black basketball shorts with no shirt on. Behind his masculine figure, his chest was rippled. Tamara slowly engaged in her mental seduction, leading him to the bedroom. There was no time to think about Dana. Tamara quickly removed her short dress, pushing Jerick onto a nearby chair. Slowly she slid over him, grinding with just enough contact to feel his flesh poking through his shorts. Tamara envisioned his hands tightly gripping around her waist, slowly moving toward her butt. The thought was enticing but not with Dana around. It would be more satisfying if it was actually happening.

⌾

Sally drove furiously, like a bat out of hell. The only thing remaining on her mind was seeing Donny on top of Valerie, both of them nude, engaging in sex, in Sally's and Donny's home. Sally was slightly dazed, zooming past two stop lights. Her thoughts whirled with anger, but mostly revenge, as tears streamed down her face.

Sally didn't make it a mile down the street before the sirens and lights flashing finally caught her attention. She glanced into her rearview mirror to find the police trailing behind her. She was clueless how long they had been trailing as she slowed down to a stop. Sally rested her head on the steering wheel. A tap on the window startled her. She lifted her head wiping the tears from each cheek, slowly rolling down the window. The lights from the flashlight were blinding. Sally screened her face, placing up her arm to the officer shining the light on her face.

Twenty minutes later, Sally drove off with a ticket for over two hundred dollars. She had an unpaid ticket from a month ago that she tried to sweet talk her way out of but tonight it caught up to her. Thank God the officer was nice enough to let her off after witnessing her crying. Sally promised to slow down and the ticket would be taken care of first thing in the morning. *What else could go wrong?* She wondered. Chad wasn't answering his phone.

⟨∽⟩

Chad's blood-covered hands were trembling as he dragged Paulette's unconscious body back to the car. He popped open his trunk, lifting her like a used tire, and then quickly slamming it. He stood motionless, out of breath, wondering what to do next. Following his first instinct, Chad stumbled to the driver's side of the car, reaching for his cell phone

⟨∽⟩

Sally darted in between traffic, hoping not to get caught again. Disturbed by Chad's frantic call, she was left figuring out the missing pieces of his scattered, meager conversation, which was still sketchy, just that it was urgent and to meet him in the back of Danielle's apartment. Either he hung up the phone, or it went dead. *What the hell was he doing and why was he at Danielle's apartment?* Thoughts stormed her mind.

⨕

Quarter after twelve midnight. Sally followed the crescent-shaped moon past town; she was less than six minutes to Danielle's apartment. Valerie and Donnie had somehow vanished from her mind. Chad wasn't being very cooperative—he still wasn't answering his calls. His struggle to breathe gave cause for worry.

Sally rushed, pulling into the nearest parking space next to Chad's car. His tinted windows were hard to see through as Sally glanced inside his car to see if he was inside. It was empty. Sally scanned the parking lot, darting toward the small, wooded jogging area. Suddenly her phone rang.

"Where are you?" Sally said as she started toward Danielle's apartment steps.

"I'm in your daughter's apartment; just get up here before I do something I regret!" Yelled Chad. Sally immediately heard the phone go "click."

Danielle's whimpering could be heard as Sally walked through the door. She tossed her purse on the table and slowly headed down the hallway, stopping at the bathroom. Danielle sat straddling the toilet, doubled over in pain. Chad stood in front of her holding a towel with blood stains on it.

"What the hell is going on?" Sally muscled past Chad and placed her hand underneath Danielle's chin, lifting up her head. For the first time, Danielle seemed to be ashamed, or she was putting on a good act. Sally was furious; the bruises and scrapes on her face and body were unbelievable. Sally turned toward Chad, her thoughts drifting as she asked herself *what would have made him do this?*

"I can't take this anymore, Sally."

"What? You beat her half to death."

"You don't know what I did!"

"You can't do this to her!" She screamed.

"Shut up! Do you know this bitch was in my house when I came home?" Sally's mouth dropped open, surprised.

"What do you mean?" She lowered her voice.

"She was in my home, Sally, in my wife's nightgown and naked underneath, drunk, waiting for me upstairs in our bedroom. This shit has got to stop!!" Chad paced angrily around the floor.

"Danielle."

"Paulette!" She screamed. "My name is Paulette." Sally was disturbed and confused by her response.

"Whoever the hell you claim to be, Paulette, Paula, Danielle, I don't give a damn! What the hell is wrong with you? You can't do this, you're messing up everything! What if Christine came home?"

"My point exactly!" Chad stormed in front of Sally's face, pointing. Sally soon forgot about Danielle's bruises; she realized Chad had given her just what she deserved, an ass-kicking. "That's not all, Sally." She watched each muscle in Chad's face grow slack. A disturbed look peered from his eyes.

"I'm pregnant! And there's not a damn thing you two can do about it!" Danielle blurted out in laughter. Sally's heart dropped; she stumbled a bit trying to catch her breath. She had never heard such a defiant tone coming from Danielle's mouth. She spoke every word with a plan to destroy.

"Pregnant! Pregnant! Over my dead body, Danielle!"

"Paulette! Stop calling me Danielle."

The play button in Sally's head suddenly hit rewind. She remembered it was in third grade: Danielle's teacher insisted meeting that day. Danielle was held in the office for misbehavior and fighting. This was the third time she had started a fight in less than two weeks. Sally was alarmed by her irate behavior and embarrassed. This time, it was different. Her teacher, Mr. Price, was concerned about Danielle's upbringing at home.

It was all a shock to Sally when she saw Danielle's school papers. The name at the top of all her stuff read Paulette Daniels. It was then that Sally requested to her husband that Danielle gets counseling. He refused, insisting that Danielle was just going through a phase. By the time she reached sixth grade, Danielle had several names and everyone fooled.

Quickly erasing the thought from her mind, Sally stormed over to Chad, swinging him around by his arm. Furious, she pointed her finger adamantly in his face. "Pregnant! What the hell is going on?"

"It's not mine!"

"No, no, you're not going to mess up what I have. You

two aren't going to mess this up! I swear to you!" Sally buried her face in her hands, trying to gather her thoughts. It was hard with everything going on, processing Chad's story how Danielle betrayed him by stealing his semen. She hated Danielle even more, but she wondered how Chad could be that damned careless? Everything about Danielle reminded her of Sally's ex-husband. She was nothing but a damn curse. *This couldn't be happening* she told herself over and over. Sally turned toward Chad. "Get out, Chad. I'd like to have a word alone with my daughter."

"Shut her up Sally or I will!"

"Get out, get out now!" Sally demanded shoving him out of the bathroom.

☙

It was almost eight o'clock a.m. The sun shone brightly through the clouds even though a string of bad weather was in the forecast for the next three days. Temps were in the low fifties, lower than normal for this time of year. Christine dried herself off with a towel after taking a long shower. Her long-time stay at home was finally ending. Trisha helped pack up Christine's clothes, making sure to leave the room just the way her parents had before they came.

Christine couldn't wait to get home. Her heart raced like it was the first time meeting her husband. She missed him so much. She wanted to surprise him; he had no idea she was coming home and that Trisha was going to be staying a while. Their five-bedroom house had more than enough room for a guest. Trisha could take one of the spare bedrooms that had a connecting bathroom. Chad shouldn't have a problem with that. Besides, she needed the help. Trisha insisted she call Chad and warn him. *That's stupid, for what? I live there, the house is in my name, there's no way in hell I shouldn't have to do such a thing!*

Her only downfall was controlling her anger. More and more, she found herself taking out her frustrations with a drink. A glass of wine soothed the pain, pain she felt physically and mentally with the loss of her baby.

She couldn't help staring at her tummy, passing by the mirror. She felt empty and angry, remembering that night; the person that caused her life to change was a hard reality to face. She really wanted this baby so badly, a baby period, how could this happen to her? Her prayers were unending. She desperately wanted that person to be caught and justice served. Thinking about the doctors and the hospital made her horribly upset. She was tired of crying; for days now, the tears wouldn't stop. Trisha always seemed to be there when she needed comfort; Christine was glad Trisha was here. Her mom was helpful, also. Some nights she'd wake up to find Valerie next to her, rubbing her back, just as she did when Christine was a little girl. Most of the time the alcohol mixed with meds was knocking her out. Her mom must have known, or felt that her pain that was endless.

Christine turned away from the mirror as the tears fell. She rubbed them off her cheeks, fighting off the anger. This time, she wanted to face the pain alone, without Trisha or her mom coming to the rescue. Christine headed for the kitchen, her mind focused only on easing the pain again.

She placed a wine glass on the counter, pouring out her frustrations.

❧

At almost eight thirty, Chad sat impatiently, waiting in rush-hour traffic. Cars could be seen for miles away. Bumper to bumper, the traffic rolled unceasingly. Occasionally, Chad glanced down at his watch, inching his way through traffic. The thought crossed his mind, but he didn't dare call Mr. Crawford; he was usually out of the office this time of morning.

Fifteen minutes later, the traffic proceeded to move at a steady pace, leaving Chad enough space to ride the fast lane to the next exit. At 8:45 a.m., Chad tucked in his tie and straightened out his suit coat, darting into the nearest elevator

It didn't take long before his mind floated back to last night. Sally had to have taken care of her daughter, for now at least. The pain about Mr. C. finding all this out was frightening. A couple of scrapes on his fists reminded him how bad Danielle's face looked. He thought about changing the locks before Christine came home, but explaining why wouldn't be easy, and showing up at her father's home with a new house key was surely going to raise some eyebrows.

❧

It felt good to be home. She sucked in several deep breaths, taking in the view. The lawn was trimmed without her having to tell Chad. She could imagine how the inside looked. Trisha drove up the long drive, pulling into the garage. Chad's SUV was gone. Christine's mom had picked out a rental Benz until hers was fixed. She parked in the same spot of their five-car garage.

She stood hesitantly at the doorway. Inside she dropped her handbag on the counter. The kitchen looked like it had never been touched; it was the same way she had left it. The door still squeaked when closing, a few dishes lay piled in the sink, the same microwave Chad claimed he was going to install still sat in the box from when they purchased it last month after the old one broke down. It was a shame she was picking out everything wrong in the house. The only thing oddly missing was the door rug. She wondered what happened to that. There was nowhere to leave their shoes.

Trisha scooted by, dragging in all the bags. Christine tried helping but Trisha refused, insisting that she relax. Relaxing with another glass of wine was right up her alley. She couldn't help snooping around. She guessed she was hoping to catch something out of the ordinary, which her husband knew she was good at. No shirt was hanging over the couch nor were several pairs of shoes lined up at the door. Chad must have really cleaned up his act.

She showed Trisha to her room on the upper floor where she placed her suitcases on the bed, plopping down, out of breath. The extra bedroom had not been used since Aunt Viv and Uncle Reese came to visit last Christmas. Christine wanted to stay and keep Trisha company but, right now, she just wanted to escape her pain without Trisha knowing. "I think you should call Chad," Trisha yelled, as Christine exited the room.

She took a deep breath. She was getting tired of Trisha telling her this. Christine grunted but kept her mouth closed. She didn't trust herself to say what was on the tip of her tongue. She decided it was best to walk away. She found herself standing in their bedroom. She sat on the side Chad slept on. Slowly climbing in, her nose hit the sheets. She took in several deep whiffs of his cologne, picturing his face over and over in her head. She couldn't wait to hold him.

Trisha's voice ran through her head about calling Chad. She stared at the phone, wondering if she should. *What the hell.* She grabbed the phone, dialing, waiting for him to answer as butterflies swarmed in her stomach. Chad sounded surprised to hear her voice and shocked to see the home number appearing on his cell phone screen.

∽∾

Danielle had been creating problems for a month now. Sally couldn't keep her quiet for long, especially after what Chad had done. Now she was demanding money, five thousand in the last two weeks. Sally couldn't keep taking out large lump sums of money; Donny was sure to question just where it was going. It was only a matter of time. This could not continue to go on. Chad paid her to keep quiet as well; who knew how much money she was receiving? The more he turned her down sexually, the more the price went up.

The weather was mild for late October. The moon was slightly hazy. Behind the clouds, a backdrop of stars lit up the skies. Sally took it upon herself to follow Danielle after receiving another threatening phone call. Sally was alarmed; the threats were made toward Christine this time. Sally had trailed behind her daughter for at least an hour now. Shockingly, Danielle had followed Christine without her knowing. *How long had she been doing this?* She was making a simple trip to the grocery store and to get her hair done, with Trisha as her chauffeur. For some reason, Danielle followed her every move, obviously being sneaky, plotting something neither Sally nor anybody else had any idea about. Whatever it was, it didn't sit right.

Christine trotted through several stores, taking in the sights of what she loved doing best: shopping. She and Trisha carried bags filled with shoes and clothes. Two hours of sifting through the finest things temporarily alleviated thoughts of losing the baby, but something always found a way to jog her memory. Christine stood in front of a window, wracked with pain, silenced by tragic memories. Trisha always found a way to snap her out of it, ending in laughter. As they walked outside, Christine's black trench coat blew in the wind, trailing behind her. At several stores, they spent a little over 30 minutes. Danielle sat, waiting across the street in a black rental 2007 Stratus. Sally grew more and more curious, each moment sitting there, wondering where and what happened to the truck Danielle was using. She hadn't driven it for months now, which was strange. Danielle had an excuse for every question she asked, claiming her car had broken down last month.

They passed several stop lights before reaching Chad's and Christine's home. Sally watched as Danielle pulled to the side to stop and wait. *What the hell was she up to?* Sally asked herself, trying to remain out of sight. She pulled way over, in front of the neighbor's driveway.

From a distance you could see Chad running out, wearing a pair of jeans and a red polo shirt. He greeted Christine with a hug and kiss. He then grabbed most of the bags, leaving her with one. Chad stopped to take a suspicious glance around as if looking for something or someone. He obviously didn't look that hard. Paulette waited with the motor still running, two houses down. She knew if she parked just right, through the brush of bushes, it would be easy to see straight through the front door of their home.

Moments after shutting the door, Chad could hear car tires squealing. The person who came instantly to mind was Paulette. He placed the bags on the floor, sucking in a deep breath, suddenly worried about Christine's safety. Paulette was a crazy bitch who didn't care about anything or anyone. Why would she be outside? Christine had just pulled in. Was that bitch following his wife? Several unanswered questions stormed his brain, making him furious. He wanted nothing more than to be able to act out his violent thoughts.

Sally followed not too far behind Danielle, who was weaving in and out of traffic like a crazed fool. She wondered if Danielle was on to her. Finally, after thirty minutes, her car veered off the highway, heading east in the direction of her apartments. *Approaching this situation needed time, and timing was everything! Danielle was obviously out of her mind.* Sally's thoughts raced with ways of putting her daughter's deviousness to a halt.

The call came as a surprise to Donny; Detective Alexander was on his way to meet him at his office. Donny stood in front of the mirror, tightening his tie. He ran his thumb and index finger across his slightly graying mustache. He tucked his dress shirt over his stomach, dusting off his suit coat, running his hand through his graying hair and tucking it in place. It was a way to kill off his nervous mood. Detective Alexander expressed the importance of meeting him now, it wouldn't wait. Donny sat attentively, full of suspense, wondering what was so important. There were a couple of new leads in the case.

Donny glanced at his watch, his patience growing thin. Suddenly there was a knock at the door. "Come in."

Donny kept his eyes on the door until it opened. A short old man in a gray suit appeared. He flashed his badge. "I'm Detective Alexander." His hand extended to greet Mr. Crawford.

Donny responded with a firm grip, shaking his hand. "Have a seat. Would you like a cup of coffee?" Detective Alexander helped himself to a seat on the comfortable lounge chair.

"Yes, Mr. Crawford."

"Just call me Donny."

"Donny, I'll take some coffee, black. I'm going to need it after all the work I've been putting in at the office." As he poured the coffee, Donny wondered if he was speaking about their case specifically. "Just a quick question: who do you know that would wanna kill your daughter, Mr. Crawford?"

Donny's hand slipped; the hot coffee ran onto his hand. "Shit!" He muttered trying to shake off the burning sensation. He handed over the cup, still looking confused.

"What do you mean, who would want to kill my daughter, Detective Alexander? What the hell kind of question is that?" Donny raised his voice, concerned. Detective Alexander took a sip, setting the cup on the desk. Donny paced the floor, confused.

"Mr. Crawford, I guess I'll just break the news. This was no accident."

"What do you mean this was no accident!" He questioned hysterically. Donny could feel the muscles in his legs going limp, just like at the hospital. His thoughts were whirling with who the hell would do something like this to Christine. Chad crossed his mind several times. *Perhaps Christine's multi-million dollar life insurance policy?* Donny thought. *That bastard wouldn't be that stupid! I'd kill him.*

Detective Alexander studied Donny's facial expression. His anger could visibly be seen. Donny was suffering a meltdown, along with an untimely blistering headache. He sat traumatized, dazed, with thoughts of almost losing his only daughter to a deliberate act.

"We're not sure just yet about the car. The evidence Mr. Roberts, who claims to know Danielle, was a little sketchy."

"What do you mean?"

"Calm down, Mr. Crawford, we're working on it. We know for sure that the car involved was an old black 1990 Suburban."

"What about the damn license plate?"

"Well, there's a problem." Mr. Crawford gave a stunned look, waiting for the answer. "The plate on the car doesn't match. It was reported stolen a week before the accident. It belonged to an elderly couple, Mr. & Mrs. Whitfield. They noticed their plate missing and called it in that morning. Good thing they did. We've run a check on every body shop in town. There's been no one with that type of vehicle and that amount of damage that's been repaired. There are hundreds of thousands of backyard mechanics who can fix up a dent. We checked the body shop close to Miss River's apartment, we checked and got nothing."

Mr. Crawford let out a deep sigh as Detective Alexander gave a full description of the year, make and model, which none seemed to register.

"I want you to bring Mr. Roberts in again."

"If we need him."

"If?"

"Well..."

"This isn't good enough!! Damn it, this is my child!" Mr. Crawford responded, using strong hand gestures, pointing, demanding the information be found. *No goddamn plates! This person didn't want anyone to find them. Christine has an enemy to plan a crime this skilled! They were doing their best to keep this secret!* He shook his head from side to side. Donny's headache had taken on an entirely different track, a quick curve into a migraine. His temples were throbbing in pain as different vehicles floated across his mind; not one was a match to the description Detective Marsh gave. He sighed, feeling helpless inside. *This was nothing but disappointment* Donny thought to himself. It felt like taking a sip of water after being stranded in the desert for days, realizing there was no more water, and now everywhere you turned, a mirage of false realities appeared, leaving one still thirsty for the truth, and wanting it now. The officer was telling the truth.

Detective Alexander shook hands with Mr. Crawford, promising to put his best men on the job. Alexander wasn't going to stop until the unknown person was apprehended and justice was served.

❧

It was another day of waking up with some strange man. Tamara turned over, glancing at the clock. *12:05 p.m.* she thought, rolling toward a limp, sweaty body next to her. She frowned after taking a look at her pick-up date. He was old, fat and his hair was thinning at the top. He snored like a beached whale, trying to breathe. Each time, his belly moved up and down. Tamara reached over quietly, grabbing her clothes. Most of her things were strewn throughout the room. She had no recollection of what happened, just that she was offered some drugs by some guy at the bar. She did-n't hesitate to follow him to the back room where she took several hits of cocaine which mixed with the three glass of hard liquor already consumed.

How this guy came into play, Tamara had no idea. She couldn't remember a name let alone place where she had met him. She snooped around in his pants, grabbing his wallet which was tucked away in his pocket. Tamara ripped through it in search of money; she exhaled and smiled, tak-ing two hundred dollars and stuffing it into her bra. Tamara glanced at his license. His name was Mitch Hardson. *What an effed-up name* she muttered, calculating his age in her head. *Sixty two, what the hell! Oh, my gosh!* Tamara frowned. She searched the rest of his pockets for drugs, turning up empty-handed. She fiend for a fix. Tamara looked down at her trembling hands, and then over to Mitch. He was still sleeping, and snoring like a chainsaw.

Tamara didn't bother taking a shower. She slipped into a skirt and top, tip-toeing around, afraid he might wake up. Tamara took a glance outside the window to see just where she was. She had no idea but the place was slummy. A bunch of guys stood outside, gathered together, up to no good. As one of the boys passed something off he noticed Tamara's face in the window. She backed away, afraid. There was no way she was going out there alone. Her first thought was to wake up the old fart. Instead, she tore through her purse, grabbing her cell phone.

Tamara waited quietly in the bathroom. She glanced

around at the walls; pieces of plaster were missing and the sink made a long, hollow sound before the water came out. She squatted, sitting on the side of the dirty tub, glancing at her watch, waiting for time to pass.

Tamara couldn't wait to leave, especially now after getting the wind from a good friend Kira, that Dana was dating Jerick Russell. She was furious. That would explain why Dana refused to hang out anymore.

Tamara grew worried when the snoring stopped. She hopped up quietly, holding the door knob, twisting the lock button. Slowly she backed away from the door, waiting. *Hurry up Kira*, she mumbled to herself. Mitch must have stumbled around the room for ten minutes. He bellowed his anger after checking his wallet. Tamara could hear the words bitch and tramp coming out of his mouth. Relief came after hearing the door slam shut. The window in the motel room shook. Tamara took a deep breath and crawled toward the door, listening to make sure he was gone.

"I gotta get outta here and find out what's the real deal with Dana. Looks like she's been holding back."

⚜

"Man, that's the girl you cheated for? Your wife, Joyce, is a hella better." Stan gave a sarcastic laugh, thinking to himself, amused, staring at a photograph. The way Julian bragged about this girl, she wasn't all that worth the time. He didn't dare tell him he knew that trick from several of his boys that were screwing her. *What the hell was he thinking?*

"What do you think?" Questioned Julian, waiting for Stan's answer. Stan sat close to the window, quickly locking his eyes on something that would keep him from having to tell a good friend the truth.

"How long has this been going on?" Julian avoided Stan's eyes. "Well?"

"Two months," He sighed.

"Two months. I thought you and Joyce were working things out?"

"Maybe, maybe not." He sighed again.

"Does she know this? Does she know about your wife, about the marriage thing?"

"Well, dumb ass, if she knew about her, she wouldn't be living right now, she would be in the hospital."

"Your ass is gonna end up right next to her!" Stan chuckled aloud, glancing at the picture, wondering in thought. *What the hell did Julian see in Tracy? Yeah, she had a bangin' body, but there was something off about her.* Word around town she was a crazy bitch, disguising herself with different names. Julian had no idea what this girl was capable of, besides, he knew Brian said her name was Paulette Daniels and that she was nothing more than a golddiggin bitch. The only thing different was that hair change and the name change. Anyone could have dyed their hair from blonde to black, what the hell! It could even be a wig! The girl in the photo had the same tattoo on her neck. Julian was being played by the most devious female. The strange thing was the obvious bulge in her stomach.

Stan couldn't think of one thing that made her attractive. Joyce, on the other hand, had a professional job. She was well kept. Joyce was a little heavy, but attractive. Her short haircut lined her oval face and her olive complexion made her skin glow. Julian had made mention of her weight gain, but he was the one knockin her up, and after five children, Joyce didn't look bad. Stan studied Julian's movements as he continued gloating, asking questions, like a kid in the candy store.

"Man, she's not worth it! Trust me."

"It's just a little harmless fun."

"Harmless! The harmless thing's real name is Paulette Daniels, not Tracy and she's a real head case. Have you thought about your losses?

"Why? She won't find out and I knew her real name!"

"Man, yo butt is blind! I've heard about this girl. How much money have you given her?"

"Not much. Why? It's all hush money."

"No, it's dumb ass money! You think that's gonna keep her quiet? I understand you might be a little pussy whipped cause she's willing to do whatever you want! But man, she's like that with everyone! If you were going to cheat with a black woman, you've cheated with the wrong one! She's not a woman, she's a monsta skeezer."

Julian let out a deep sigh, holding back his anger. "Is that all your ass is going to do is criticize?"

I know *this dumb ass didn't just ask that question, and get mad. It was useless, he wasn't listening.* "Man, just take me home."

Julian drove through town to Stan's apartment. He

spent the entire ride lying to Joyce and making plans to meet so-called Tracy that night. The last thing Stan wanted was to be in the middle of his mess when Joyce found out. He was playing 'em both for a fool, but what was worse, he was playing with the joker.

Julian slammed on the brakes in front of Stan's apartment. Julian could tell Stan didn't have two words to say. Stan knew it was best to leave, saying very few words. He would soon find out the truth the hard way.

"Later, man," Stan said, closing the door. Julian sped off, just as he expected with no response. Laughter escaped from Stan's mouth while standing there; disgusted, he shook his head.

❧

That night, Julian arrived at Tracy's apartment, anxious and ready for sex. Everything Stan had said went in one ear and out the other. He was so anxious he had forgotten to draw out some money. Maybe Tracy would forgive him this time, plus he was good for it. It was eight o'clock. He had told his wife that his business meeting had gone over. He trotted up the stairs like a child, fantasizing their endless night of blissful sex. He knocked several times before she answered.

Smiles graced her face and his as she stood with a long shirt and robe on, revealing a little of her breasts. She welcomed him in, pushing him against the wall. He welcomed her tongue into his mouth, ripping off her robe. Her hands went straight to his manhood, unzipping his pants. She ran her hands up and down, sticking her tongue deep into his throat. He explored every inch of her. He quickly reversed roles, slamming her against the wall, dropping to his knees. Softly she moaned, rubbing his head. He was lost in a moment of passion and nothing else mattered. Tracy dropped to her knees to give him a mouthful of satisfaction. My gosh, it felt good.

He reached into his pants pocket to pull out a condom. Tracy insisted he should not use it and besides, he really wanted to feel her. They violently kissed their way over toward the couch where he bent her over face down. The condom lay on the floor next to his pants. His second thought was: *what am I doing?* But his first was *I'm getting what I came for.* Tracy's moans turned him on more as he thrust her harder and harder. It was time to switch it up for more action, things his wife wouldn't allow him to do to her. Tracy loved it and so did he.

They ended up on the couch, hot and sweaty and out of breath. Laughter escaped her mouth and Julian joined in. There was no way he could go home like this. He continued kissing and caressing her. He ran his hand down her stomach, something he should have done before engaging in sex. The bulge in her stomach caught his attention. Everything Stan said ran across my head. "Tracy, you're not pregnant are you?"

"What! She ripped his hand from her stomach, jumping furiously from the couch. Tracy paced the floor, spewing out profanity. Julian was shocked. What the hell do you mean am I pregnant? We have sex and now you ask me that! Who the hell have you been talking to?" She screamed

"Tracy, calm down, I didn't mean ..."

"You didn't mean what? You are such a lame ass! You suck at sex! I pretend to enjoy it but you're a goddamn loser!" Julian's ego was crushed. Just when he thought he was doin' something. He couldn't believe she was acting this way.

"And you're nothing but a damn whore bitch! Tonight you won't get paid! Not by me, damn it!"

Julian rushed to put on his clothes. Tracy leaped onto his back clawing and screaming. She made sure to rip her nails into his face. Julian grabbed her arms, shoving her hard onto the floor. He fought to hold her back with one hand, trying to put on his clothes. She was out of control, screaming "Give me my money or else!"

Julian shoved her back onto the floor, toppling over her. "You crazy bitch!" He screamed, wrapping her arms around her head. "We're done, no more!"

Tracy looked into his eyes, and with her words, ripped away his soul. "I'll tell your wife." Those were the last words Julian wanted to hear. "I'll tell her and I damn well mean it!"

He held his hands in a tightening grip around her neck. "You mention anything or come near my wife, I swear I'll kill you, bitch!"

Julian rose up from the floor in search of his jacket, stomping over toward the front door. He looked back with one last threat. "I damn well mean it!" He said, before slamming the door.

Outside, Julian sucked in a deep breath. He felt the side of his face. Blood stained his fingers. There was a long gash. His heart was crushed, wondering why wishing he could take it all back. Sirens approaching brought fear. Julian rushed to his car, speeding off. *She couldn't have called the police?* He questioned himself fearfully. "No, this can't happen, no!"

He could only thank God that even in his moment of sin, the cops passed him. It gave him something to think about, that was for sure. Right now he had to get cleaned up and head home and pray that Tracy didn't find out anything about him and his family. Everything Stan said traveled through his mind. Julian hated to say Stan was right.

❧

Paulette sat on the floor, crying. There was another man gone. She was furious. "You won't get away with this, I swear!" She screamed over and over, banging her head on the floor.

"I told you, you won't win, Paulette, Tracy, whoever you are."

"Shut up, Danielle, shut up!" The voices in her head pounded.

"It's going to end horribly for you; all you do is hurt people around you."

"Shut up! I hate you, I hate you, damn, you're weak and stupid!" Paulette screamed at the top of her lungs, gripping her hair, pulling tight. She dashed into the bathroom, ripping through drawers. "I'll show you, Danielle." She pulled out a straight edged razor. "I'll show you!" Paulette watched as the blood pooled onto the floor, laughing as she cut deeper into her breast. "No one will want you now, bitch! No one!"

⌥

The day had turned out hot and sunny, that is, it was until a familiar face was spotted. Trisha and Christine exited out of the coffee shop, stopping.

"Isn't that Danielle?" Trisha questioned Christine, staring at the reflection in an outside glass window of Fifth Avenue.

"Where?"

Christine glanced over her shoulder. Her eyes darted through the crowd of people. She tried not to look obvious. "I still don't see."

"Right there, she's wearing a pair of blue jeans with a pink jacket. Can't believe she's dressed decently for a change. It's a little low-key for Danielle. Oh no, is she coming this..?" Trisha chuckled. Christine didn't have time to figure out the direction Danielle was approaching in.

"Hi, Christine and, um ... ."

Christine's eyes broadened, shocked.

Christine and Danielle hadn't spoken in years. After Danielle's spells of rebellion in front of the family when they were younger, Christine fed her with a long handled spoon. She had caused enough embarrassment.

"Trisha."

"Oh."

Oh, my ass. Trisha though with a distasteful look on her face.

"So how is life treating you, Christine?"

"Fine, and you?" Carefree words slipped from her mouth.

"Oh, it couldn't be better." Judging from the scars on Danielle's face someone had taken out a good well-deserved ass whippin' on her. *I hope life was getting better for her after the fact* Christine thought to herself

Trisha picked up on her snooty attitude quickly. She was anything but classy, in every way. She smacked her lips, swinging her hips from side to side, like some hoochie momma. Trisha continued studying her body movements, wondering why she couldn't stand still. There was something strange like she was almost bragging.

"I hear from the grapevine you're pregnant." Christine took in a deep breath; her fake smile remained plastered on her face. The last thing she wanted to let Danielle know is the truth. Trisha fought back her words of anger, turning the other cheek.

"Yes, Chad and I are expecting a baby." Christine let the words flow from her mouth. She watched as Danielle's exasperated attitude turned into an uncertain look of shock, obviously trying to withhold her anger. It was like old times, watching her moods come and go; her facial expressions changed almost like she was another person. Christine was shocked. She didn't ask anything about the accident or being hospitalized.

"Well, I'm expecting, too."

I feel sorry for that poor bastard, Trisha thought to herself, turning away, chuckling.

"Well, that's nice, Danielle, good luck." Christine's hopes of ending the conversation weren't going the way she hoped.

"I thought I told you two my name is Paulette, so please don't call me that other name." There was a look of shock on Christine's face.

"Okay Paul ... l ... ett," Trisha replied smiling. *That name, yeah, she's crazy. Right now I just want to punch her in her damn face. Give her another ring without the diamond,* she thought.

"I'm so excited, it's my first, too, you know how that is. I can't wait; I hope it's a boy. I already know what I'm going to name him," Danielle boasted, forcing her way through Christine's heartache as each word tore into her, making matter worse. She stood silently in another world, as Danielle's words faded. Christine flashed back to the night of the accident, the hospital, bits, and pieces of Chad's conversation, the baby. Christine's eyes snapped back to reality, disappointed to find Danielle still rambling on.

"Okay, I think we have to go. Bye." Trisha interrupted her bragging, grabbing Christine by the arm and rushing by, making sure to go the opposite way.

Paulette was appalled, after being left standing alone. She watched Trisha and Christine disappear through crowds of people.

Once out of sight, Trisha pulled Christine close by her

arms. "Christine, don't pay attention to anything she said." Trisha could tell each word had hit Christine hard. It was as if Danielle was trying to hurt her. "Christine." Trisha waited for a reply, trying to get through to Christine's gazing off in another world, calling her name several times.

Christine reflected on what she remembered that night. She remembered seeing a black truck speeding off. The car airbag deployed. After flipping over several times her eyes became heavy. Blood trickled from her forehead. Disoriented, she tried searching for her phone but it was nowhere in sight. *If it wasn't for the air bag. My baby*, she thought. Tail lights dimmed through a tall brush of grass. Footsteps approached, stopping. Christine lay helpless and crying. Faintly she screamed for help, fighting to free her leg from the dashboard. The person stood there … whoever it was turned and ran away … didn't bother to help. Something was pushing against her stomach. Christine remained unable to speak until she exhaled deeply, her trance-like state disappeared. Trisha was checking to see if Danielle was anywhere near.

"I hate that screwed up bitch! I hate her!" Christine screamed, drawing attention to herself.

"Shh, we're in the coffee shop."

"I hate her." Christine lowered her voice after noticing everyone staring. "That's one bitch I wish would just fall off the face of the earth."

"I know, I feel the same way. Danielle's got some issues, too many to count. I wanted to tell her I feel sorry for whoever got her pregnant." Christine and Trisha laughed.

"Let's get a cup of coffee to take a load off."

It didn't make any difference. No matter how much Trisha spoke badly about Danielle, something didn't sit right with Christine. *Why did she, after all, these years, make a point to tell me she was pregnant? The timing wasn't right. Did she know about the baby? How could she? Only Chad knew, and my parents would never tell her. Sally didn't even know. What was her motive?* Christine thought, blocking out the world.

❦

Tamara had fallen hard after watching Dana go out once and make the right catch. Someone Tamara had tried years to get was taken by a friend; one she didn't think had the right stuff to attract someone like Jerick Russell. Dana and Jerick were now the hot item tearing up the red carpet. Tamara could barely get through the doors at the club now without being made to wait like the other females in line. It wasn't too long ago she remembered being the one who lead the pack into the club, the one who sucked up all the attention. It was the opposite now. She felt like a side-line hoochie who had lost at playing the game.

❦

The word on the streets was Whitney was dead. Tamara didn't want to believe it but she had been missing two and a half weeks now. It wasn't like Whitney to stay away from her kids this long without a phone call. The two guys she left the club with were never seen again; no one knew anything about them. Bartley denied having any involvement in her disappearance. Tamara found that hard to believe given Bartley's tyrant ways, knowing he was abusive and controlling. She confessed to Detective Rice about Whitney not being able to leave the house without him knowing all; she was a street walker for him. "It wouldn't be a shock if Bartley lined Whitney up," Tamara told Detective Rice. "Nightly he lined Whitney up with older guys wanting sex in exchange for money." Tamara had no proof, it was her word against Bartley's. As far as being a witness, she continued, she would possibly be discredited. Most of the witnesses from the club said Tamara was doing just about the same, searching for rich men to have sex with for money.

❧

It was devastating enough hearing the horrific news of Whitney Steven's last month. Her disappearance splashed the third page of every newspaper. For weeks, the unidentified body was known as Jane Doe. Whitney disappeared without a trace and there was no evidence left behind to track what actually took place. Motives too many to count and numerous suspects grew daily along with a host of angry wives and girlfriends. The list continued to grow. The only thing left behind was Whitney's car, mysteriously abandoned in a parking lot out of state. The door had been left open with her keys still in it. There was no sign of a struggle. Her case was growing old and cold.

The police were currently investigating her husband, Bartley Stevens. His air-tight alibi kept officers in the dark for the time being. If he had anything to do with his wife's disappearance, there was no way to tell. Bartley had already replaced Whitney with another young woman. It was obvious he didn't suffer any mental distress.

Several plastic and cosmetic surgeons who saw Whitney were being subpoenaed. Their testimony was crucial to solving the case. Whitney left the club with some guys from out of town and was never seen again. Last month, an older lady in her sixties noticed a piece of clothing sticking out of the ground. She went to grab what she thought was a loose piece of clothing. The fresh soil collapsed revealing an arm.

❧

After nine years of giving everything I have and trying to dig my nails into the right man's wallet, nothing paid off, just a highway to hell. The men in my life were coming and going faster than flies on shit. A few lingered around, the old ones and the ones wanting just sex with no strings attached. The game was getting old and tiresome.

Her sleazy schemes had become an every night ritual at Hot Babes Club. She had now taken on a job at the hottest strip club, taking her clothes off for money. The every-night bumping and grinding against men was followed by her drug addiction to cocaine or whatever she could get her hands on. Once high, she did anything for money; she was a complete wreck without it. Coke was controlling her entire life, what little she had left. She owed money to everyone and tried to avoid most of them. Some of the guys she could give sex to or a head job to pay what she owed; the others wanted to get paid. Her body was weak, she was used up; most of her time was spent taking off her clothes and getting high.

Tamara sat in front of the dressing room with her head down. She avoided staring at the image in the mirror. The bitter truth was hard to bear. Tamara's peevish ways could only be controlled through her addiction, and once high, her trickin began.

A dark hand with a shiny gold platinum watch slid in front of her. In his balled up hand a package was left underneath a gold necklace, Tamara quickly unwrapped it. The room was spinning and so was her life, out of control. The high only took seconds to set in. A regular customer promised drugs in exchange for sex whenever he wanted it. That was right up her alley since all the money made was going to him. An old drug-dealing friend, Trevor, demanded all of her earnings and kept tabs on how much Tamara made.

❧

Dana's name appeared on her screen. It was the last person she had expected to hear from. Her heart raced once she heard the voice. "Jerick calling again about Dana's stupid surprise party!" When he spoke his name, she literally jumped out of her seat. *Dana didn't deserve him, I spotted him first!* Tamara attempted to keep him on the phone. Jerick reminded everyone about the party keeping his conversation short to the point and brief.

She was ashamed - her inner jealously controlled every

vile thought of Dana and Jerick. She wanted to vomit. Thinking of them left a bad taste in her mouth. Jerick was the one she was trying to hook up with at the party. Miss Goodie Two Shoes and her so-called Mr. Right. Why did he call from Dana's phone? Smart. Probably so she didn't get his number.

Tamara sat, looking in the mirror, fantasying. She ran her hands down her body, releasing a soft moan. *It's not too late* she thought. Tamara rushed toward the closet and pulled out a short backless dress. This was for sure going to catch his eyes. *This is my one and only chance to steal him away from Dana. Dana will finally realize who she's messing with once Jerick gets a taste of this, there's no turning back.* Tamara smiled, filling herself with confidence, quickly showering.

⤫

Her heart was racing; everywhere you looked, people stepped out of luxury cars and SUVs, dripping in money. Jerick's house was everything and more a woman wanted. Tamara made sure, her recently enhanced thirty six C cleavage showed, making her grand entrance. She wanted what everyone else had on their arm, a rich man, but one specifically. Mostly everyone here was bougie. Women exchanged their fake air kisses without touching cheeks. She did her best to blend in, but most of the time the only thing she received were dirty looks from the high class women.

There he was: tall, powerfully built masculine and fine, all in one. His creamy brown skin glowed like magic. Slowly her eyes undressed him. She wanted to jump his bones now. Instead, she secretly sized him up until Dana jumped onto his arm. Tamara had to admit Dana was beautiful tonight. Her breasts seemed perkier; she was about fifteen pounds slimmer. Her gold highlights brought out her big green eyes. The two of them seemed happy together and Tamara hated it with a passion. She watched as he chuckled aloud with friends, toasting drinks to each other.

Tamara made sure to stay discreet and out of Dana's way. A soft bump took her attention away from them, in front of her stood a tall, slim, dark man. He wasn't the best looking but his money changed all of that. He spoke with an accent, introducing himself with a soft kiss on her hand. She smiled. She had never been greeted in such a way before; for a moment, it sent chills down her spine. His name was Alom.

For most of the night, Tamara remained on his arm. Still, the dirty stares continued. Her eyes followed Jerick. Her lust for him was building up inside. Alom and Tamara danced. She felt his hand riding up her skirt, softly clenching her butt. A moan escaped her mouth, feeling his hardened flesh poking between her legs. The lights were dim. She watched as others danced in laughter. Alom continued moving his hand around her backside. She stuck it out a little for him to feel more of it. One hand rested on her nipple, softly rubbing till her knees weakened. Her eyes stayed focused on Jerick the whole time, wishing it were him. Before she knew it, Alom was inside her. She straddled his legs, grinding endlessly, lifting one leg and wrapping it around his waist. "Jerick." She called softly underneath her breath, picturing him.

Tamara rushed to the restroom provided downstairs. Several women stood inside, chatting. She pulled out an ecstasy pill, popping it with a bottle of water sitting on the toilet. She couldn't believe what she had just done.

She searched the room, looking for Alom. He stood by two other guys, laughing and drinking. Tamara walked up beside him, smiling. Alom gave her the cold shoulder, pretending not to know her. His brush-off was telling her to go mingle while he got to know other people. She was so humiliated.

Jerick stood, banging his glass with a spoon, asking for everyone's attention. All eyes were on him, curious to know what he was going to say. The room stood still; Dana shrugged her shoulders, unsure.

Jerick approached Dana. Tamara's heart sank, watching as he knelt down on one knee. The proposal came as a shock, a huge disappointment to her. They were freaking getting married! Dana willingly said yes, bursting into tears. Tamara's mouth hit the floor, her jealousy overtook all thoughts after being played by Alom, Jerick and now Dana's engagement to Jerick.

Tamara couldn't help noticing how beautiful Dana's cousins were. Twins, with caramel-colored skin, long hair that hung to the middle of their backs, with piercing green eyes much like Dana's. The two of them stood 5'9" with legs and a body that could kill and stop any man.

Fingers were suddenly pointed from one of her cousins;

the disappointment was they ended up heading in Tamara's direction. She could see the dislike on Dana's face. Her approach, knowing Tamara was here, wasn't a pleasant one. In a distance, she could see Alom chatting with Jerick, the two looking and pointing, as Dana made it plain and clear she didn't want Tamara to stay. Tamara was more concerned with what Alom was saying and why they were all laughing. One of the twins ran up and whispered in Dana's ear. Whatever it was, she found it comical as well.

"This is why you don't invite tricks to high class parties!" one of the twins said, turning to Jerick and Alom. Jerick knew he had made a big mistake. Tamara vocalizing his invitation was useless. The cousin made sure Tamara was the center of embarrassment. Tamara tried arguing her way out of it. Dana stood laughing as her cousin ripped into Tamara like a feline cat.

Tamara ran outside and hid behind a tree. She stared up at the sky, crying. *All this to try and steal Dana's man and it all backfired. They all laughed my butt out of the party.*

Dana stood around, swotting five's with her cousins, toasting another drink. Her well-thought out plan worked, having Jerick invite Tamara. Trevor spilled the beans about her wanting to screw up Jerick's and Dana's relationship. Dana exhaled, thinking back to the night Tamara and Whitney ridiculed her about having no class or a good man.

❧

The night replayed over and over of Donny and Valerie. Sally felt betrayed and used. She wondered how long their affair had been going on. *I need relief,* she thought, pulling out a short freak dress from the closet. Sally pinned her hair up and hopped in the shower. She pulled out her best perfume, spraying it all over her body. Donny wouldn't arrive for hours. Sally smiled while entertaining her sexual thoughts with someone else.

⟨∞⟩

The doorbell echoed throughout the house. Sally's heart raced with excitement. Never before had she thought of being this devious, but now was the time. Sally raced to the front door, first making sure her dress was high enough. A masculine shadow could be seen through the glass doors. Sally opened the door slowly, watching as his eyes wandered straight to her revealed breasts.

"Hello, Chad." She spoke seductively, inviting him in.

"Mrs. Crawford," Chad replied, shocked by her catchy outfit.

"Sally."

"What's the hurry? It sounded urgent." Sally glanced down the long drive, praying Donny wouldn't show up early.

Once inside, Sally offered to take Chad's jacket. He knew it was the last place to be, at another woman's house when he was so horny. Chad stared at Sally's curvy shape, fantasizing, unable to retain his sexual thoughts as Sally rambled on about Danielle and then Christine. Danielle was the last name he wanted to hear right now and Christine was far off the mind.

It didn't take but a minute before he felt Sally's hand moving up his pant leg. Like anyone shocked, he smiled, laughing it off, but unable to move. He couldn't wait for her to grip his manhood. When she did, a breath of relief escaped his mouth. He watched as she ripped into his pants like a whore in heat. Her tongue softly passed over his ear, inside and out. He was hard as a rock. It throbbed as she stroked every inch of him. Sally's soft wet lips enfolded the head of his penis. He couldn't believe what was happening! The wetness of her mouth covered half of him. He helped to shove her head up and down while she sucked harder. She was amazed at the size, all the while marveling at how sexy Chad was. He shoved her back almost to the point of climaxing. He didn't care whose wife she was, she was getting it now! Sally moaned as he caressed her breast. He made sure to suck hard while his fingers slid in and out of her. He quickly ripped her dress off, placing her over the couch. He had never had a woman this old but it felt good, and she loved every inch of him. He listened to her moan as she spread her legs open, allowing him to penetrate her deeply. A loud moan escaped Chad's mouth, it was time to climax. Sally pulled him out unexpectedly and dropped to her knees.

"What the hell! That really hurt, Sally!"

"What the hell are we doing?" Sally blurted out. It was good, and he was young, firm and handsome, but she didn't want Chad to know it. She enjoyed every minute of him, wanting more.

"This isn't helping, the heap of shit was already in! Oh, man!"

"Let's tone it down for a while."

"Sally, this can't happen again!"

"What's done is already done, Chad! Donny's wife has screwed his son-in-law and you have screwed your father-in-law's wife! And you're screwing Christine's step-sister! What more do you want, Chad?

"I really don't need to hear this shit right now! This can't happen again."

"You will not be able to hide the truth, Chad."

"You want me to hide it with Danielle! What's the difference now, Sally? What kind of game are you playing with me, damn it?"

"Danielle's different! I just need you to make me feel wanted when Valerie's around. Just a little sex here and there won't hurt."

"You're using me as a sex toy?"

"What do you think what we just did was all about? No different from you using my daughter as a sex toy, now is it? I can be good for you." Sally ran her fingers down the front of his pants, softly stroking him.

"No!" He shoved her hand away, confused. *She's worse than her damn daughter!* He placed his manhood back inside his pants, gently wiping sweat from his forehead. There was no taking this moment back. *If Christine knew the real me, it would rip her apart.* As he stood, out of breath, several thoughts swarmed in his head. At the moment, they didn't think twice about what they had done. The reality quickly set in as he walked out the front door. He couldn't believe he had just screwed Christine's step-mother.

Once Chad was gone, Sally knew she had gotten even with her husband by screwing her stepdaughter's husband, and it wasn't going to be the last time, especially if Valerie was still going to be welcome in her house.

◈

She waited days for Chad's call. Like that would ever happen. She wanted him to apologize. She was losing her control over him all because of his wife. *Chad wasn't going to get away with this, I'm carrying his child!* Paulette told herself the things she wanted to hear while staring at herself in the mirror. She glanced down at the plastic stick she left sitting on the dresser from taking her home pregnancy test. Paulette fantasized about what she wanted. The plus sign lying upright brought a smile to her face. The doctor's office had been calling non-stop for weeks now; she refused to answer, ignoring the name on the screen. Paulette refused to let Doctor Hanner know she was pregnant. Truthfully, it was the only thing making her happy. Paulette fought her way out of denial again.

"You're lying and it's all going to catch up to you." The voice in her head spoke clearly.

"Shut up, you bitch. I'm keeping it!"

"You're making a big mistake, you're going to lose."

"Shut up, Danielle shut up! I'm Paulette, damn it, and I'll do whatever the hell I please!" She grabbed the end strands of her hair, pulling several pieces out of the scalp.

Paulette tossed herself onto the floor in a fit of rage, fighting the voices. She screamed aloud at the top of her lungs until the voice disappeared. The strands of hair clenched tightly in her hand fell to the floor before she took in several deep breaths. Paulette picked herself off the floor. She glanced in the mirror; pieces of her scalp showed. "Damn it, I won again, Danielle. Paulette's in control so why don't you just stay in your place. Besides, you really don't exist!"

"I *do* exist! And I will be in control!"

Paulette raced to the closet, ripping down several boxes of shoes, to a box hidden in the back. She pulled out her favorite wig. Blonde, tightly curled. "Now that's better," she said, taking a look at herself in the mirror.

Tonight I'm passing the time with a few other guys. Tank and Raymond. Raymond was her usual lay-up whenever Chad refused to show up. She used him sexually in order to get her rent paid and other things she needed. Twice-a-week sex or a head job pacified his wants like a baby and kept him happy with his wife.

She couldn't help but wonder why Chad didn't want her out of all the men willing to leave their wives for her. She didn't want any of the men offering. She wanted to be with Chad. *I love him, but why doesn't he want me?*

"Cause they only want sex from you."

"Shut up, Danielle! You're nothing but a damn goodie two shoes. Stay out of this, damn it! Get out of my head! I hate you!" *That tramp Christine wasn't gonna have him, either, if I can't.*

❦

She was on a sexual high tonight. She didn't give a damn who she screwed, she just wanted to get laid. She could care less if he was married or had a girlfriend. She was on the prowl again, searching for satisfaction in the worst way. She had to admit her sexual high never was satisfied unless it was Chad. It had been a month now since they had been together; the only thing she had were memories of the two of them and that wasn't enough.

Paulette walked into the bar with one thing on her mind, surveying the area which had a few select good-looking men. She paced the bar like a lion in heat, making sure her skintight jeans revealed her butt. Her shirt was tight, revealing half of her breasts, a great catch for any man, she thought. Disappointment struck: most every guy appeared to be hitched up with someone. *Maybe one freak would want to share tonight. There was always a chance at that.*

Like most places, the women outnumbered the men, which meant she had to work extra hard to get the attention she wanted. That wasn't a problem; these hussies weren't going to ruin her action tonight.

She felt like a bitch in heat, ready to pounce on the first sucker ready to screw. Just then, she noticed her first catch - a dark-skinned brotha who couldn't stop staring. She tucked a few hairs back into place, relieving one last button on her blouse without him noticing. She pushed her chest forward, proudly displaying her sexual longing with no shame. Dirty stares and glares from women came from all over. She didn't care, they were just jealous.

It didn't take but a few minutes of seduction. He was all game and ready to leave after staring at her breasts as they talked.

Her insides were ready to explode. Once they hit her apartment door, her shirt was already off. She ripped into his pants, pulling out what she wanted. Her heart raced, and he moaned in excitement. Her pants were ripped off and thrown somewhere on the floor but she didn't care. She lay on her back and opened her legs, helping him find his way in, moaning aloud like she'd never had it before, grinding out her anger nonstop until reaching her climax. It was good for the ten minutes it lasted. Tonight she was getting hers first. She begged him to stay; she wanted more later on that night. While laying in bed with a man she hardly knew, her mind raced with thoughts of ways to destroy Chad and Christine, and she knew just how.

❦

Christine knew healing psychologically was going to take a long time, mentally even more. Four months of feeling a little life moving inside and in a split second, the life was gone. Christine sobbed alone, locked in the bathroom. Slowly she ran her hand across the emptiness in her stomach. "Why, why did this happen? Lord knows how much I wanted this baby." Her soft cries intensified, staring at herself in the mirror. The agony of losing her first child ripped her emotions into shreds. Doctor's orders were to wait awhile before trying to get pregnant again after such a bad miscarriage. *Just my luck I'd lose the baby Chad didn't want! This was all bullshit!* She made up her mind not to wait. She was going to get pregnant again.

She hopped in and out of the shower quickly, reaching into her stash of perfume, layering her body with an irresistible scent, one that was sure to make Chad go crazy. There was no need to dress. Chad was still sleeping in the bed. It was six in the morning. *Nothing like morning sex.* Slowly she lifted the covers, positioning her nude body next to his. Her touch made him squirm as curiosity woke him. She instantly took control, stroking him lightly, kissing his chest, sucking hard on his nipples. She moved downward. Chad stopped her unexpectedly, flipping her body around. He placed her legs around his head. She trembled in blissful pleasure as his tongue moved fast and slow. The sex between them was so powerful; she loved every minute of it. The thought of some other woman getting what she was getting made her furious. Chad's forceful stroke erased the thought from her mind. They were now grinding in harmony. She could hear him calling her name. Her insides tightened. Chad began to grunt. She opened her legs wider as he shoved harder, soon releasing what she prayed would knock her up again.

Chad rushed into the bathroom. He had twenty minutes before leaving for work. She could hear him singing in the shower, obviously overjoyed as much as she was about getting some. She lay, staring at the ceiling, rubbing her stomach, hoping his sperm would meet her egg. It was seven o five. The home phone rang twice, stopping before she could reach it. His cell phone rang. Quickly she reached over, grabbing it. There was no name on the screen, only a number. The shower was still running.

"Hello." She could hear someone breathing. "Hello." She hung up since no one answered. The call came through again. Her thoughts were whirling now. "Hello? Who is this, damn it!"

"The other woman." Christine's heart raced; she was speechless. The voice was unfamiliar.

"What the hell do you mean?"

"I'm screwing your husband, bitch!"

"That's a fucking lie! How did you get this number?"

"How do you think? From him, bitch! You think you got something special? You don't!"

"Don't call this damn phone anymore, you whore!" Christine shot up from the bed, reaching for her robe. "I don't believe you! You're just some desperate whore trying to get money! Well, you won't!"

"Chad has a scar above his pelvic bone. The only way you can see it is if he was naked, and we both were."

Christine stiffened up, her heart skipped a beat. No one could know that. The shower stopped. Christine stood confused. She quickly grabbed a piece of paper jotting down the number. "Don't you dare call this phone anymore! Hello? Hello?" There was no answer. She was ready to cuss Chad out, but she knew now wasn't the time. She couldn't look him into the eyes. He approached her with a kiss. She nudged him off with an excuse to leave the room. She couldn't shake the conversation from her mind. She couldn't wait for Chad to leave. She reached for a glass and a half-filled bottle of wine. The anonymous number lay on the counter top. She felt relief gulping down a glass, quickly filling another. *The baby and now this.* She was going to find out who this whore was!

❧

Paulette returned to her apartment. The side she could not control was growing stronger day by day. She felt good inside, bouncing off the walls, overjoyed. Paulette seemed to be winning over Danielle's good side. The phone call to Chad's wife was just the beginning. Paulette shoved Danielle out of her mind, allowing her altered ego to take over. "I'm five months pregnant with Chad's baby. There's no way they'll be able to trace that phone call back to me! Thank God pay phones still exist." Paulette laughed aloud.

It was finally done. Christine and Chad both knew the truth. Paulette didn't care about messing up their fairy tale-fake ass marriage. She told Chad she was keeping the baby and that he was going to be with her. She was already five months' pregnant and there was no changing her mind. Besides the support payments she'd receive from him, he would have to come running back. Paulette cracked a devious smile, forcing back any ill feeling of remorse for Christine losing her baby. *My plan worked!*

Paulette chuckled aloud, rubbing her vicious hands together. *I've finally got what I wanted and won. That trick lost that baby because of me,* she gloated, rubbing her hands across her stomach. Paulette's mind replayed the sequence of events that night. Sitting outside Christine's job, waiting anxiously, staring at a silver car she knew was hers. Paulette couldn't wait to finish what she had started.

The sun had just gone down. It was after seven. Paulette became antsy as seven thirty passed. "Come on!"

If it weren't for me running her off the road this would never have happened, having Chad all to myself. Now she could rub this in Christine's face. Her father's Benz was parked next to hers. Paulette remained hidden in the adjacent parking lot in an old black suburban. She sat, idle. The windows were a dark tint, making it hard for anyone to see inside. Minutes later, Christine was spotted giving her father a huge kiss on the cheek before getting into her car. Paulette's adrenalin pumped hatred and jealousy. She made sure to keep a distance behind Christine. She had no idea someone was following her. Christine had at least a half-hour drive before getting home, and the last fifteen minutes was down a long dark road. From a distance, Paulette could see a light glowing inside her car. She was obviously calling or talking to Chad. Fifteen minutes passed. Paulette sped up as Christine's silver Benz turned onto Clarkson Road. A flash of a silver car flipping over was all Paulette was able to see.

I did it! I got her, Paulette boasted to herself, laughing.

"You're gonna regret this." An unexpected voice popped in her head. "Chad will hate you even more now."

"Shut up, Danielle! Leave me alone, damn it! You don't know what the hell you're talking about!" Paulette screamed, nearly swerving off the road. "Get out of my head now!"

"I will have control over you in the end!" Danielle insisted.

"Never! Never will I allow you to be in control again! Danielle, you have been nothing but trouble!"

"No, Paulette, it's you!"

"No! Shut up!" Paulette cried, drenched in tears.

"This is war, you won't win, Paulette! You're playing with fire and you're gonna get burned."

"Shut up, bitch! You never won anything! You've always been afraid to take it or give it. That's why it was taken. Remember, Danielle, your mother's creepy old boyfriend and not to mention..."

"Shut up!"

"Mother didn't believe me! I had no choice but to become who I am now! Paulette gets what she wants!"

Paulette continued fighting with her multiple personalities. She drove recklessly, trying to shake Danielle's voice out of her head. There was a loud ring followed by silence. Paulette wiped away her tears, happy that Danielle was gone. "She always runs away!" Paulette shouted, ripping her black wig off, tossing it onto the floor of the truck. "Shut up!"

❧

Paulette opened the door, shocked to find Chad standing outside. She broke out in a nervous fit, holding the door slightly shut. She left enough space, revealing a portion of her living room. In an instant, she felt her world crumbling down. "What are you doing here?"

"I need to speak with you now!"

"It's not a good time." Paulette thought of a quick lie. "My apartment is a mess, besides ..."

"Bitch. I'm not here to sleep with you. That shit is over."

Paulette fought to keep the door shut, falling backward onto the floor as Chad surprised her by shoving his way in. Paulette pushed herself off the floor, trying to shove Chad back out the door.

"Get out, please, just get o..."

"Is everything all right in there, baby?" The man's voice echoed through the hallway. Chad let go of her arms, peering around her to see if his mind wasn't playing tricks on him. Paulette dropped her head. He approached wearing only a towel. Chad's laughter could be heard everywhere, generally to Paulette. Chad looked him up and down. He had to be in his late fifties, out of shape and, worse, had more gray hairs than Mr. Crawford. "Is there a problem?" The man asked.

"No, he was just leaving," Paulette mumbled with her head still held down.

"Naw, man, you have the problem, not me," Chad chuckled. Chad lifted Paulette's head, looking her eye to eye as if reading her lost soul. "And you claim to be pregnant," he whispered. Paulette tried fighting his tight grip. "You better blame this old bastard cause I will never confess or own up to you blaming me. I never slept with you, you crazy bitch.

It was all your imagination." Paulette slapped Chad's hand away, angry.

"I slept with you and you know it! And it is your baby!" She screamed.

"Wait! Hold on, you're pregnant?" The man questioned, confused.

"Tell him, tell him! You probably lied to him like you're doing to me. Did you steal his money? Oh, that's right, he paid you because he's married! Damn, Paulette!"

Paulette refused to answer, dropping her head again. The man disappeared into the bedroom. Chad's laughter echoed; Paulette's tears were endless. The man returned, fully dressed in his suit. Without saying goodbye, he shoved his way past her, leaving. Chad followed behind him.

Paulette slammed the door shut. She slipped down, falling to the floor, wailing out her sorrows and humiliation.

❦

Chad thought it would be a good idea to pop into Mr. Crawford's office. He stood hesitantly outside a large set of doors, exhaling. Before opening it, he overheard Sally's voice. Judging by the sound, she wasn't happy. Her cries echoed just outside the hallway. Mr. Crawford spoke in a low tone. Chad placed his ear against the door. Unable to make the voices out, something about Valerie; Sally was furious. Mr. Crawford was his usual calm self. He assured Sally he wasn't cheating; she was making a big deal over nothing. It was silent. Chad placed his ear closer on the door. Faint cries became what sounded like muffled moans.

Sally's outburst of "I love you" could only mean Donny was gettin' it in on the job. A short flash of he and Sally having sex crossed his mind. A moment's jealousy was quickly shot down. Chad jumped at the sound of the door twisting; his feet remained frozen unable to move.

"What the hell are you doing outside my door?" Mr. Crawford shouted angrily. Chad swallowed the lump in his throat, unable to speak. Sally poked her head over her husband's shoulder. She was alarmed to see Chad standing there, wondering how much he heard.

"I … I just got here, Sir, Donny, I mean, Mr. Crawford. Sorry, I wanted to personally hand you the reports firsthand." Mr. Crawford took a quick glance. "I'm sure you'll be pleased."

"Yes. from what I've seen, but I don't have time right now, it will have to wait. Thank you." He shot a glance at his watch. "I have a meeting with Detective Alexander; be back shortly."

Lightly, he pecked Sally on the cheek, dashing through the open spot provided. In the blink of an eye, he was gone. Chad exhaled a sigh of relief. Sally shut the door behind, ushering him by the arm down the hall.

"What were you doing?

"What were you doing, doin' it?

"That's none of your damn business!"

Chad hated to ask this of her but Danielle was out of control.

"Please, Sally, I need you to speak to Danielle for me." Chad pulled her aside to the nearest corner.

"That is your damn problem, damn it, not mine! How could you?"

"How could *we*? You had the same damn urge. You didn't hesitate to jump all over me. What's the difference?" Chad spoke. "Maybe 'cause Valerie and getting back was the only thing on your mind."

Sally sighed. "I don't care to deal with her, you know that! Danielle has some serious mental issues! It's bad enough she thinks she's someone else!"

"I had no idea she was Chris's step-sister! I just wanted to get laid!"

"You should have thought about that!"

"Did *we*? Your damn daughter is gonna mess up everything! Everything!" Chad pointed his finger in her face, whispering, "Your marriage and mine!" Sally shook her head "no" in denial. "Wake up, damn it! It's just one more step away from Valerie to steal your man!"

"Shut up! Shut up, damn it, I can't lose Donny! Never! Not over Danielle, you, or anybody!"

"We need to come up with a plan before the shit hits the fan. She's been blowin' up my phone every day and all morning, leaving twisted messages and text after text."

"How come you didn't use protection?"

"We did. I know for a fact Danielle's sleeping with eight different men at the club. She cannot pin this shit on me! She's nothing but a thirsty hoe and everyone knows that! Sally, words are starting to leak about this child being mine. I won't be the laughing stock of the town! No way in hell!

Chris will run to Valerie and Valerie will run to Donny! And guess where that leaves us!"

"Okay, that's enough, damn it!"

Sally charged passed him, bumping into his shoulder. An urgent text lit his screen up. "Speak of the devil, guess who?" His heart skipped several beats. "She couldn't have! She better not have, damn it!"

"What?" Sally swallowed the lump in her throat.

"If any of this gets to Mr. C. We're both done for!"

⚜

Saturday morning, Chad felt like Christine was timing his every move. She was more inquisitive than before, which made him worry. It was another day of dodging Danielle's crazy tail and hoping she kept quiet. Right now, Chad was a nervous wreck, left wondering what all Chris knew. She wasn't being herself and neither was Trisha.

⚜

Donny sat impatiently, waiting downtown in the police station. The man who witnessed the accident, Joe Richards, was back in town. Detective Alexander was in taking his statement again. Donny was anxious to find out what was being said. He wondered if there were any leads. Finally, after thirty minutes, the door opened. One of the detectives stepped out. Mr. Crawford watched the witness, a young white male, exit in the other direction. The smile the man gave was reassuring; he was trying. Detective Alexander didn't have to usher Donny in; he helped himself into the office.

"Hello, Mr. Crawford."

"Well, what do you know?" He questioned before the door shut. "Please tell me you know something."

The detective sighed. "Have a seat." Donny rested his discouragement in the nearest seat, waiting. "Mr. Crawford, all I can tell you based on the evidence and witness, someone was trying to hurt Christine intentionally."

"What! What the hell!" Donny shot up from his seat angrily.

"Calm down, please. Months of evidence have led to an obvious, deliberate attack."

"Calm down! The person responsible almost killed her, they killed my grandchild, damn it! My daughter lost her baby!" Mr. Crawford leaned in over the desk, yelling. His short temper was fused. He turned, pacing the floor.

"Trust me, I'm on this day and night. We have several leads and, trust me, we have two of the best detectives working nonstop. Thanks to your fifty thousand dollar reward, it's given us more leads than ever. The vehicle possibly involved looks to belong to a man named Vernon Rivers. With that match, we'll be on our way. Joe's statement is really paying off. Thank God someone was there to witness it or we wouldn't have a damn thing to go on."

❦

Bartley had repeatedly retold the same story about his wife: that he was with the kids all day and night. He sat contentedly behind his attorney, wondering what was being implied. Toxicology reports run on Mrs. Stevens proved heroin being in her system. The cause of death was strangulation with the obvious marks around her neck and bloodshot eyes. The suspect had raped and beaten her black and blue. Surveillance cameras in the club made it hard to identify both men Whitney left with. One appeared to have been in his late thirties, 5'9", a possibly Hispanic man with long black hair. The other was an African-American in his late fifties, 6'2" and bald. No one at the club had ever seen the men before. Her phone records showed Whitney had just placed a call to her husband before leaving with the two men. Detective Rice studied each file carefully. Everything was out of the ordinary, especially the prior call to Bartley. Tamara was discredited as a witness. Bartley stated that Whitney's infidelity began three years ago, that she promised to stop, and that he had no idea who the two men were. Rice leaned back in her chair, dropping her head against the back side.

Forensics proved several things in Whitney's case. After four months of a long-awaited criminal investigation, someone was finally on the hot seat. The prime suspect for her disappearance and murder was Bartley, her husband. Detective Rice studied Bartley's alibi report. His story was inconclusive. "How come no one noticed this?" The story about being with the children had fallen through the cracks after questioning more people. "How could this have been missed?" Detective Rice questioned, swallowing back a large gulp of black coffee. She sat back, exhaling. Bartley stated he left town on the fifth of January with the kids. Reenia, the live-in nanny, said she had been running around those same days with the children and that was on the fifth and sixth of January. Miss Larkson, the elementary school teacher, said the oldest attended school on both those days. Someone was lying here. Bartley claimed Whitney left with some friends of hers out of state and that she was only leaving for two days. A week later, Bartley filed a missing person's report, leaving enough time to cover his butt. He claimed to have not seen Whitney or had contact with her in a week. Semen traces and DNA proved different: The tight line around her neck meant she was strangled from behind. It was time to get a warrant. Bartley had a lot of questions to answer.

❦

Chad never once questioned me about my baby. It felt good feeling it move, but I was still in pain. They weren't gonna get away with this - Julian, Raymond, or Chad and last but not least, my so-called mother. Paulette paved the way for destruction everywhere she went. Raymond had finally shown his face after all the threats: sex in exchange for eight hundred dollars to pay rent. Raymond showed his face just after getting engaged. Paulette refused to give up, using the information she had to get what she wanted.

❦

Paulette drove around in search of the nearest pay phone, pulling over at the first one she saw. She dialed, waiting.

"Hello?" It was Christine. "Hello."

"I've been in your home," Paulette whispered.

"What? Who is this?"

"I made love to your husband on the cream couch." Christine grew furious but more heartbroken, listening to the muffled voice. "Who the hell is this? You've gotta be a sick, twisted bitch, you call yourself a woman!" Paulette hated Christine's reaction; the strength in her voice made her angry.

"I guess we're both having babies 'cause I'm pregnant by Chad. Your marriage is over bitch!"

"Over my dead body, I swear I'll kill you, hoe, you and that bastard child of yours!" Christine rambled on, screaming into the phone hysterically. Trisha rushed downstairs, concerned, overhearing her distraught screams.

"What's going on?" She snatched the phone out of Christine's hand, pushing her aside. "Hello!" Trisha yelled into the phone. "Hello." She placed the receiver on the base, confused.

"Chad! He cheated on me!" Christine screamed, frustrated, trembling as tears fell down her face. "He cheated! She said she's pregnant! She's pregnant and she's been in this house!" Trisha grabbed a hold of Christine, holding her tightly, angered by her pain. Trisha couldn't believe what she was hearing. She helped Christine over toward the den area, laying her on the couch. It was time for encouragement.

Trisha spoke to Chris, brushing away her tears. She assured Chris she would find out the truth, softly rubbing her fingers through her long hair. "Don't let this break you, Chris. We don't even know for sure if it's true. It could be someone playing a huge prank. My cousin works at the phone company. With your approval, I'll have the number disconnected and changed tomorrow. I swear I'll get Chad if it's true. I promise!" Christine nodded yes, cuddling up underneath the covers.

❧

Paulette dialed the number again hoping to finish what she had started. "I'm sorry, the number you have reached is temporarily out of service."

"What! What the hell!" Paulette slammed the receiver violently on the base over and over, shattering the head. She sped off furiously, squealing tires.

❧

Donny was out of his usual hideout: the study. Sally noticed his cell phone lying on the desk, ringing back to back. Donny only left his cell phone home if he had too many things on his mind. That must be the case. It was Christine. Curious Sally took it upon herself to answer it. Christine's voice was distraught, you could hardly understand with all the crying as she rambled, assuming Sally was her father. Sally's heart sank; her blood was boiling after hearing it all. "I didn't know when to cut in so I took the next moment of silence. I'm sorry, Chris, your dad's out of the office." I hated to interrupt." Christine was shocked.

"Where … where is he? I need to speak with him. It's urgent."

"He's in the meeting, you remember, with the Kingston Company."

"Oh, I forgot."

"Is there anything I can help you with?"

"No! I'll try him later." The phone hung up without a goodbye. Sally hopes failed on getting more info. *Danielle had to be causing Christine's hysteria. As if things couldn't get worse …* An unexpected knock caught Sally off guard. She rushed to the front door. To her surprise, it was the last person she wanted to see. Danielle rushed by, inviting herself in. "No, no you can't …"

"Shut up, momma!" Sally's eyes widened, amazed. Her mouth hung open. She wondered what the hell Danielle was talking about.

"Don't come in this house talking to me … " She spoke, raising her voice.

"You just couldn't leave him alone! It's bad enough you two are in cahoots together."

"What the hell are you talking about?"

"You're screwing Chad!"

Sally tried fighting off the accusing look. She continued hiding behind the truth, in denial. Sally was fed up with Danielle's outburst. She violently grabbed her daughter by the arm, swinging her back. Danielle barely caught herself from falling.

"You don't know what the hell you're talking bout! You crazy bitch! You don't even know what the hell your real name is! You're just a crazy, psycho bitch who's unhappy and sleeps around to get satisfaction." Danielle pulled away from the tightening grip, yanking away. "How dare you come here accusing me of that bullshit? The nerve of you! When does it ever end with you, Danielle? Everywhere you go you bring trouble, and now this! You have really lost your goddamn mind!"

"I hate you! You and that Christine have always taken what I deserve. I deserve Chad! Not her! You sleep with Chad because Donny's sleeping with Valerie!" Sally was shocked she even knew about Donny. She was right but there was no way in hell Sally was going to admit it. "I'm not stupid, mother! You screwed Chad out of revenge! I'm telling!"

"Shut the hell up and get the hell out of here! Your threats mean nothing to me, everyone knows you're crazy and you'll lie and cheat to get attention! You've always been that way, Danielle!"

"My name's not Danielle!"

"Oh give it a rest, damn it, I know what the hell I named you! And you try telling, it will be the last thing you do!"

Sally shoved her out the door, pushing her down the steps. Danielle landed on her hands and knees, looking down at the cement, humiliated.

"I don't just drop my panties for anyone like you do. I'd be stupid to screw that boy," Sally screamed. Danielle quickly rose up, storming toward her mother without warning. Sally didn't have enough time to shut the door. Danielle's nails dug into her face, clawing like a cat. Their anger had turned violent. Sally fought to pry her daughter off, grabbing her by the hair, shoving her off the porch again. Danielle slowly picked herself up off the ground. With tears in her eyes, she dusted off the gravel rocks stuck to her arm and knees.

"Get out of here and don't bring your psycho tail back here!" Sally screamed hysterically, peeking through the door.

"I'm telling! I'm telling Donny and Christine!" Danielle screamed through the closed doors.

Sally stormed to the phone, picking it up. She started to dial 911 but hung up. What good were the police going to do? Thank God Donny wasn't here to overhear her. It had to be fifteen minutes before Danielle finally left. Sally overheard a vehicle speeding off. *How did she find out?*

Sally remembered it was sometimes long ago that Danielle acted this same way: ten years ago when she was eighteen. It was just after her father passed away; they were at the Church after the funeral. Another side of her reared its ugly head. Danielle hated hearing all the positive talk coming from people. Danielle's embarrassing reaction to Sally's speech shocked the entire congregation. Sally rambled on about how good a man he was like everyone else, his good job, being a family man and his love for God. Danielle knew he had only gone to church a few times in his life. There was no use telling the truth, not while her husband had suddenly died. Danielle expected someone to spill the beans, inconsiderate to the timing. That day Sally could see the disappointment on her face. Danielle screamed out of nowhere "Liar!" and then stormed down the aisle. Sally stood in front of a confused congregation, trying to cover Danielle's mess, again blaming it on mental illness.

That same strange subdued voice had taken control. Profanity escaped her mouth out of nowhere, blaming and accusing her father of molesting her. Sally grabbed Danielle's mouth while several family members helped to drag her out the door downstairs. She was out of control, fighting, kicking and cursing everyone, most of all her mother. This wasn't the first time she had blurted out these insane accusations. Danielle seemed to be blaming every-one for everything but herself. Sally refused to listen to any of her daughter's lies. Out of all the men in her mother's life, she accused all of making her do sexual things to them, and blaming her father was just preposterous. Sally refused to have anything to do with Danielle for years. Danielle had a different story to tell for any fool that would listen after the behavior she exhibited in church, and on top of that, claiming her name was Paulette.

Sally stood out of breath, angry, staring at the phone. The loud sudden ring coming from another room startled her.

Sally couldn't believe what she had just heard. The phone call from Chad left her baffled. She stared into space for a short period, feeling her anger shoot up like a rocket. Sally rubbed at her aching temples with her free hand. *There was no way she was going to get away with this. Not this time.* Sally grabbed her purse and stormed out the door.

⟨☙⟩

Chad was furious. Paulette was threatening to meet Christine and her parents and tell her everything about them this evening. There was no way he could continue keeping her away from Christine. Most disturbing, she threatened to spill the news about the day she came over when Christine was in the hospital. *How could I be that stupid? I can't let this bitch destroy everything I've worked hard to get. Christine had already lost the baby and this bitch was claiming she was pregnant. Hell, no, no way in hell am I allowing this mess!* Chad paced the floor, getting satisfaction from the morbid, tempestuous thoughts running through his mind. "Screw her!" He yelled out, rushing over to the window, looking out. There was nothing to see but heavy rain pouring; the windows were foggy. Thoughts began to run maddeningly through his mind, speeding up his heart. His dull anger had ignited into a sudden fury of someone else, someone scary.

⟨☙⟩

Twelve forty-five a.m. Bartley was brought in again for the third time for questioning. He wasn't being charged with anything or under detention, Rice explained. Bartley didn't have to answer any of the questions if he didn't want to. Rice hoped he did. She listened as Bartley spoke highly of his wife. He had more experience with life than Whitney's twenty-five years. What the hell was a fifty-nine-year-old doing with someone that young? Bartley was way too nervous; his hands trembled badly as he drank the paper cup of water given. He could barely place his mouth on the rim. Sweat began to seep from his armpits through his shirt. This was surely an unusual response for someone who claimed to not be guilty. After ten hours of interrogation, Bartley started to break. Tears overwhelmed him, and fear of more questions. Detective Rice didn't understand. Bartley could willingly walk out, no one was detaining him. Guilt rambled from the tip of his tongue. Rice sat up in her chair glancing over at the tape recorder. Bartley rubbed his forehead; he leaned forward, his hands dangled between his legs.

Rice and Nash had Bartley placed at the scene of the crime. A huge piece of evidence, hair and carpet fibers from the Stevens' home, were taken from Whitney's hair. Bartley was breaking out of frustration as more evidence placed him as the primary suspect. Bartley's confession came as a shock. He rambled off a list of women used for prostitution. A stillness hovered in the room. A missing person's case they had worked on three years ago was unexpectedly mentioned. Kimberly Cartwright, a twenty-three-year-old female had been found with the same identical marks. Bartley confessed to murdering two different women.

❧

Sally rushed over to Chad's office, forcing her way in, out of breath. "We're in trouble!" Chad leaped up from the desk toward Sally, curious. Tears flooded her face with an outburst of anger.

"What, Sally?"

"Christine called, crying. It's Danielle. She had to have told your wife something!" Flashes of Valerie laughing at her floated in and out. Sally viciously paced the floor, nervous. Chad's heart sank, his body slumped forward, confused. He remained speechless.

"It's just a hunch but a strong one. Christine called Donny's phone and something told me to answer. Donny left his cell phone on the desk. I knew it was important. She called over and over again, so I picked up." A deep sigh escaped Chad's mouth. "She was hysterical, Chad, and crying about some woman!"

"Let's not jump to conclusions; she's been doing a lot of that lately since the loss of the baby. Danielle's playing with her and this is no time to be playing games!"

"Come on, Chad!" Sally tugged on his suit looking him in the eyes. Chad rushed over toward the sound of his cell phone. He sighed. It was Paulette, texting message after message. Chad stood, hesitant, slowly opening the first text.

Paulette: I really miss u Chad, I love u and I know I can treat u better than yr wife. Plz, I'm carrying yr child. We need 2 b 2gether.

"What's she saying?" Sally stood by, curious.

"Talking crazy as usual."

Paulette: I haven't heard from u plz call me?

Chad: Paulette I have nothing 2 say 2 u! I told u 2 stop calling me and texting!

"Wait, Chad, Sally interrupted, placing her hand over his phone. 'Don't upset her. We have to play by her rules."

"What?"

"I know what I'm talking about, Chad. We can't trigger her, not now! She can't explode."

Chad rolled his eyes carelessly. "What should I do?"

"Play into her hands, please! We have to stall or she'll tell everything and ruin us all."

"I don't like this idea!"

"Neither do I, but what choice do we have?"

Chad: Danielle I'm sorry.

"Sally, I don't feel right lying about this."

"You'll do it if you wanna save your marriage," Sally spoke.

Danielle: My names not Danielle, its Paulette!!!"

Chad: ok Paulette please don't do anything crazy? We'll talk. I need to see u. I've been thinking a lot about u lately, and the baby. I have to get back to work, we'll talk soon.

Chad felt he had to lie to keep her on a string in hopes of nothing more happening. "This isn't right, Sally."

"Let see if you and I could get all the nice things owned by ourselves! That car, house! You better play into her hands. Tell her what she wants to hear without the sex! At least until we figure out a plan!"

"She's your daughter, can't you control her?"

"And your sex slave, you should have controlled your dick!"

"Look who's talking, the lady who seduces Donny for his money."

"So what, Chad! This shit all started with you!"

"No, you! You had that crazy bitch, not me! Something was going on long before me being in the picture!"

"You slept with her! We can go back and forth, Chad, pointing fingers. The real truth is, if this leaks, we're both done for."

Chad hated admitting that was Sally right. Chad was beginning to realize that Paulette was Danielle. Danielle was a self-destructing time bomb, ready to explode at anything.

⟡

Paulette's eyes lit up, her heart quickened in excitement reading Chad's words. She was overjoyed, reading it over and over, almost memorizing each word. Thoughts of her and Chad marrying were delusions in her head. *I have him now!* A loud laugh escaped her mouth. *I knew it, I knew it!*

⟡

"Now what?" Chad asked, turning toward Sally, his mind saddled with misfortune.

"I don't know, but critical information is in the wrong hands!"

"We have to do something, quick!"

⟡

There was a huge lead in the Crawford-Richards case. Several reports of a woman being seen that night were called in. Description: late twenties, 5'5", pumping gas in the same identical SUV. Detective Alexander slowly put the pieces together but was left clueless. Hours later the big break came from officer Canton, an out-of-state cop. He stated that he pulled over the same identical vehicle that night for speeding roughly around two in the morning. The camera on his car revealed the same woman. She was given a citation for speeding. The only thing different was the license plate; it was different from the reported one. That threw another loop in the case. Detective Alexander had a gut feeling it was the same vehicle involved. Proving it was going to take more time. He stared at the name on the citation paper. "Danielle Rivers? It's time to pay her a visit."

❧

'This is one messed-up family," Marsh spoke. "I can't believe she's screwing her own cousin, Vernon Rivers."

"That's messed up."

"Do you think he's in on this?" Alexander questioned.

"No, not at all, but Vernon had to know we were going to find out their relation. Might be why he's been so cooperative and eager to get us out of his face."

Chad crept up the drive, paranoid, slowly thinking. His worst fear was Chris's dad being here. He planned out several lies as a backup. *What had Danielle done?* Chris wasn't herself lately, she seemed withdrawn, she was deteriorating. After entering the house Chad removed his shoes at the door. Slowly he walked past the dining area picturing Chris on the couch waiting like a watchdog with sharp teeth, growling, ready to attack.

Christine sat her half-empty glass down on the table. After four glasses she was barely coherent. The room spun as she staggered upstairs into bed. She had drowned her sorrows in another bottle of wine attempting to block out everything, especially the phone call.

Trisha paced the floor, waiting for Chad's arrival. Her eyes darted to the clock on the wall and back at her watch. She practiced everything she was going to say since Chris had no strength to face him. Trisha took a deep breath, quickly escaping to the bathroom.

Chad stood, momentarily visioning Christine running through the doors. The thought was quickly erased when seeing several empty wine bottles in the trash. He never thought twice about Chris having a drinking problem; the empty bottles had been going on for a while now. Chad gathered each of the bottles, placing them on the counter top. Trisha unexpectedly bombarded her way in, publicizing her assumptions, while approaching Chad. She was angry. Chad stood troubled, unsure of what to say. He listened to her ramble on about some girl calling.

"Danielle?" he thought. It had to be."

"Tell the truth, Chad? Have you been cheating?"

"No, I wouldn't." He had no choice but to lie. He had always been powerless to sex. Most of his past relationships were destroyed by sex and him sleeping around. "Trisha, you have to believe me."

"I don't have to believe nothing! Plus this whore claiming to know a lot. She even said she was pregnant!" Chad's mind instantly shot to Chris, and how she was feeling hearing it all.

"Trisha, please you have to get through to Chris." Chad placed one hand on her shoulder. "I can't lose her."

"I don't know. You should have seen her lose control, trembling and screaming at the top of her lungs. You're in deep shit if any of this is true!" A vision of Mr. Crawford approaching, boiling with anger, crossed his mind. Chad quickly shot down the thought.

"Trisha, I found these empty bottles of wine in the trash. They weren't here yesterday. Haven't you noticed how withdrawn she's been?"

"Only when you're around, Chad, and that makes it your problem!"

"As a live-in friend, it's yours as well!"

"Oh, hell no! Don't put me in your guilty mess! No, I won't be a fool! You got three days Chad, three, to clear up your shit! Or I'm going to Donny myself!"

"I didn't do anything!"

"Prove it, Chad! I'll calm her down for now, but that's it! If any of this is true ..." Chad watched as Trisha stomped towards the door. She turned back. "You can kiss this all goodbye!" Trisha escaped, holding a cup of black coffee. Chad's body slumped over looking at everything.

A day passed and Christine remained distant. She did her job as a housewife and the drinking continued. No one ever witnessed Chris drunk or buzzed; she hid it well.

Dinner was strange that tonight. Chad's mood was more subdued, Christine's was hyper, laughing and yakking about her childhood and the things she and her family would do. Trisha remained transfixed on Chad, giving dirty looks. He wondered if she was on to him and how much she knew.

Silence rang loudly while getting ready for bed. Christine took all day in the bathroom. Ten minutes later Chad couldn't resist her rubbing him down. She hopped on top of him, nude and emotionless. Chris tore into him like the dessert on the table. It didn't last long; she came in a matter of minutes, afterward rolling over for bed with nothing to say. Hours later Chad lay awake dumbly staring at the ceiling waiting for sleep to come. Chad's inner guilt was taking over, making him feel horrible inside. What was going on inside Chris's head?

Detective Alexander arrived in upper New York at Paulette's apartment. The sun beamed through the windows of his car as he thought about Christine's case.

Detective Alexander knocked three times, listening to the footsteps approaching. The door opened. He held one side of his suit coat back. A tall dark male stood holding the door open after calling for Paulette. As she approached she noticed the badge on the side of Detective Alexander's waist. By the look on her face, she seemed shocked. She stammered over her "Come in." He watched as the man exited her apartment in a hurry.

"What do I owe this visit, Officer …?"

"Detective Alexander." Paulette feared his presence.

"Ok, Detective, what can I help you with?"

"First of all, I need to know where you were the night of Thursday, May ninth." Paulette's heart beat fast.

"Do you have a warrant?"

"No, I'm not searching anything, just questions."

"I don't have to answer, then?"

"You will if you don't wanna be drug down to the station for suspicion, and then be interrogated for hours. We can do this the easy way or the hard way, Danielle."

"Please call me Paulette."

"But your name is Danielle?"

Paulette sighed, rolling her eyes, fighting back her anger.

Paulette/Danielle fit the description of the woman that night and all Detective Alexander needed was to pin her to the crime. For some reason, he knew she was guilty as sin. Detective Alexander scanned the living room. On the wall, he noticed several photographs bunched together, nothing unusual until spotting Danielle posing next to a black SUV in a photo. It showed only the tail end but had the same custom-made taillights. "I'm just here for questions."

"I was with my mother," she blurted out, drawing back his attention.

"Your mother?"

"Yes," she sighed, "Sally, Sally Crawford."

She owed me, damn it! Paulette thought to herself. "I had a fight with my boyfriend, you know? I needed her comfort." Detective Alexander knew the Crawford's and they never mentioned a daughter named Danielle.

"OK, Danielle, Paulette, thank for your time. We'll talk soon."

Paulette watched as he left. She tried calming down the beating of her heart, plopping down in a chair and exhaling deeply.

"I told you, you wouldn't get away with it Danielle." She

violently threw her head into the top of the chair banging harder.

"No, no, I'm pregnant and no-one, not even the damn Detective is gonna stop me from having Chad! He wants me now, and I'm gonna have him!"

"You'll never have him," the voice in her head spoke softly.

"Shut up, Danielle! Go to hell and leave me alone!" she screamed, at war with herself, digging her nails into her arms.

❦

It was a beautiful Saturday morning. Donny was in the study sitting in his swivel chair behind a big black desk, on the phone, as usual, taking care of business. Sally noticed his radiant mood, which meant no call from Chris or he had just slept with his ex-wife. Sally made sure to stick close by him most of the day, hoping he wouldn't ask about his phone. It was wrapped tightly in a shirt tucked deeply into the couch.

The doorbell rang loudly throughout the house. Sally wasn't expecting anyone unless it was Valerie. She rushed to the front before the second ring. To her surprise, someone in a suit waited outside. Sally looked around making sure Donny was nowhere in sight exhaling. Slowly she opened to see a thin middle-aged white man standing there. Her heart dropped when he flashed his badge. "Mrs. Crawford?" a lump of saliva stuck in her throat and she was slow to answer.

Something was definitely odd about this, Detective Alexander thought. *This is Donny Crawford's residence. Why were pieces of evidence leading me here? Donny never made mention of Sally? Only Valerie.*

"Yes, I'm Mrs. Crawford. Are you here to speak with Donny?"

"No, ma'am, I'm here to speak with you." Sally tensed up, her heart raced as sweat formed in her palms.

"Oh." Sally stepped onto the porch closing the door behind her. "What a surprise. What do you want with me?"

"I have a couple of questions for you."

"Me? I don't understand?"

"Your daughter's name is Danielle, right?"

"Yes." She took a short glance at the beautiful landscaping and tall fenced-in yard, snapping back to reality. Sally felt every muscle in her body weaken. "She sometimes calls herself Paulette," Sally chuckled.

"We have reason to believe she's been involved in something horrible."

"What? What has she done?"

"I don't want to get into that right now but the evidence we have has led us to her. How's the relationship between Christine and Danielle?"

"Umm … I don't … are you saying my daughter's responsible for the accident?" Sally asked hysterically. Detective Alexander's words muted out as silence rang a loudly Sally stood dumbfound, thinking. "Danielle, it can't be, she can't be!"

"Was Danielle with you the night of Thursday, May ninth between ten and eleven o'clock?" He waited for an answer.

"Mrs. Crawford?" Sally's heart raced out of control as his questions flooded in and out, making her angry.

"Mrs. Crawford. Mrs. Crawford?"

"Yes. Yes!" Sally blurted out unexpectedly behind all the confusion. Detective Alexander took Sally's word as a confession while she remained dazed.

"We will be in touch, Mrs. Crawford."

Sally looked down at her hand. She was left holding a card with his name on it. "Wait! No, Wait!" she screamed, stepping off the porch. Detective Alexander was half way down the long drive. Sally watched as his car disappeared. *What have I done?* A whirl of thoughts floated through her mind. If Danielle was the cause of the accident and Christine losing her baby, it was over for them all. Sally stood on the side of the house, crying, wishing there was a rewind button.

Hours later, Sally waited at the corner in her car. She was furious. Behind an apartment complex, she pulled underneath the canopy. Sally sat impatiently, inattentive to a black car waiting in the distance. Detective Marsh noticed a black male running toward the car, then getting in.

Judging by Sally's tear-soaked face, the news wasn't going to be good. Hysteria came out of her mouth, as she spoke about losing everything. Chad's heart was crushed; a Detective had seen at the Crawford's house. He shook his head in denial, wanting it all to go away. His anger fueled, learning Danielle might be the one responsible for his wife's accident and the loss of a child. Chad banged on the dashboard repeatedly, spewing out words of profanity and leaving a dent. Sally was wailing in tears, rocking back and forth in her seat. "She ran my wife off the road two months ago! I can't believe this shit!" Chad repeated angrily.

"I messed up, Chad!" Sally shouted.

"Messed up how?"

"Danielle obviously gave him my name as an alibi."

"You didn't!"

"I didn't know! I wasn't thinking. By the time I'd realized what I had done he was gone. What was I supposed to do, call the detective and tell him I made a mistake?"

"How the hell could you not know, bitch, you covered for her! I swear Sally that ho is going down!"

"What difference would it make, Chad? She screamed, looking him in the face. "I blanked out. Honestly, I didn't know what I was saying! Before I knew it he was gone. Besides, if Danielle gets locked up, guess what all's coming out!"

"How could you be so stupid?"

"You should have kept your dick in your pants in the first place!" Chad gave a perturbed look trying not to come undone.

"If Donny finds out all of this... I don't even wanna think about it, I'm dead, I'm so dead."

"We all are, with it being my child, and what we did. For now, it buys us a little time. Hopefully, they don't arrest her right away."

"It doesn't buy us much time." "Danielle's not the only suspect, Chad, so don't get all worked up."

"I can bet you she did this, and if she did … Chad let out a sigh. "You don't think Detective Alexander is on to us?" Sally burst into tears again.

"We need to do something now before Donny finds out!"

The Captain nodded to Detective Alexander without speaking, motioning him to sit down. He pulled up a chair, moving it so he was face-to-face. Captain Baker made it short and sweet. It made a lot of sense keeping it quiet for now. With Donny so eager, any wrong move could trigger more people to be involved who aren't. Captain Baker insisted Detective Alexander keep whatever information about his step-daughter from him.

The call came as a shock, not even an hour before leaving the Crawford's. Detective Alexander braced himself by sitting down, grabbing a pen and paper. Vernon had an airtight alibi that night since his work log showed he was there. That excluded him. He admitted to dating Paulette six months ago saying he couldn't deal with her personalities but now they were friends. The black SUV with dark tinted windows was gone. He had allowed his cousin to borrow it for a week and he had left for Texas a day and a half ago.

"It was another dead end!" He spoke aloud.

"Not so soon." Detective Marsh walked in closing the door behind and told him about Paulette.

Detective Alexander's ears were ringing after hearing

Marsh's evidence. Why the hell would Sally rush to meet Chad, Christine's husband?

Detective Alexander knew he was going to have a warrant for someone by the end of this week if not several warrants.

"There no way I'm going to jail!" Paulette screamed, trotting through her apartment. "Momma better have covered for me, I know that! That detective can't come back here!" Paulette thought back to whether or not she covered her tracks. Vernon had no idea she had made an extra set of keys to his SUV. After refusing to let her borrow it another night Paulette stole it the night he was working. Vernon owed two different vehicles, the SUV he hardly drove was always parked outside under the canopy at his apartment. "How did the detective trace this back to me?" Still, they had nothing because the license plate she was sure didn't match.

Detective Marsh rushed in Alexander's office, holding a tape in his hand, waving it in the air like a crazed psycho.

"We got her, we got her! You gotta take a look at this!" Marsh shouted, rushing over to show the tape for viewing.

"Could it be?" Alexander questioned. He waited as Marsh pressed the fast forward button to the night of the incident, pausing at a familiar face. "That's her!" shouted Alexander. She was partially hidden behind a large black hoodie not even two miles from the accident.

"What was she doing in that part of the state when she

lives in upper New York?" Marsh questioned. "Only problem is the truck with a different license plate, the custom taillights are the same."

"I noticed that. We'll have to pay another visit to Danielle, Paulette, whoever she is," Detective Alexander spoke, twirling his pen around in his hand. "Find out from Vernon who this cousin is and where he lives in Texas." Marsh nodded his head yes in return. "I have a hunch someone's been doing a lot of backstabbing. Marsh, continue your surveillance."

"Yeah, I will."

"Meanwhile, I am placing a call to the Texas police department. I have a nephew on the force there that can get answers about the SUV."

Sally grew worried, entering her husband's study. She made it a point to stop by from time to time hoping to determine his mood and if he had found out anything new. She approached carrying some coffee. A faint smile she kept plastered on her face, overhearing his idle threats. Drips of coffee fell to the floor; she tried covering by wiping them into the carpet using her big toe. In a sedated trance Sally mistakenly made a light sound with the cup. Donny's eyes cut into her like a knife. Sally backed away terrified as he resumed his conversation. Before leaving she overheard something about a private investigator and paying him top dollar. Suddenly it was hard to breathe. Sally thought about the alibi she mistakenly admitted to. Donny was meeting the investigator today. Sally rushed to the nearest corner crouching down to the floor.

Two days had passed Christine tried pulling herself together out of her slug mood. The bright sun beamed through the curtains down to the floor of the cracked blinds. Chad had already left for the day, Trisha's room was empty. Coffee lingered at the very top of the stairs. Christine took in a long sniff; instead of wine, coffee sounded better. She sat at the table, reminiscing until she heard a knock at the door. Curious, she rose from the table, heading towards the door.

"Dad." She stood shocked holding open the door. He rushed in as if upset.

"I've called you and so has your mother! What's going on with the home phone, Chris?"

Christine felt her mouth flop open, forgetting she had allowed Trisha to change the number. Now wasn't the time to explain about some girl and Chad; her dad would fire him.

"I'm sorry, Dad, I forgot, I've just been goin' through a lot of changes, you know with the baby and all. It was a last minute change. I should have told you. Sorry."

"I've been calling you whenever I have free time. I noticed you haven't called."

"That's a lie! I called you the other day, remember you had the Kingston meeting." *As hysterical as I was you mean to tell me Sally didn't tell my dad?* Christine thought to herself, finding it suspicious.

"Hysterical why? How come your name doesn't show up on my phone? I recently found my phone mysteriously tucked in my couch. I had been searching for it. You know very seldom do I use this one, only my business cell.

Christine visualized Sally tucking it between the couch after speaking with her.

That bitch! She thought. "Sally answered," Chris quickly blurted out, angry. She watched her dad's eyes widen; he quickly became agitated, searching through his phone.

"What do you mean she answered? Sally knows better than that," said Donny.

"Just that, dad, as a matter of fact, I called several times." Chris suddenly felt the need to pace the floor, wondering why Sally never told him. "That's strange, Sally never mentioned it?"

"What did you want, honey?" Chris longed to spill everything; instead, she gave a fake smile with a lie.

"Nothing, Dad, plus I forgot it was two days ago. Oh, it was probably about the number change."

"Hysterical about a number change. That makes no sense Chris." Christine turned away from her dad's questioning stare.

To avoid any more conversation she quickly grabbed a pen and paper, jotting down the number and passing it to him. He pulled her close, wrapping her in his arms with a light peck on the forehead. *I just wish Daddy could wipe all my problems away.* The moment Christine felt so secure in was cut short by him rushing off with nothing but business on his mind. "Bye, Daddy," she whispered, watching him back out of the drive. *One sure thing I am going to find out is why Sally never mentioned me calling.*

Chad was out of his office. In a moment's glance, Christine scanned his desk. There lay a pile of messages. She skimmed through a couple curiously. *Who the hell was Paulette?* Most of the messages were from her. She couldn't shake the uneasy feeling, or was it instinct? Christine could hear Chad's voice approaching, it grew louder. She was quickly taken aback, overhearing Sally's voice. Christine quickly crept over toward the door. Danielle seemed to be the topic of their conversation, something about a truck. *Gosh, I can't hear. If Donny finds out? What the hell were they talking about?* Christine tried moving closer, losing grip of her purse. The two of them were alarmed by it hitting the floor. "Damn it!"

"Christine?" Chad spoke, shocked. The look on Sally's face was priceless. *I bet they're wondering what all I had heard.* "Baby, what are you doing here?"

"Hi, Christine," Sally spoke softly, watching as Chad embraced her.

"Honey, I'm so happy to see you out and about." He smiled looking Chris up and down.

By now her blood was boiling and she was tired of damn secrets.

"How long have you been here?" Sally questioned.

The nerve of her!

"What kind of question is that, Sally?" Sally shot a

glance at Chad, confused, their nervousness reeking of guilt. Chad cleared his throat.

"I ... I just asked."

"Long enough!" Both of their eyes widened. "I have a couple of things I'd like to discuss!" Christine spoke with attitude. Sally felt her heart beat rapidly. Chad swallowed the lump in his throat. "First of all, Sally, why didn't you tell my father I called him?" Sally stammered over her words making sure the right one came out, rendering back some lame excuse about forgetting. *Ok, I'll let it slide* Christine thought to herself. "Don't allow it to happen again, Sally. If you're going to answer his phone, learn to relay messages!" Sally's mouth hung open embarrassed. Shocked, she remained silent as Chris grimed her. Christine gave a light fake peek on Chad's cheek, rudely brushing by Sally.

"Chris?"

"Not now, Chad. I have way too much on my mind, I don't need the stress!" Chad stood wondering what she meant.

"Baby ... " Chad spoke, cutting in. He backed away after seeing the look in her eyes. He knew she was pissed.

"What's this about Danielle, and my father never finding out?" Sally dropped her head remaining silent. There wasn't enough time to think of a lie. "You know her twisted daughter?"

"No. I ... I don't really, I was just giving Sally some advice."

"Some advice, huh? Well if you two are gonna play games, you're messing with the wrong woman damn it!"

"Christine, Baby, we're not!" Chad whimpered.

"You know how I feel about her. I swear if she comes around if won't be pretty! And you can tell her I said that Sally, and I damn well mean it!" Chad backed away, drawing his thoughts about everything. He was unsure what triggered Christine's mood.

"Honey, what's wrong?'

"Nothing, I've noticed you two have gotten awfully chummy-chummy!" Christine let out a sinister laugh.

"We work together," Chad spoke confused.

"You have a lot of messages from a girl named Paulette, Chad?"

I can't believe I didn't throw those away. If she finds out Danielle is Paulette she'll blow a gasket, Chad thought, keeping calm.

"Chris, it's business. What's … what's wrong?"

"Whatever, Chad!" She turned, coldly walking away.

"Christine, Christine wait, please!"

Christine was cold as ice. An arctic freeze left Sally and Chad still chiseling their way out of a dead-end. Sally placed her face into the palms of her hand, resisting the urge to cry. Chad backed his back against the wall of the hallway sighing deeply. Tension filled the air, watching as Christine tooted her nose in the air, disappearing around the corner.

Since when did double trouble become so friendly? Christine thought. She didn't have time to think about it. Trisha wanted to meet for lunch in fifteen minutes at her favorite restaurant uptown.

"I don't know what your wife knows right now, but we

have to calm Danielle now!" Chad stood dazed at the horrible thought of the two of them becoming more distant. Sally snapped her fingers bringing him back to reality.

"This is no time to feel sorry for yourself, damn it! We need to play into Danielle's hands.

"What? I can't!"

"You will if you don't want Donny to find out! He'll have your balls on a platter with blue cheese!"

"And I guess he'll have your ass on it too, feeding Valerie."

Twenty minutes had passed as Christine stood in line waiting at the grocery store. She sent a quick text to Trisha saying late, I'll tell you about it. She stared at her cart filled with several bottles of wine, salad fixings, milk, and a variety of meats, wondering what to take out. There was a voice, a voice she had heard before. Christine kept her back turned as she floated passed with some tall lanky man trailing behind. His pants sagged down past his butt, and he wore a black t-shirt. Danielle's voice made her angry. Christine was calm as can be on the surface, deliberately counting each of their moments. Her heart was pounding, making it hard to catch a beat. Christine leaned toward the display, grabbing a book, plastering her face in it. For a moment, sheer panic threatened to overwhelm her. Danielle rushed over into the express lane. The guy in the wife beater spoke with a deep and husky voice which made it carry. Some layers of numbness seemed to fall away. Christine felt another quiver of alarm overhearing him calling her Paulette. Her eyes widened with disbelief. Suddenly it was hard to breathe. Christine moved back, stumbling slightly. Her mind drifted with no ending, her feet froze to the floor unable to hear the cashier calling next.

She rushed outside. The sun shined, blinding bright, spattering its rays all around her. She felt herself breaking inside again. A couple of ladies stopped to see if she was all right. Unsure, she nodded yes quickly, walking away, shifting the tears from her eyes. Chad lied, and so did Sally. In the moment of her pain, a voice rang out. She hated to turn around. In an instant, her anger floated through every blood vessel she had.

"Keep it short." Her boyfriend spoke pushing a cart toward his car. Paulette gave a sassy look, ready to feed her dirty intentions.

"Danielle," Christine spoke, wishing she would just get the hell out of her face. A forced greeting came out. Danielle stood looking like some ghetto whore, wearing a short dress revealing all the tattoos on her arms. The bump in her stomach she continued rubbing like she cared. Chris quickly packed away her bags, slamming the trunk until hearing Danielle speak.

"How's Chad?" Christine turned slowly.

"What business is it of yours, Danielle?"

"My name is Paulette, Chris!" Her heart skipped a beat thinking back to the messages left. Her best interest was to leave, but she couldn't.

"Paulette, huh? Since when?" Christine chuckled aloud.

"That's none of your business, Chris!"

"Then why are you here talking to me, Danielle, oh I'm mean Paulette! Whatever the hell your name is!"

"I told you my name is Paulette, not whatever the hell, damn it!

"I have to go!" Christine abruptly turned away refusing to fall for her game.

"Tell your husband I said hi." Paulette stood smiling. Chris tossed her keys into her purse quickly, whisking back around.

"What the hell is that supposed to mean, Danielle?"

"Paulette!"

"You've got something to say damn it! Say it!"

"My name is Paulette!" she yelled, approaching angrily.

Christine was ready to defend herself this time. *If Danielle knows what was good for her she would step out of my space now.*

"Yes, damn it, I have something to say! Ask your husband, ask him!" she shouted.

Christine rolled her eyes. "I don't have time for pissy games. People are starting to stare and I'm not the one for attention." Danielle moved closer standing in front of her. Christine asked Danielle to move back. She refused, taking a step closer. "I don't have time for this!" Christine shouted shoving her hand up between them turning away. Danielle grabbed her hand unexpectedly, forcing her back around. Christine quickly became filled with rage. She violently yanked her hand back shoving Danielle hard against the car next to them.

Danielle grabbed a hold of Christine's hair, tugging, screaming. "I have you bitch!"

Christine slammed Danielle to the ground, losing her balance, tumbling on top of her. Outraged, she punched Danielle several times in her face, gripping strands of her hair, slamming Danielle's head against the cement. *I wanted her dead!* Christine thought, feeling a grip on her arms. She was tugged off the ground by a stranger. Christine shoved her hair from her face, breathing rapidly, ready for more. Her boyfriend had a firm grip on Danielle's arms. Christine watched as Danielle kicked and screamed, trying to break free, threatening her.

"I'm pregnant! I'm pregnant with your husband's child!" rang aloud in Chris's ears. Danielle continued making a fool of herself, cursing. "I've been screwing your husband, tramp!" she yelled, laughing aloud.

"Tramp! You sound like a complete dumb ass! You can have that low life son of a bitch! Especially since you both like screwing everything! You two are a lot alike. Yo hoe ass is with another man, bragging about fucking someone else's husband. Bitch, you're a real class act, ya head case!"

Danielle continued yelling as she was being dragged away by her friend. He attempted to place his hands over her mouth to mute her foolishness.

I might have gotten my hits and last words in, but I don't feel any better. Chris pulled her keys from her purse, quickly getting in her car. A whale of tears escaped her eyes, sorrow and pain made her tremble. She felt herself breaking into a nervous rage, unable to catch her breath. She dialed her father's number. After speaking with him, she called Trisha, hoping she'd make it here first.

Mr. Crawford was expected to be in a meeting in less than an hour. Once hearing Christine's uncontrolled crying, everything was on hold. Donny was unable to calm himself; Christine didn't make sense. Donny heard Chad's name and cheating with Sally's daughter. He rushed out of the office to his car.

Christine stared at her trembling hands. She couldn't believe she had just hit a pregnant woman. Deep inside she didn't care. Vile thoughts of killing her crossed her mind. Christine cracked open some wine, drinking large gulps and then tucking it back into one of the bags. Several people tapped on her window asking if she was okay. It all made sense now, Sally, Chad, their conversation, the look on their faces. Trisha's Honda was spotted pulling in, abruptly stopping across from her car. Christine unlocked her doors still drenched in tears. Trisha held her in her arms. Her question of "is it Chad" faded away. Christine loved that Trisha felt her pain; through it all, they could cry together and somehow end up laughing. Not this time, the wounds were too deep.

The call from Donny came to Valerie. He gave her direct orders, demanding they be done now. Valerie scrambled around, searching through the phone book, stopping at movers. Donny was willing to pay top dollar to have Sally's ass removed.

"It's over for everyone!" Paulette chuckled. "I can tell the police Christine attacked me!"

"Not with cameras and witnesses all around in broad daylight," spoke Kevin.

"Shut up, what do you know!"

"I know you screwed up a good plot! Why the hell would you do that? Do you know how much money we coulda had? You just messed up! Damn it, Paulette you don't think!"

"Christine's not going to get away with this!"

"Neither are you if you keep letting your anger control your every thought! Now you really have trouble."

Paulette lifted her head, shocked, following in the direction of his pointed finger. A whirl of confusion stormed her brain. Two detectives stood outside her door, waiting. Paulette's heart sank. Paranoia and fear kept her glued to the seat.

"This can't be, no, no!" she whispered.

"Looks like the heat is on you, Babe. Kevin waited for Paulette to exit his vehicle.

"You're not staying?"

"Hell, naw!"

Twenty minutes later Donny and Valerie arrived to pick up Christine. Valerie rushed over, hopping into Christine's car. Trisha stepped aside watching as Valerie embraced Christine. She brushed back pieces of hair from out of her face, wiping away her tears with a cloth. Donny assured Christine everything would be OK, taking the time to embrace her. Valerie thanked Trisha for showing up ahead of time. Tears escaped Chris's mouth. Donny became angry, feeling her body trembling. He pulled her closer to his chest, rubbing her back while listening to Christine's mumbling. She made mention of Danielle while slowly entering the car. Donny's eyes widened, curious.

"What about Sally's daughter?"

"She slept with my husband!"

"What? What the hell do you mean?" Donny raised his voice shouting over Christine's crying. Donny slammed on the brakes pulling over to the side of the road.

"She says she's been with my husband, Dad! She's the one who called! That's why I had the number changed. She's been threatening me!" Valerie couldn't believe it. She noticed the scrape marks on Chris's knuckles. "Did you two get into a fight?" Christine nodded her head yes. Valerie bellowed, "Donny I don't care what you do, fix it and fix it now!"

"She calls herself Paulette."

"Who?" Valerie questioned.

"Danielle, she calls herself Paulette!"

"Damn her!" Donny's mind shot through a slew of horrible thoughts. One was kicking Chad's ass. All of the messages left at the receptionist's desk dating back to months ago from a Paulette. Chad's lie was that she's a client he was working with. Donny became more inflamed thinking about the lies. "I'll fix this! I promise I'll fix everything! Go with your mother. I have some business I need to take care of." Christine nodded, rendering a hand as her dad helped walk her to the car.

"What's going on?" Valerie questioned.

"Take her to the house! I'll talk to you later!" he shouted, rushing off.

"Donny, don't do anything stupid!" Valerie screamed, watching as he ran off. She released a short prayer as he took an abrupt U-turn in the middle of the street, his tires squealing as he passed.

Donny imagined his sinister plan, anxious to get to the office. *Someone has a lot of explaining to do.* He couldn't shake the thought of Danielle, Chad and the possibility of them sleeping together.

This evening nothing seemed to be working out right. Christine was a drunken mess, ready to destroy anything in sight. *Chad and Sally were going to pay for hurting me. Danielle tried killing me over him! She made me lose my baby! I don't care what daddy does, I know the shit is about to hit the fan, mainly for Chad. Momma will take care of Sally.*

Hesitant and filled with doubt, Paulette stepped out of the car. Her friend quickly drove off. The last thing he wanted was to be involved with the police. Paulette paused in the sunlight for a moment, trying to think clearly, hoping to not look guilty. Two detectives, Marsh and Alexander, stood anxiously waiting. One was tall, masculine with broad shoulders, the other chubby with a medium build.

Paulette hesitated a moment after inviting them in, slowly moving forward. She wondered what they wanted this time. Paulette was in control, there was no sign of Danielle. Once inside each of them bombarded her with questions. She felt herself breaking mentally. The detective who spoke to her last time could see it. Stories contradicted themselves, leaving Paulette confused. Marsh hammered away like he knew she was already guilty. Her palms were sweaty, focusing seemed difficult. *Come on Paulette! Don't you dare let Danielle take over! They'll find out everything! No! No!* Alexander knew she was lying. Paulette tried remaining calm till they mentioned Vernon's SUV, questioning how she knew him. Another shady lie escaped her mouth. *I'm not losing him!* All she could think about was Chad and having him to herself.

"I told you my mother's my alibi, why are you here?"

"We're here, Danielle …"

"Paulette!" She raised her voice quickly readjusting herself. *Don't fall for their games. They're only trying to trick you.* Paulette thought.

"I'll call you what's on your birth certificate!" Marsh spoke, authoritatively. Paulette gave him a dirty look, angered. "I don't have time for games! We're seconds from pulling you into the police station on evidence proving you were at or around the area of the accident!"

Paulette took several deep breaths. *He's bluffing,* she told herself. "You have nothing on me!"

"That's where you're wrong," Detective Alexander spoke lividly. Paulette's heart beat rapidly, she quickly became worried. "You said you were with you mother, Danielle, between nine and ten. Evidence shows you driving the same SUV with a different license plate pumping gas at Mac's service station. It was around ten, the accident happened at 9:45 p.m.

Suddenly she felt a headache coming, she was sick to her stomach hearing it all. It was like looking through a shimmery piece of glass, replaying that night. The more they spoke the more her head spun out of control. She could feel what felt like little kicks hitting inside her stomach. She couldn't respond quickly enough. Detective Marsh clobbered her with questions. He promised to work 24/7 to bring the person to justice. He assured her it was only going to take one more piece of evidence. She was shivering with fear. Her mind floated to several different things he could be talking about. All that ended when Marsh mentioned a name she didn't want to hear.

"Vernon," he spoke, rubbing his thumb behind one ear. "Hmmm? He had the same last name as you, Rivers? Correct?" By now Paulette was smoldering in guilt. Detective Alexander had a smile on his face. Laughter was on the tip of his tongue. Both detectives stood at the door, smirking behind what they knew. "We will be back very soon, Paulette Danielle, or Danielle Paulette. I promise you that," Alexander spoke, exiting with Marsh.

Paulette sighed, slamming the door behind them, rushing into the bathroom. Tears stained her face, anger shot through her blood. "I'm gonna lose, not this time! Not ever! I'll show you, Danielle!"

Paulette searched for a razor. Once in her hands, she cut deep into her arms, laughing as blood dripped to the floor. "I'll finish you, Danielle!" she screamed.

"Once my nephew calls back, we got her ass!" Alexander spoke with determination.

"This is one messed up family," Marsh spoke. "I can't believe she's screwing her own cousin, Vernon Rivers."

"That's messed up."

"Do you think he's in on this?" Alexander questioned.

"No, not at all, but Vernon had to know we were going to find out their relation. Might be why he's been so cooperative and eager to get us out of his face.

⚛

Sally was looking for acceptance anywhere; having the lavish life, designer clothes, and exquisite taste was all about to run out. Word quickly spread around the office that Donny was here, and he didn't appear to be in a good mood. Chad and Sally squirmed with fear, wondering what to do. She glanced at her cell phone, slumping over with anguish. As if matters couldn't get any worse …

"Valerie texted me Chad!"

"Saying what?"

"Both of our asses are done for!" Sally paused, tearing up. "Danielle got in a fight with Christine!"

"What! Is Chris all right?"

"The question is, are we going to be all right? Donny's on his way here. I'm sure everything is out now, about Danielle, us, we are done for. My daughter just made Valerie the happiest woman."

"And what about you?"

"I know you're not talking! All this shit started with you!" Sally pointed her finger in Chad's face.

"You had her!"

"This is no time to point blame!"

"Yeah, because truth be told, we're all guilty and now we have to face the devil, Donny Crawford, himself!"

"Damn it - why! Why? Why?" Sally blurted out.

Donny paid no attention to the office environment. He was livid, asking anyone in his way where Sally and Chad were. Seth pointed in the opposite direction to borrow some time. He ran the other way, up two flights of stairs, breathing hard.

"Donny's looking for you two." A tall, dark man poked half-way in the door. He paused shortly, searching the hall. "He's pissed, big time!" Seth whispered, lightly closing the door and darting down the hallway.

Sally and Chad looked at each other, fearing the outcome. Chad aimlessly paced the floor, wiping his sweat-filled hands on his pants. Sally floated in and out of reality, trying to calm her beating heart. She felt her knees weaken when the door slammed. Donny stood there, furious. He brushed beads of sweat from his forehead, gritting his teeth together. Unsure whether to run, Chad's feet stuck to the floor. Sally had no strength to move. She swallowed several times, feeling tears falling from her eyelids.

Donny stood without a care in the world, breathing rapidly. Behind the brownness of his pupils, there was no emotion in his eyes, only coldness. Donny's approach made Chad weak. He stumbled backward, avoiding eye contact as Donny's toes met his. Sally squirmed into a corner, out of the way. In a matter of seconds, Chad's back smashed against the desk. Donny's grip tightened around his neck.

All the wrong he had done to Christine floated through Chad's mind.

"You son of a bitch! I know everything!" Donny's cold eyes ripped away at Chad's soul. His grip tightened; it was hard to breathe.

"Donny, please!" Sally begged.

"Shut up, bitch!" He pointed. Chaos erupted in a blink of an eye. Donny's violently swept his across the desk, throwing everything onto the floor. The computer monitor hung by the cord dangling off the side of his desk. Donny reached for Chad and threw his body over the desk where he landed on the floor. Chad's failed attempt to get away had him back on the floor, with Donny hovering over him. His foot remained pressed on Chad's chest, holding him down. The pressure made it hard to breathe. Chad didn't dare lay a hand on him or give a dirty look.

"You're outta my daughter's life, damn it! You hear me, jackass? I don't wanna see you or hear your name. If so, I swear I'll kill you!" Chad nodded, wiping blood from his face with his sleeve. Angrily, Donny turned toward Sally. She stood numb, sobbing, trembling. "You knew about your daughter screwing my daughter's husband!" Donny screamed.

"No, Donny, please!" Sally shook her head no, backing as far as she could before Donny grabbed her violently by the neck, backing her into a wall. "Please!"

Karen, the receptionist, stood outside the door, carefully taking in an earful. She was shocked by it all. She disappeared, with enough to spread around the office.

"That whore daughter of yours screwed my daughter's husband! Did you know this, damn it?" Sally refused to answer, pleading for her life, feeling Donny's hand tighten around her neck. "I want all of your shit outta my house tonight, bitch! I'm done with you and that whore daughter of yours!"

"Please, Donny, I need you, don't leave me, please!" Sally's tears were endless. "Donny, let go," she begged.

"Valerie's packing your shit as we speak! I don't care where the hell you two go, but don't bring your asses back to my business or home or I swear you'll have hell to deal with!"

"You don't understand! Please." Sally face contorted with anguish, falling to her knees. Donny rendered a detestable look, and then lifted a brow, laughing, as if the situation was comical.

"You're both fired!" He screamed. "I want all your shit cleaned out of my offices today!"

Inquiring ears and eyes wanted to know more about why Mr. Crawford was in such an uproar. Word had spread quickly. Karen sent texts to all she knew at her desk, updating them about Donny's outrage regarding Sally and Chad.

※

Once the ruckus died down, Seth returned, asking every now and again what happened as he helped Chad pack his things in a box while a security guard waited. Chad refused to discuss it, embarrassed that everyone might soon learn about this. Little did he know, word had already leaked.

Seth continued prying; from the looks of it, he knew Mr. Crawford had whipped Chad's butt. Why was still a partial mystery to the curious minds of those who hadn't heard the story.

Vile thoughts of Danielle crossed Chad's mind. He knew she had said something. He couldn't wait to get out of there to give her a piece of his mind. Facing the worst wasn't over yet: there was Christine and the fight she just had with Danielle. Chad sighed deeply, focusing on the pain in his heart. Everything he had lost was over some whore. A tear fell as he turned to take his last look out the window. *I had it all, and I messed up. How could I be so stupid?* Chad bowed his head, ashamed. He made sure to take the back way out of the office to avoid the rush of questions he knew everyone wanted answers to.

❧

Paulette wrapped her wounds in bandages, slightly looking at the reflection in the mirror. The thing deep inside she hated about herself called for peace. Paulette was unwilling.

❧

Sally hung her head in shame, watching as two movers packed and loaded her things. Valerie stood griming, a devilish smile etched her face as she crowded the door.

I had every right to go in and get my things. For some reason, I couldn't move. The lavish life was gone. She and Donny had been married for four years. Sally stared at everything for the last time, crying. Valerie slowly made her approach. Her long black hair flowed behind; in her eyes, she carried the look of revenge. Sally grabbed her cheek from Valerie's slap that came without warning. Sally rubbed it slowly until the stinging went away. Valerie held her intimidating stance, griming Sally. She made sure to publicize Sally's dirty laundry, sharing it with the movers as they loaded her things. It all seemed quite comical to them as they laughed. "This is what you wanted all along, Valerie! You have him now!" Valerie turned with hostility brewing.

"Tramp, I had Donny all along, in your bed, in your home, whenever I wanted and don't you forget that!" Sally was appalled. As Donny walked by, delegating what the movers needed to remove, Sally tried calming her kindling flame. She realized Valerie didn't matter, she was losing Donny.

❧

It was about 10:00 p.m. A strange car sped up the drive. Sally stood, blinded by the headlights, backing away. The car suddenly stopped in front of her. Danielle staggered her away out of the open door. Sally exhaled deeply; anger shot through her like a rocket. Danielle's sinister laugh caught Sally's and the movers' attention. Thank God Donny and Valerie were in the house with Christine. Danielle marched up to her mother, cursing, and swearing, calling her a thousand names. Danielle spewed her hatred like a time bomb that had exploded into a million disturbed pieces. Sally fought to shove Danielle back into her car.

"That's what you get mother, all of you! Yes, I tricked Christine's husband into sleeping with me. He had no idea Christine and I were step-sisters! I was getting back at you and her! You always treated her better than me, damn it! Like she was some freakin' princess! You ignored your own daughter, Momma! Even when I told you about father raping me when I was ten, you never listened! All you did was tell me to shut up and stop lying! How could you? I had to destroy you and everyone around you!" Danielle laughed aloud. "I stole Chad's semen out of the condom we had just used to have sex! I made sure Christine lost her baby, there was no way she was having Chad's baby!"

Sally couldn't believe everything Danielle was saying. She had destroyed everything. "This is your fault, mother! It's all because of you! Do you like what you've sown, a rotten seed that's spewing venom to everyone? I was raped twice, Mother! By your husband and ex-boyfriend! You had to have known something was wrong with me back then. Remember grade school when Mrs. Price came and spoke with you? No. No, you were too self-absorbed in your fucked-up relationships to pay attention, me being fondled by your ex-boyfriend's son at nine. All of them hurt me and you did nothing! I grew to hate you, especially after telling you and you ignoring me! Now it's time for Donny to know that you fucked Christine's husband like I did." Paulette let out a sinister laugh. "Yes, Donny, my mother screwed your daughter's husband." Laughter escaped her mouth. "Who did I learn this behavior from? You, Mother! You!"

Sally was furious and finished listening to Danielle's

babbling; it had all gone too far. Sally grabbed Danielle by the throat, tightly squeezing watching her lips turn blue. She thought about everything, bursting into tears. Danielle fought to free herself, kicking and clawing her mother's fingers away until her grip loosened. *Not now, not now with all these people watching,* she told herself. Thank God the movers had gone back inside.

"You get the hell outta here, you crazy bitch before I kill you myself!"

Danielle's body fell to the ground. She coughed her way back to breathing normally. Sally walked away, numb. Danielle picked herself up and got into her car.

My hands still trembled from almost killing her. Embarrassed, Sally waited for them to finish packing her things. Donny wouldn't even allow her back in the house. Valerie assured Sally all her things would be packed up. Everyone was inside. She sat alone in her car, humiliated and heartbroken, wondering what she was going to do next. *It isn't over just yet, Danielle.* Sally expressed her anger, wiping away her tears.

❧

No matter how many times Chad apologized to his wife, it didn't accomplish a thing. It didn't matter she didn't believe him. Chad was forced to pack some things and was told to get out of the house by the weekend. She couldn't stand the sight of him and neither could he, for that matter. There was no coming to agreements with anything. Trisha stood like a guard dog, barking at him all through the house on how fucked up he was. She made sure to take the key from the key ring before he left. The slam of the door still echoed. His life was shattered into pieces.

Chad moved back in temporarily with his best friend William. *He owes me,* Chad thought, *he was the one who hooked me up with that tramp.* That night Chad developed a plan. Danielle was gonna pay for what she had done and he was going to make damn sure of it.

❧

It was the biggest break yet in the case. Thomas Kindle, Vernon's cousin, was pulled over twenty minutes ago. Officer Kent caught him speeding fifteen miles over the speed limit, heading back into town. Thomas had tried giving a fake name along with a fake I.D which didn't pass. With his arrest and the search of the vehicle, they discovered a license plate wrapped tightly in a shirt. Thomas swore he didn't have anything to do with it, saying he never knew it was there. Once the license was run, it turned out to belong to the elderly couple who had reported it stolen a while back. Which only proves Paulette/Danielle is lying.

❧

It was cold and dark. The last thing Danielle remembered hearing were several faint voices arguing in the background. The unknown shadows brought terror to her heart. Uncertainty slowly unmasked itself. "What are you doing, following me?" The two masked faces silently forced themselves on Danielle, shoving her into her apartment. "Get out! Get out of my apar….." The dark glove muffled her yelling as she fought, landing on the floor. "You can't do this to me, you can't do this to me!" The blow to her head sent her spiraling. The dark shadowy figures stood over her, making sure it was the last time she spoke. Her body fell forward, slamming against the floor. All Danielle knew was she was stuck several times from behind with a blunt force object. She fought to move her arms, but couldn't. She was weak. A pool of wetness surrounded the back of her head. She hoped it was water. The smell of death was fresh in the air. She lay staring up at two blurred masked people. "Momma? Chad? Danielle can't win. Paulette … Paule .. w … won!" she cried softly, searching for more names of people who hated her. Danielle's eyelids quickly floated to the back of her head. The coldness took moments to travel across her body, shivering, taking her last breath. Paulette never gave a second thought to what she had done.

❧

It was a chilly night. The moon slowly crept from behind the dark, cloudy skies, appearing as a waxing crescent shadowed by darkness. Detectives Marsh and Alexander sped through the streets, sirens blaring, after hearing the dispatch report of a possible 240 at an address they knew. Marsh looked at Alexander with concern. Deep in their hearts, they knew. Their attempt to make an arrest was shattered. NYPD, along with the paramedics, arrived. A frantic call from a neighbor had overheard the yelling and screaming. It seemed to go on for hours: people trafficking, loud noises and banging at the door never ceased. People from the neighborhood gathered around, curious to see what happened. The apartment door was open to Danielle's place. Detectives Marsh and Alexander entered the crime scene. Marsh's feet stopped at a pool of blood. His eyes followed the bright red stains to the kitchen as he walked slowly. The paramedics rushed by Marsh. One leaned over in search for a pulse. The woman paramedic noticed a lump on her stomach and realized she was pregnant. She was instantly heartsick, wondering who would do this. Quickly she knelt down by the woman's stomach, hoping to feel something. Something wasn't right. She lifted her shirt, surprised. Danielle's body lay in a pool of blood. Alexander shook his head, shocked. Surveying the bloodstains on the walls and countertop, it appeared someone had dragged Danielle here to finish the job. There was no sign of forced entry or any footprints.

"Is she pregnant?" Marsh blurted out.

"No!" The female paramedic spoke.

"What do you mean no?" Marsh and Alexander both questioned confused.

The woman chuckled. "Oh, you mean this?" She pulled out a fake silicone padded belly from around Danielle's stomach.

"My gosh, this girl had a million tricks under her sleeve," Marsh spoke.

"Yeah, well, seeing the marks on her arms, she was obviously abusing herself quite often."

"How do you know that?" Alexander questioned.

"They're suicide marks," Marsh spoke. "Most cases of self-abuse you can tell by their marks."

"I guess our 240 has just been upgraded to an 187, homicide," Alexander replied shaking his head confused.

"Damn it! We were just on our way to arrest her! So much for that! Now we are investigating an entirely different case."

⌘

From one piece of evidence to the next, Detective Marsh studied what he thought was credible. He read over several disturbing facts in Danielle's diary. She was obviously suffering from some mental disorder. Paulette stressed over and over again how much she hated herself, Danielle. Marsh carefully glanced over each word, jotting down names. Chad's was mentioned an awful lot throughout and her love for him. As Marsh continued reading, he soon realized there were a lot of people who had motives to want to kill Danielle.

⌘

The detectives were thrown for a loop again. This time, Detective Alexander made sure he was the first to arrive to speak with Sally. He stood in front of the large glass doors. Uncertain but curious, he rang the doorbell.

"Detective Alexander?" Donny spoke curiously, shoving a piece of toast in his mouth. Donny extended his hand to greet him. Alexander rendered his hand with a smile.

"Mr. Crawford. I didn't expect to see you."

"I do live here. Is this about the case? Come on in."

"Actually, Donny, it's not. I really need to speak with your wife, Sally. The two of you, to be exact."

Donny lowered his head saying the first thing on his mind. "She's not here, I'm sorry."

"When will she be back? It's urgent."

"She won't."

"Huh? I don't understand. Mr. Crawford, I'm not one for pulling teeth."

"I had her and all her things moved out last night! What's this about anyway?"

"Moved out? So let me get this right - she no longer lives here?" Donny obviously knew about Chad.

"No! She and that damn daughter of hers have caused enough problems! I don't care to see either of 'em again!" Donny exploded.

"You won't, at least not one of them." Donny's eyes widened, confused. Detective Alexander scrambled around searching for the right words.

"What the hell is that supposed to mean?"

"Mr. Crawford, I'm sorry to tell you, Danielle was found dead in her apartment early this morning." Donny crunched his eyebrows together taking in a deep breath. He looked in the opposite direction, toward the stairs.

"What do you mean? She's dead? How?"

"That's a long story. I need to speak with her mother."

Donny sighed. "I can give you her number. I don't know where she's at." Donny reached into his pocket, pulling out his cell phone. "I don't believe this." He rattled off the number making sure Detective Alexander got it. "I don't know what to say, especially after almost losing my daughter. It's horrible."

"That's another thing I wanted to talk to you about."

"Yeah, what is it?"

"We were on our way to arrest Danielle."

"What? Why?"

"We're pretty sure Danielle's the one responsible for Christine's accident." Donny's heart quickened; agitated he paced the floor.

"She tried to kill my baby over that bastard!"

"Just what's that supposed to mean, Donny?" Alexander questioned, curious about his outburst.

"That damn Danielle, she's been harassing my daughter, calling, claiming she's sleeping with Christine's husband! And now she's pregnant." Donny spoke as if Danielle was still alive. The list of suspects was growing. "She's pregnant and my daughter lost her baby! That's bullshit!"

"I'm so sorry, Donny, but things aren't always what they seem. Danielle wasn't pregnant at all; she wasn't carrying a child." Donny placed his hand over his forehead confused. "She was wearing something that made her appear to be pregnant."

"I don't believe this!"

Christine stood at the top of the stairs, listening. The more Detective Alexander spoke, the angrier she became.

"If you don't mind me asking, Donny, where you were last night?"

"Me?" Donny pointed his finger at his chest. He uttered

a short laugh. "You don't think I had anything to do with Danielle?"

"It's just a question, you can answer, or you can wait, but eventually I'm sure one of us will get the chance to question you soon."

"I have nothing to hide. I was asleep outside by the pool. I remember Valerie woke me up shortly after eleven."

"Valerie?"

"Yeah. My ex-wife."

"About what time did you go outside?"

"I ... I guess twelve? Look, I had a few drinks, took a swim, drank some more. I guess I must have passed out."

"Anyone else sees you?"

"Well, yeah, Rita and Marie, our maids. Hell, Rita served me my drinks."

"Can I speak with the two of them?"

"Sure, come on in," Donny called each maid. Two short Hispanic ladies approached. Alexander questioned them individually. Each of their stories remained consistent.

"Okay, Donny, thanks for your cooperation." Detective Alexander quickly crossed Donny off the list of suspects.

❦

Speaking to Sally didn't go too well. She showed up at the police station causing a scene by her fussy behavior. She insisted the detectives arrest Donny and Valarie on her suspicions of them murdering her daughter. Her display of mixed emotions made it hard to identify how she was feeling. One minute she sobbed, the next she sat staring into space, followed by another outburst of tears. Sally seemed agitated by all the questioning and where she was that night. She wondered how dare they ask such things after losing her daughter. Little did she know Danielle's diary stated over and over how much she hated her mother and wished she was dead.

"Did you know that Danielle stated in her diary that she was allegedly molested twice?" Sally's eyes widened. An unexpected laughter bellowed from her mouth. Both detectives looked confused.

"One thing you don't know about Danielle is her mental illness and she's a habitual liar and it doesn't excuse what she did!"

"Are you speaking of what she did to you?"

"Everyone!"

You just lost a child and this is the remorse you show? Alexander thought to himself. "What kind of mental illness did Miss Rivers suffer from?"

"Schizophrenia. She was diagnosed at ten. We did counseling for three years, she was medicated and doing fine during that time. Things shifted quickly; she refused to take her meds … it got horrible between us. Her behavior was irate and unruly. When she became sexually active it changed for the worst."

"Did you ever have Danielle tested for sexual abuse?"

"No. Danielle lied and cheated to get whatever she wanted! What don't you understand?"

"What if she was? She stated that her father …"

"Please!" Sally interrupted, throwing up her hand. "I don't want to hear this shit!"

"Well, it needs to be talked about."

"For what? To make me look bad?"

"You just lost your daughter and you're still making this about you!" Detective Marsh stood shaking his head. "Did you know that your daughter was cutting herself?"

"I didn't mean it that way and nothing shocks me anymore. You really don't know Danielle! I love her but she was out of control."

"Maybe you should have paid more attention to Danielle. Do you think perhaps she was acting out?"

"You always act out being schizophrenic!"

"Did you know she was having an affair with a Chad Stone, Christine's husband?"

"No, I did not!"

"She claimed to be pregnant by him, she never told you this?"

"I said no! Shouldn't you two again be arresting the Crawford's for murder?" Sally hopped up, pissed.

"As soon as we gather the information needed, but right now we're trying to piece together a case and we have no evidence to make such arrest," Alexander spoke.

"Why the hell not? Oh, let me guess: because of his damn money!"

"Did you not hear what I just said? We don't have enough evidence." Alexander felt angry.

"Well, get your shit together then!"

Sally expressed her anger in so many words before grabbing her purse and storming out of the police station.

"Is it a wonder why the daughter is crazy seeing how the mother's acting out?" Alexander spoke, exhaling.

"I thought I'd seen it all," Marsh spoke, watching her walk out of the police station. "One thing right about Danielle's diary, she was right about her mother's selfishness," Alexander said.

Once outside, Sally took a deep breath soaking in tears staring up into the sky. Detective Alexander stood watching from the window. Sally pulled out her cell phone, one hand wiping away tears. It was obvious by her hand gestures she was yelling at someone as she walked to her car. Sally sat for at least fifteen minutes, chatting with the unknown person. Her alibi that night was a little leaky. Sally claimed she stayed at a hotel all night. Only the receptionist saw her, once when she checked in.

Detective Alexander made sure to keep Sally, Danielle's mother, as the prime suspect. Something about her didn't feel right. Now it was time to question Chad Stone.

⟨∞⟩

I can't believe my daughter is dead. It was the last thing I expected to hear the detective say Christine and Danielle being involved in her accident and the loss of her baby. How could someone fake a pregnancy? She lied about everything! The pain slowly crept into her heart. Visions of Danielle's childhood floated in and out. Sally hated the person, rethinking her childhood. She couldn't bring herself to feel the pain for too long. Looking back over her own childhood she realized she was a lot like her own mother. She hated the person she had become but couldn't find it in her heart to take the blame. She had always put a man before Danielle to get what she wanted. Her passing haunted Sally day in and day out, night sweats and visions of her face pressed against her thoughts. Dreams of fire, of screams, replayed. Her dreams were the only thing piercing her heart with pain. Danielle was her only child! *Now I have nothing!*

Danielle's funeral was lonely and hard. Only a handful of people came to show their condolences. Mostly everyone hated her since she had left a bad taste in everyone's mouth, lying, cheating, stealing, sleeping around with everyone. *I hated to say this but the reoccurring dreams I'm having are screams of her in hell and the constant torment of her burning for eternity.*

Sally stumbled across a notebook in Danielle's apartment. Once she arrived home, she read it. More of the truth came out reading over a journal Danielle kept at her leisure. Her confession was as plain as day about Chad.

"He approached me, wearing a suit; his voice went straight to my heart. He ordered me another drink, giving his name, Chad. I smiled with delight, wanting every inch of him. We laughed and drank. Chad continued staring at my thighs, licking his lips. He was turned on and so was I. We danced, like close grinding, like we had known each other for years. He continued telling me how beautiful I was. Chad suggested we go somewhere quiet, like my place. I was all in. We were in a

hurry, unable to keep our hands off each other. He followed behind me to my apartment. The two of us rushed upstairs into my apartment. I loved the attention he showed me. Chad was affectionate. He undressed me slowly, unlike the rest of the creeps, kissing me from head to toe. My body trembled with passion. He stood before me, nicely built, with rippled abs … could this be heaven? Erect and ready, I leaned forward, softly stroking him. The night ended in both hard-core sex and heartache. He told me either he was married or had a girl-friend who couldn't give him what I could. Chad talked about how much he enjoyed himself, lightly kissing me. There was that sudden look on his face. He jumped up, saying he needed to leave. I begged him to stay but Chad refused, rushing to put on his clothes. He kissed me on the cheek, promising to meet again soon.

We have continued meeting for sex on a regular basis. I have him where I want him! We text each other sex messages and photos on days we can't meet. My love is growing for him … three weeks in. Chad is giving me everything I need and money on the side.

Things have changed … he has become distant, hard to reach. I'm not letting this one slip away. Chad arrived tonight when he was finally free. Full bliss began at the door. Chad pulled out a condom. I hated that he used them. My screams of lust ended the thought. Chad opened every door to my heart, pounding harder. I watched him remove his condom, tossing it into the trash. He checked the time, rushing into the bathroom. It wasn't a surprise that he was leaving again. My anger shot from zero to twenty. I reached over, grabbing his condom. I stuck the condom inside me with the end open, squeezing his liquids inside me. I'm pregnant! I'm pregnant! I'm the only one for him!

Heart shattered. Chad's married. I found out when I followed him home. She walked out and my mouth hit the ground. It was the one person I hated besides my own mother ... Christine Crawford. I hate that bitch! Damn goody two shoes!

Disappointment. I failed my pregnancy test! Damn it! I need him again without protection! I begged repeatedly, Chad refused ... is he on to me? I need to get pregnant now!

My doctor has said it wouldn't be a good idea ... she has been calling me daily, asking me to come into the office ... No! I am doing this my way!

Sally flipped through more pages of the journal.

Chad is spending more time with her! I hated it! He was weak, my plot worked after ramming her.

I showed up at their home unannounced. Chad opened the door, excited to see me. He told me how much he missed me. We rushed into foreplay. He pulled out a condom. I begged him just this time not to use it. He refused, slipping it on. Chad insisted I take it or leave it. I took it just to have something to rub in Chris's face, maybe he'd leave the condom lying around. Three minutes later, I watched Chad disappear into another room. He had obviously removed the condom. I heard the toilet flush. Angry, I stole a pair of gold earrings from the table. I begged him to leave Chris. Chad forced me out of the house. I searched around on the internet how to fake a pregnancy. There it was—a silicone belly. It would work perfectly.

My bitch of a so-called mother! She never backs me, only cares about money and men! Always has the reflection of me in mirror image and she's too stupid to see it. Denial!

Sally flipped back through several more pages, refusing to read any further about Chad and the many pages that Danielle wrote about hating her mother. She stopped at the night of the accident. Danielle had rammed Christine's car from backside as she was turning the corner. Sally continued reading.

I stole Vernon's truck without him knowing. I waited outside Chris's job, counting down the minutes for her to leave. I laughed as I watched that bitch's car flip. I thought for sure she was dead. I ran up to see, afraid to look down. I could hear her crying for help … she wasn't dead. I stood for a moment thinking of ways to kill her … nothing came to mind plus I needed to get out of there before someone showed up.

Sally noticed the dates in the book. Some were dated years back. Different numbers were written in large print at the top of some pages, seven, ten, thirteen, fourteen, fifteen, sixteen and seventeen. The page written with a number seven at the top was more like a child's writing. This obviously meant Danielle's age at the top of the page was age seven.

Sally struggled to read Danielle's handwriting. Her mind reflected back to her first husband. She smiled softly, stroking her hand over the top page, gazing into space. Sally remembered falling so in love she would do anything for him. Of course, momma didn't approve. It was always "He's too old and wiser." *Momma always said I was just a pretty face and sexy.* Her warnings of John wanting younger girls went in one ear and out the other. John always gave money after sex.

Sally remembered dinner at her mother's as a teen. Johnny stood up and proposed. She was shocked, but more so overjoyed. Momma had a distasteful look on her face that could kill someone dead. Only 16 and Johnny age 20, she knew it was a clear and present dangerous relationship. Momma yelled out, "Don't ever have children, especially a girl!", storming out of the room angry. Sally was hurt. Johnny whispered," I love you, and you're the only girl for me." Dinner hadn't even been touched but Johnny had other things on his mind. He continued whispering how much he loved her, sliding his fingers between her legs.

"Not now," she had responded as his fingers slide deeper and her legs opened wider, allowing him in. He placed her hand on his lap. His hardened flesh poking through his pants turned her on even more. She undid his pants, unconcerned where her momma was, sliding her hand, searching for his manhood. Her hand slid up and down his shaft, fast and slow. He wanted more.

And then Momma had walked in, asking where Sally was. He replied, "In the bathroom," while cutting a piece of his steak. Sally continued sucking him, down underneath the table. Her momma's feet disappeared as Sally was still giving what he wanted. She could hear momma yelling, "She's not in there." Johnny lifted the table cloth to watch, both of his hands gripping Sally's head, working her faster. Her momma unexpectedly returned. Sally opened her eye after releasing his wetness in a napkin on his lap. Her momma's mouth hung open, disappointment raging inside. Sally was lost for words and so was Johnny. Sally hopped up quickly, Johnny did up his pants.

"Whore, whore, you whore!" momma screamed at the top of her lungs. Her momma grabbed Sally, tugging her hair, knocking her to the floor.

She landed on top with a firm grip, banging Sally's head on the floor. "Nasty whore, in my home!" Johnny grabbed Sally's momma, yanking her off her. She kicked and screamed at everything in sight, yelling out perverse words. "Get out, get outta my damn house now!"

Sally snapped back to reality, glancing back down at the book. "Seven years old," she whispered, swallowing the lump in her throat.

Who do I tell? So confused, help. Daddy was in my room again while Momma was in the kitchen. It was quick and painful just like the other times. I'm so confused. I need to tell someone. Daddy said if I ever breathe a word I was going to pay. I was given a spankin just to test the waters.

Again, this time in the backyard. He pulled me away from Jill into the garage. All I thought about was playing with Jill, envisioning myself as someone else again. Daddy made me wipe my tears before heading back, if not he'd spank me.

Sally's mouth fell open. The heart-wrenching truth tore through her mind. *She wrote it all down and I never believed her. No, it can't be, Danielle's lying.*

15 years old. I was more experienced with sex than any girls my age. I needed to tell, but who? I can't deal with this anymore! Momma hates me ... she hates me! I tried but momma yelled, quickly raising her hand to hit me, she called me a liar. I told her I wasn't, she slapped me and told me to shut up. I hate her! I was telling the truth, what the hell ... why not lie?? Fuck her!

Momma and I have become really distant. I can't stand the sight of her. The two of them laughing as if damn in love ... bastard! Danielle is a thing of the past. I hate her, she's weak, lets men run all over her. I need to be stronger! Paulette got what she wanted.

I hate you, Sally!

I hate you, Sally!
I hate you and that fucked up husband of yours!

Another day, momma never questioned about my busted lip. She barely looked at me. She seemed ashamed. I wanted to tell her daddy punched me in the lip and raped me.

The argument turned really messy between momma and I. Paulette's in control and I love it. Momma noticed the change. She asked what had gotten into me. If only you knew, bitch. She told daddy. They argued for hours about my disobedience.

The sneaking out at night and sometimes not returning for days. Daddy was pissed. Just as I expected late at night he came again, shutting the door behind him. While making me undress I quickly placed myself somewhere else. Paulette's here. He asked if I was seeing someone else. I lied. I'd been seeing 3 different boys, some on the same day. I didn't want him to feel special like he was the only one getting it. Fucking asshole slapped me after making me give oral sex. He said his dick was burning. I kinda thought it was funny. Come to find out I had chlamydia. He beat the hell out of me. He knew of the boys and threatened to kill each one of them.

Another day. Daddy's strong hand gripped tightly around my neck. He straddled over my nude body tightening his grip. Imam tell was the wrong choice of words. He made me pay sexually.

I hate you, Danielle!

I hate you, Danielle!

You weak Bitch I hate you!

I think I'll be Tonya tonight when he comes in.

Sally flipped through scanning in disappointment. *I can't read this anymore,* Sally said to herself. She slammed the book shut, gazing into space.

✧

The pain sunk in, deeper and deeper, as she thought about the past. She had spent most of her time in church learning about Jesus, and accepting the Lord as her savior as a pre-teen. *Things turned horrible and confusing when the pastor invited me into his office. I hate going back to that place in time! I was too young to know better. I did what he wanted sexually. My grandma would never believe me, so I couldn't tell her the truth. Grandmother looked up to that man and his wife. I was only ten.* The same age the sexual abuse happened to Danielle as a kid. She didn't want to believe Danielle was going through the same thing, so shutting out the world was best—or at least so she thought. *To be honest, I don't know whether to cry or be happy with the horrible destructive path Danielle left behind. My marriage is over, my security is gone! Danielle wasn't going to be causing any more pain, not ever! It's a selfish way of thinking, but Danielle is not going to wind up ruining my life! There's an-other man out there somewhere who would love to have a*

*woman like me. If it's the last thing I do, I will find him! She
won't ruin my life from the grave!*

❧

Sally had expected to receive a call from Donny to express his sympathy for her loss. Unfortunately, it never happened. Donny finding her and sending divorce papers was
the only communication, and that was by his attorney. The
small lump sum of money Donny provided helped Sally get
into her own apartment. She used everything of Danielle's
to refurnish her new home. Due to the pre-nup, Donny had
tricked her into signing, Sally had no alimony. She remembered being tipsy and that she and Donny had just made
love. Afterward, he asked for her signature on a few papers.
He promised to explain in the morning but never did. She
didn't remember a thing.

She had filled to fight it in court but soon got death
threats, and with the murder of her daughter, she didn't
bother provoking Donny or persuading her attorney about
the issue. She knew Donny and Valerie would drag her ass
through the mud until she came crawling out, covered in
shame, and broke. She was defenseless to deal with people
with that type of power. She and Chad never spoke again
after telling him that her daughter was dead. He avoided
phone calls and eventually changed his cell number. Could
she blame him? She didn't care how much he blamed her,
he was at fault too. For now, Sally decided that her search
for someone well-off was high on her priority list of things
needed now.

⌘

Whoever murdered Danielle made sure to wipe clean any evidence that was left behind. CSI and the local detectives were unable to find a single fingerprint in or out of the kitchen. It was like someone flew out of the sky, landed outside the window and climbed in. So unrealistic, not even a shoe print was left. Whoever did this had the master plan to not get caught. Without a murder weapon, it made figuring out the case even more impossible.

Forensics showed Danielle was murdered by several blunt forces to the head. In the back was a large hole from which she obviously bled to death, which meant she might not have seen her attacker. Most disturbing were the scars all over her body. She had semi-open cuts as well as old ones that must have been from years ago. She also had recent cuts on or around her arms and breast area.

⌘

Nearly five months had passed by. Not a single witness for the case of Danielle Rivers had appeared. Christine claimed to have been with her mother. Valerie kept her at the house, consoling her pain. Donny's maid, Rita, said they never left the room and the last time she saw Christine was 12:01 a.m. where she was fast asleep in her old room. Chad Stone had an air-tight alibi; cameras showed him at Lucky's until 3 in the morning, drinking with some friends. After ten drinks he was drunk and unable to drive anywhere. His friend William drove him home.

❦

After six months, the detectives were still at a dead end. Not a piece of fabric or fiber, not even a hair follicle could place anyone with the murder. Her case had unfortunately gone cold.

❦

I had finally gotten what I tried so hard for. Christine stood rubbing her belly, looking at herself in the mirror. A smile crept across her face. She wished it didn't have to be this way: six months pregnant and no husband. Donny had made sure she quickly got a divorce. A part of her was so happy. Christine was having her first child, after all, she had been through. After dealing with Chad's bull, she had unfortunately given up on men. She and Trisha were live-in lovers for only a short time. Christine loved her and Trisha proved she'd do anything for Christine. Trisha had been with women before, but it was Christine's first. She thought after all the alcohol and pain, it helped to induce a sexual relationship with her. She didn't dare tell her parents about their love affair, afraid of the ridicule. Her daddy would blow a fuse. He was already lining up Mr. Right.

It didn't last long between them. When sobering up, Christine really had a chance to focus, and this wasn't the lifestyle she wanted her child around. It was against everything she believed in but had used it as a way to escape pain. Trisha took it hard. She even threatened to tell the police everything because of their breakup. She must have forgotten that she played a bigger part in it all. Trisha calmed down once she came to her senses, apologizing. Christine still loved her as a friend, but her love was more toward Chad. She couldn't take him back, even with all the flowers and begging. He had lied and cheated with some whore that killed their first baby! She couldn't forgive him now, but she wanted him back. Her pride was too strong and there was no way. She had other things to worry about.

For now all, she could ask for daily is repentance. Her anger, resentment, and bitterness, along with many other demons, were her only way out for now. She prayed to have all her sins thrown in the sea of forgiveness. With the case gone cold, it gave her a sense of relief. She would die to live with this horrible secret. There's nothing like getting away with a crime because nobody would ever think Daddy's little girl was capable of doing something like that. It's now the end of Christine's old life and the start of a new one.

⎯⎯⎯

Years had gone by, Jordan was now three and into everything. Every time she looked into his eyes, her focus went right to Chad. His curly afro matched Chad's, along with his big dark brown eyes. They had been divorced for three and half years now and Christine was still madly in love with him. They had a weekend agreement for Jordan to stay with his daddy until Monday, provided he was in a stable church home and no other woman around their son. Chad did everything to abide by her rules, or so she had thought.

She arrived early to pick up their son due to a sudden

death in the family. She stood at the door, knocking until her knuckles ached, waiting for Chad to open the door. She had called earlier and he had said Jordan would be ready. She banged on the door until it swung open.

"Can you please stop banging on the goddamn door?" Her heart fell to her feet, taking in several deep breaths. She had beautiful light brown skin with a weave straight to her butt, but shockingly a tanned white girl. Christine watched as she flung her hair around, questioning who she was with an attitude. She was curvy in all the right places with perky breasts peeking through her see-through gown.

"I'm Christine." A whisper of pain came from her mouth.

"What, who?"

"Christine! Jordan's mom!" She couldn't let this woman intimidate her. The strength in her voice came from nowhere. "I'm Jordan's mother! Where is my son?"

"I'm coming, Christine!" Chad yelled, scurrying behind the door. Her devious smile told it all as Christine tried to murder Tamara with her stare. "Sorry, I lost track of time, Chris."

Chad appeared, lightly shoving the girl out of the way. Christine watched as they mumbled back and forth, something about "you better tell her." She couldn't help but stare at his nicely built chest. Her mind shot straight to them in the bedroom in a heated moment.

"I'm sorry, I was in the restroom and didn't hear the doorbell." Christine knew that was a lie as she stepped out of the heated moment and back to reality. "Jordan, come on, your mom's here." Chad was unable to make eye contact with the evil glare she was giving him. Calmness came seeing Jordan's big brown eyes, but anger shot from one to ten, seeing his hair braided to the back. "Are those braids in my child's hair?" She knew Chad couldn't braid, and what the hell was this woman doing touching her child! She ripped Jordan from Chad's arms, kissing his cheeks, as he burst into laughter, all the while trying to conceal her anger. Jordan and Christine hugged, exchanging "I love you" for a brief moment.

"I need to speak with you now, outside!" said Christine to Chad. She packed Jordan in his car seat in back of her Mercedes, slamming the door. "You know I hate braids, Chad! What the hell is it doing in our child's hair?"

"I can explain, I didn't know!"

"What the hell do you mean you didn't know? I don't do ghetto bullshit like this Chad and neither does my father! It's coming down and I don't want to see it again!"

"I fell asleep, Chris. When I woke up his hair was braided. I think it's kinda fly." He had told too much. His only way out was to lie. If she ever found out he left Jordan with his new girl, she'd claw his eyes out.

"You didn't bother to take them down knowing how I feel about them, especially his grandpa, and what about the agreement to no women around our child, Chad? Huh? You just had to bring someone else around, didn't you?"

"Look, don't tell me how to run my house!"

"You mean your apartment."

"Whatever, Chris! Isn't it time you started living for you and not your father?" Chad leaned forward, pointing his finger in her face. "I didn't say a damn word when you were sneaking and getting' your freak on with Trish, did I? In a damn lesbian relationship, pregnant with our son!"

"I never! I was never in a damn relationship with Trisha! Never! How dare you say that to me!"

"Liar, you damn liar! You were 'cause she threw it in my damn face to stay away from you!"

"She was lying only to make you jealous. I was never in a relationship with her. How dare you, Chad!" She felt the emotions and tears building up as Chad continued stabbing her open wound with the truth. "She's lying and your stupid ass believed her!" Chad continued shaking his head, insisting that she was lying. "I don't have to take this from you, Chad. It's bad enough after all these years we still can't get along." She pulled his firm grip from around her arm, racing for the car.

"Christine, wait! Open the door." Chad banged on the window, following her, as she backed away. "Christine, wait!" *Damn it!*

She took off, squealing her tires, billowing in tears. Chad was the last person she wanted to know about Trisha. She couldn't believe Trisha would brag to him about that. Tears streamed down her face. Her cell phone rang. It was Chad calling. She ignored it, tossing it to the floor of the car. Jordan's soft voice continued calling "Mommy" until she answered.

By the time she reached home, Jordan was fast asleep. She carried him to the front door, staring into the house, wishing someone was in there. She reached for her keys, quickly opening the door. In a quick fantasy, she envisioned Chad greeting her at the door, whisking Jordan from her arms as laughter flourished, his lips blissfully greeting her with a long kiss. Each thought made her heart heavy, knowing he was too busy doing that with his new ghetto Barbie. Inside, she placed Jordan in his bed, lightly kissing his forehead, telling him goodnight.

She was due for relief, letting the water from the shower head sprinkle down. She lathered up with her favorite shower gels, sniffing the aroma. *If only his hands could be wrapped around me. I gotta stop tormenting myself.* That was the end of the shower. She grabbed her towel, drying off. She noticed a few missed calls on her phone but didn't bother to check. The doorbell caught her off guard. She raced to put on her gown, wondering who the heck it was. She looked through the peek hole quickly, stepping back.

"Come on, Christine, it's me, Chad, I know you're at the door, peeking. Let me in."

She had to get control of her beating heart. Since moving, Chad had never been in her new home. She took a quick glance, making sure everything was in place. "You shouldn't be here!"

"Let me in, please."

This wasn't a good time, not with her hormones going crazy. "Can we talk later?" Her hand rested on the door, hoping he'd say no.

"No. We need to get some things straight now!"

She knew once he entered she was setting herself up for

sex. The door opened slowly as Christine peeked through a small crack.

Chad lightly shoved open the door barging in. Christine was looking hotter than ever and Chad missed everything black about her. Sexual thoughts ravished his mind.

"This really isn't a good time, Chad. I think we said enough tonight."

He stood dressed in jeans and a nice fitted shirt as he walked in she took a long whiff of his cologne, calming her heart.

"Nice place you have here, Chris. I see you've taken in some of your mother's elegant touches."

"Yeah, I learned from the best. It's late, Chad, and you shouldn't be here."

"Look, I wanted to apologize. I had no right saying that to you. We need to act like parents."

"Don't worry about it, okay? And you're right."

"Well, I am, and it's heavy on my mind. I had to come. This is no way to act in front of our son. I haven't seen you in forever, Chris, not without your mother or aunt being present when taking our son. There are things we need to discuss, Chris. I'm sorry for what I said."

"I'm sorry for screaming at you."

Her heart beat out of control. He was hard to resist. As he moved closer, she felt her body tingling inside.

"Do you forgive me, Christine?"

"Yes, I do, Chad."

"Okay, well, I better get going." Chad walked toward the

door. Christine followed, trying to think of a way to keep him longer. He opened the door.

"Wait, ummm ... " Christine paused. She didn't know what to say. He slowly shut the door. Her chest heaved at a rapid pace as he moved closer.

"I can stay if you want."

"Yes, please. Please stay."

Chad's hand moved lightly across her lips. Her tongue followed behind the darkness of her eyelids. She felt his lips press against hers, sending her heart into overdrive. His tongue slid around her mouth, feeling his hands grip around her butt. He ripped open her gown, his tongue exploring her body. Her moans became louder as he took his time exploring, something she had missed. She quickly unzipped his pants, pulling him toward the table. She leaned back, waiting for him, as he pulled her forward, plugging himself into her. "I love you, Chad" is all she could yell as he filled her, lightly stroking faster. She felt her stomach tightening, and his moans became louder. Chad gripped her hair, squeezing her tightly to his chest. His breathing increased as he blurted out, "I miss you, Chris." They both went into a blissful moment. Chad lay on top of her, both breathing rapidly.

"I've missed you, Chris."

"I've missed you, too, Chad."

Inside her bedroom they lay in each other's arms, reminiscing about the good times. She couldn't hold back the questioning brewing deep inside any longer.

"Who's the girl, Chad?" He sighed lowering his head.

"She's my girlfriend, Chris."

"What? She laughed. What the heck are you doing here then?"

"I guess we still care about each other. I mean, I couldn't get to you with a ten foot pole with your family around to tell you anything! She wants to get married, she keeps pressuring me and I'm tired of it!"

"Have you cheated before?"

"No, no I haven't."

"What's her name?"

"Tamara."

"She has a last name?"

"You don't need to know all that, Chris," he chuckled, blowing off.

"She's very pretty. Are you going to marry her?"

"No, I'm not ready to get married again. I wasn't ready when we married."

That was a relief hearing Chad say he wouldn't marry her. "Those damn braids came down before meeting the family. Mom questioned why Jordan's hair was so wavy, all the while giving her I already know stare. I don't want to see them again!"

"Okay. Can we sleep? I'm very tired. Jordan's a handful." They both laughed.

Christine and Chad cuddled like old times. She fell fast asleep. In the midst of his thoughts, Chad lay there, staring at the ceiling, puzzled. One lie had led to another, it was so easy. *My love is strong for Chris, I'm still in love with her, but I could never go back to that family.* His life was at rock bottom, and he needed money. No job could compare to what Mr. Crawford had been paying him: 75k a year. He was suffering the consequences now. He made a mere twenty thousand with a helluva lot of overtime. Tamara and Chad shared expenses down the middle. If Chris only knew, Chad's testosterone was still raging and sex seemed to control him. He hated to say it but Tamara reminded him of Danielle, just a little classier.

They had met inside a club called Hollywood. Tamara was one of those white girls trying to be black. Her curves took him into overdrive. She wasn't ashamed of showing what she had. They danced the night away, almost having sex on the dance floor. Everything around him was sex - he wanted it now! Tamara invited him back to her place. It was his first time having sex with a white girl. She did things to him he would never tell anyone. He was hooked from that night on. Their sexual encounters became stronger; anywhere and everywhere they took advantage of the moment. She didn't have a college degree, only a few terms of college, and had a simple nine-to-five clothing store job. Tamara would never meet up to Christine's standards and that was fine, he didn't have to compete with the money. Tamara would do whatever he wanted her to do, without having her parents hovering over them, without the evil father. Chad had never even met Tamara's father, nor did she make mention of him. Her mother was more laid back, too concerned about men, booze, and her cigarettes, and whatever she could get her hands on. "I need Chris right now, so if this is what it takes, but with Tamara … I made a commitment. I have to keep this from Christine."

Weighing his pros and cons, he was still stuck in a position of allowing his manhood to control him, and now he was between two women again.

My clothing reeked of Christine's body spray. How am I going to pull this one off? How the hell am I supposed to get her smell off?

Chad sighed, getting into his car, trying to think of a way to sneak in without Tamara knowing. At 3 a.m. she had to be worried. Chad pulled off the side of the road swimming in thoughts. He reached for his cell phone, sighing, preparing the quickest lie on the tip of his tongue. Her phone rang twice.

"Chad, where the hell are you? I've been trying to call you, even sent texts!"

"I'm on the side of the road, honey, I blew a tire. I thought I had it all under control until I looked in the back trunk - no spare! I was so pissed off I didn't feel like talking."

"I can come get you, you know! It's three in the morning. You don't need to be on the side of the road this time of the morning."

"No, no, don't worry about it. The tow truck man should be here any moment."

"Are you sure?"

"Yes."

Well, you remember my high school buddy, Trevor?"

"Yeah, what about him?"

"Well, he stopped by for a moment. He was looking forward to laughing with you, you know, your stupid jokes and all. You should have called; he's been here since eleven." Tamara chuckled. "Are you sure you don't need me to come get you?"

"Yes, I'm sure Tamara."

"Okay, I love you."

"Love you, too."

∽∾

She and Trevor sat in the bathroom, locked in, shooting up the last bit of heroin. Tamara's mind shot back toward the first hit. She wished for that same feeling over again but could never achieve it. They laughed at each other's jokes, and then he reached into his pocket pulling out a blunt. He said, "We got time, whacha think?" Before she could take a hit, Trevor lifted her up, forcing her over the sink. "You gotta pay for my service, honey."

"Chad could walk in any moment!"

"I don't give a damn, my shit ain't for free B!"

"Come on, Trevor, please."

"You better make that asshole contact his rich baby momma. 'Cause you gots back pay that you owe and yo sex ain't payin' the cost to be the boss."

"All right, all right, I will. It's just taking a little time! It's bad enough I have to deal with that little fucking brat of a child! I'll get your damn money!"

"You owe now!"

Trevor ripped off her panties, ignoring her begging to

stop. Her body was weak from the high, unable to fight back. He stood behind her, forcing himself inside. Her hip bones slammed violently against the bathroom counter top as he gripped her hair, yanking her head back. "I want my money, bitch!" is all she heard, as he rammed harder, pushing her face into the sink. Her skin was on fire, burning, as he tore into her with no protection. Just when she thought the torture was over, Trevor forced her on her knees. Her begging did no good. Her eyes focused on a few bumps on his penis, but only a glimpse, as he forced her mouth over him. She did what she had to, to knock down the payment and keep his mouth shut in front of Chad. She owed Trevor over fifteen thousand dollars for high supplies and he was a dealer that wanted his money. Trevor slowly removed himself, tucking it away. "I'll be back next week," he spoke, out of breath. She raced for the sink, turning the faucet on high, bathing her mouth in warm water, spitting out the residue.

"You don't want me to tell yo little boyfriend," he laughed, hanging it over her head with a devious smile.

"Trevor, please don't tell Chad. I'm begging you, please! My high won't last until next week, Trevor, imma need more!"

"Well, you know what you have to keep doing, bitch! Next imma bring my boy! That dumb ass, don't he know yo ass is strung out on heroin?"

"No, and I prefer it remains a secret, damn it!"

Trevor's hand came fast across her face, knocking her to the floor. He stood over her, pointing his finger in her face.

"I'm sorry, I'm sorry I won't do it again! Please!"

"I see you need some more discipline, hoe! And imma teach yo ass a lesson fo-sho!"

Tamara pried herself off the floor, listening to his footsteps as they faded away. The door slammed, sending relief. She limped over toward the tub, slowly turning on the shower. The smell of weed lingered heavily in the bathroom. Tamara grabbed a can of bathroom spray and light body spray, spraying around and down the hallway. Trevor's headlights dimmed as he backed away, squealing off. The little supply of getting high he left came with a huge price. Money was needed, and now to continue supporting her habit.

❦

Thirty minutes had gone by. Chad scrolled through his phone, stopping at Christine's number. It was too late to call, plus she'd probably be mad. He glanced at his watch; she had to be sleep by now. No matter how much he didn't want to ask her, he was going to have to. He was two months behind on his car payment and a month on rent. *Christine has more than enough to give. I just don't want that bastard dad of hers finding out or her mother and aunts so they can boast and throw it in my face about not being about to maintain on my own. Not a chance! There had to be another way. Money around the house was going too fast. Everything Tamara got, it was gone.*

He pulled in the driveway quickly, turning off the headlights. From the window, he could see the living room lamp still on. Normally it was left on when they were asleep. There was no movement, not even from the bedroom window curtains. He made sure the keys didn't jiggle upon opening the door. Tipping lightly through the apartment, the smell of fresh body scent hit his nose. Tamara had to be asleep. He rushed to the bathroom, locking the door. He ripped away each layer of clothing, tossing them into a pile in the corner. The bathroom floor was a little damp. Inside the shower, he made sure to wipe himself clean of Christine's perfume and sexual scent.

∽

She awoke the next morning to Jordan's little voice calling for her, his blanket held close to his chest. Reaching for her nightgown she slowly scooted out of bed. Chad? Her eyes darted around the room. The spot next to her was empty. Besides, Jordan would have made it known if his father was here. Outside the bathroom she waited until Jordan went potty, feeling the guilt starting to suffocate her. In hopes of him maybe still being here, she made sure to steal a peek in every room of the house. Jordan sat in his favorite chair, singing. Her mind was totally gone in a place of wanting to be with this man. She had to get over this feeling.

∽

An urgent meeting was called today at the office. Christine rushed into the conference room a couple minutes late to receive her daddy's deathly stare. A couple higher-ups sat waiting, each sipping on coffee. "Hello, Dad." She rushed over, pecking him on the cheek. Dad stood stern in his Italian tailor-made suit, announcing her name with a brief introduction. His eyes seemed to rip right through her, today out of all days. Did he know? She sat gazing out the window, wondering what Chad was doing, only to be interrupted by her daddy's deep voice calling her name. Each one of the men stared, waiting.

"Your presentation, Christine," her dad spoke.

"Oh, yes, I'm sorry," Christine spoke quickly, slapping on her business face, with an introduction of the new proposal for investing in small businesses.

"Thank you, Christine." Her dad went into the final ending, capturing each one's attention.

The meeting was another success from the smile on her dad's face and firm business handshakes. He approached Christine with a very handsome, well-built black man. She shied away from him, her lust glowing.

"Very nice proposal, Christine." They shook hands catching eyes for a moment. Her heart sank when seeing his ring finger. *Damn it! The ones I'm attracted to are always married!*

"Thank you, ummm ..."

Donny rushed in with a well-rehearsed welcome introduction. "Sorry, this is Mr. Russell, he's a well-known business man."

"It's very nice to meet you, Mr. Russell."

"Likewise, Mrs. Stone."

"Please, Ms. Crawford."

"Not a problem. Sorry, it's short notice but my wife and

I, we're having a little get together to celebrate our three-year anniversary. I'd love for you and your husband to join us."

For a moment she was lost in the word "husband," hurt was more like it. How the hell was she supposed to respond?

"Sure, Christine would love to join you all," her daddy interrupted, pulling her out of the dog house. "I might even join you all myself and accompany her."

She glanced over her shoulder, hiding her despair, gritting her teeth, wishing her daddy had never said that.

"That would be awesome, Mr. Crawford! Ms. Crawford, I'd love to introduce you to my lovely wife, Dana.

The smile told it all as he cheesed from ear to ear, saying her name briefly, describing her. He was truly happy with her. "I ... I'd love to meet your wife, she sounds very beautiful."

"All right. Well, I'll see you both tonight. Looking forward to it." Mr. Russell turned toward Donny, giving another firm handshake.

"We will be there, sir!"

"Nice meeting you again, Ms. Crawford."

"You, too, Mr. Russell."

Donny walked away, carefree. Furious, Christine trailed behind, following him into his office.

"Daddy, you have to stop doing this!"

"Doing what, Chris?"

"Talking for me; I can do that myself."

"Oh, sure you can, like at the meeting, you staring off

into oblivion, daydreaming about God only knows what! If I hadn't snapped you back to earth you'd still be staring into Pluto!"

"I'm not talking about the meeting, daddy! He assumes I'm married and expecting me to bring..." Christine froze, refusing to let Chad's name come out of her mouth. "... Someone" came from her mouth in a low tone.

"Why were you late? These are clients, Chris, unlike that damn ex of yours, that brought all that drama inside the office."

"And Sally didn't?"

"Don't you contradict me, Christine Crawford! That son of a bitch caused more pain and drama." Donny mumbled under his breath, cursing Chad's name. "You didn't answer the question: why were you late?"

"Jordan, he ... he wasn't feeling very well, Daddy."

"That's what the nanny is for, for no excuses and you're to be at work on time."

"Yes, Daddy."

"Pull out your best dress. We will be attending that party tonight."

"I'm not really in the party mood, Daddy. Besides, he thinks I'm still married. How embarrassing!"

"Too bad, honey, if I left it to you, you'd be sitting in the damn house drowned in sorrow. We're Crawford's, Chris, we bounce back after anything. You hear me? We're Crawford's and we don't take no shit! You get out, mix and mingle, find someone."

She didn't know why her daddy was going into all this.

If he found out Chad was at the house last night, she wouldn't live it down. She didn't want anyone else. Her daddy's last demand was for her to be ready by seven tonight and they weren't going to be late.

"Oh, yeah, Trisha called the office."

Her heart sank, like cement hitting water. "Did she say what she wanted … did you speak to her?"

"No, she was actually looking for you. She said you changed your cell number and she didn't know it. What's going on with that, Chris? You two were like best friends and now, nothing."

"You know, Daddy, we get older and things change."

"She bragged about her new girlfriend. My mouth hit the floor. Did you know she was or is now dating women? So badly hurt by men she decides to sleep with women! Don't you ever think your mother and I will accept that type of behavior? I'd cut you from everything! Oh, she had the nerve to ask me how Sally was doing. I guess she realized her mistake, apologizing. She switched it, asking how your mother was doing."

Christine could feel her heart skipping a beat; sweat beads poured from her pits. Her lungs felt caved in, watching him pace the floor, condemning Trisha. If he ever found out about Trisha, she had more than enough over Christine's head. What the hell was she doing, asking him about Sally? She couldn't worry about this right now! *I need a drink! No, no, no! I can't and won't go back to alcohol!* What was she doing? Paranoia sat in every pore of her face. The attempt to calm her breathing wasn't working. Her daddy meant what he said, he'd cut off all money. *What have I gotten myself into? Right now I need an excuse to leave.* Donny brushed by her, tapping her on the shoulder. *I'm going crazy … Dad's mouth moved; I thought he said Trisha, Chad, Danielle.*

"Christine… Christine!"

Her mind was playing tricks on her. Looking into her daddy's mouth she thought she heard him calling each name, but it was her guilty conscience.

"Christine Kay Crawford, I'm talking to you!"

"Yes, Daddy, I'm sorry! I just don't feel good right now. My stomach is turning. I think I'm coming down with something."

"You just kick whatever it is and be ready by seven tonight! By the way, Trisha said, call her."

"Yeah, yeah, okay."

Christine rushed out of the office, her eyes fixed on the walls, avoiding eye contact with anyone passing. The piercing stare of her dad stung her backside as she refused to turn around. Alone in the elevator, Christine leaned over, gasping for air. Waiting anxiously for the doors to open, Christine burst through before the doors could fully open, racing for the parking garage. She glanced at a familiar car, hoping it wasn't … It couldn't be. Christine walked around back, staring at the license plate, mumbling the word "Trisha." Furious, she scanned the parking garage; there was no sign of her. Was she with my dad?

"Hello, Chris." Christine hated to turn around.

"Trish … Trisha, how are you?"

"I'm really good, and you?"

"Ummm … what are you doing here?"

"Well, you changed your number. As far as we go back, I'm appalled that you wouldn't give me your new number."

"It's not like that."

"You're that ashamed, I get it! Plus daddy controls all, even your life."

"Trisha, please. Why would you ask my dad about Sally?"

"Honest mistake, really." She laughed like it was nothing. "I totally forgot."

"How could you forget? She wasn't a memory that could be easily erased."

"You sure had no problem erasing us, and what we had. I love you, Chris, more than you'll ever know."

"Trisha, you know I don't agree with being with another woman! I don't have anything against you. It's just not for me!"

"Yeah, you told me that time and time again, damn it! You weren't disagreeing when we made love, were you? You enjoyed every minute of it!"

"I was drunk five days a week, Trisha, miserable, Okay? And why would you brag to Chad about us!"

"Chad is what got you into this shit! And you're still fucking him! Does daddy know? I bet he doesn't. Little daddy's girl with all her fucked-up secrets and the biggest one of all!"

"Shut up, Trisha. Enough is enough! Is this what you're here for, to brag in my face?"

"Seems like I'm always coming to your rescue, Chris. Yeah, I bragged to Chad. You wanna know why?"

"No, I really don't."

"Well, I'll tell you anyway. I ran into Chad and his new wife."

"Wife?"

"Oh, you don't know, Chris? Chad got married again right after you." Trisha's laughter pierced her ears, more so hearing the word "wife." She clenched her fists in anger, blocking tears.

"He's not married to her."

"Yes, Christine he is, and guess what? From what I heard, she's worse than Danielle. I guess Chad can't escape his demons, huh? Oh, and his new wife was teaching your son to call her "mommy." When I heard it, I was upset. They both stood looking stupid like their world had ended so I tore Chad a new asshole because the shit he's carrying doesn't seem to be leaving quick enough!"

"Why are you doing this to me, Trisha? Why? Why are you hurting me?" Tears of anguish billowed from her eyes, dripping down her chin. She felt herself breaking.

"Chris, you overlook the obvious. Chad is the one hurting you, not me."

"I can't handle this, I can't handle this! I need to leave." Chris turned around, furious, slamming face first into her SUV.

"Christine! Oh God, I'm sorry."

"Let go of me, Trisha, let go of me!" Christine fought as Trisha tried to hold her, giving in. Inside her arms, Christine's tears soaked her shirt. Trisha apologized over and over.

"The least you can do is let me drop you off. You can't drive like this, Chris."

"No, I'll be fine."

"No, you're trembling."

"Okay, I just wanna go home."

❧

Trisha was a pro at games. It was all a trap and Christine fell in, waist deep. She stared at the ceiling as they lay next to each other in Trisha's bed. Her father's threats filled her head. She was in a no-win situation where she had to give in, to both Chad and Trisha.

It was five forty two. Trisha drove Christine back to her car. She didn't have much to say but goodbye and thank you. Trisha had wormed her way back into everything Christine was attempting to bury.

"I'm sorry about everything, Chris, but I love you. If you need me, just call." Christine gave Trisha a quick nod since she was trying to get away from there as quickly as she could.

It was a little after six. *Dad is going to kill me if I'm not ready*. A quick shower, body lotion, up-do hair, nice red, re-vealing gown and heels. The only thing missing was … *nope … nope … I'm not going to think about him. Trisha had to be lying! Chad wouldn't, he wouldn't … no … no … I can't keep doing this to myself*. She reached into a long hidden stash tucked in the back pantry. Her pain said yes, but her spirit said no. Just like everything else, she ignored them all. She cracked the top off an old brand of wine, sniffing the aroma. She didn't hesitate to pull down a glass. *Just a little.* The taste hit her mouth, sending her into alcohol bliss. She filled the glass, gulping it down, holding the glass up waiting for the residue to drip into her mouth. She was tempted to pour another glass, the doorbell echoed through the house. It was ten to seven. She placed the wine back into her stash, just a little closer for easy reach.

"I'm coming, Daddy!" He stood outside with a smile, commenting on her beauty, how much she looked like her mother. She felt so secure in his arms, a place she never wanted to escape from.

Nothing but luxurious cars lined the driveway of the Russell mansion. There were women in glamorous dresses, butlers serving hors d' oeuvres and trays filled with wine. Christine felt like a teenage kid in love, sharing her first kiss, high on adrenaline. The vigorous feeling had fallen off. It was empowering, being back in the game of fortune. Expressions of the lusting lifestyle poured out through her confident walk, grasping the arm of the one and only prestigious Mr. Crawford. Christine flaunted her newly purchased Arzu Kaprol V-neck red gown, sucking up the attention as people approached Mr. C. like he was a celebrity. The women were so dramatic; those who weren't attached to a man's arm walked around in revealing outfits in search of one. Mr. Russell stood waiting at the door, eagerly introducing his wife.

❧

Dana was so beautiful, with light pretty eyes. *There's so much of myself in her.* They hit it off right away, laughing, as she introduced Christine to several well-known people. Donny made his way over toward the food, stuffing his face. Glasses filled with wine floated passed her face. She couldn't resist grabbing one. Dana held Christine's arm, escorting her around.

"My feet are tired, Chris. Do you mind me calling you Chris or do you prefer Christine?"

"Either one is fine, Dana."

"Okay, well, let's go grab a seat. I think we made our rounds of meeting everyone. Oh my gosh!" Dana plopped down on the couch with her glass of wine. Christine didn't hesitate to follow suit.

"So Christine, Chris." They both laughed. "My husband tells me you're married."

"Actually, Dana, the real truth is I'm divorced."

"Oh, no, I'm so sorry, Chris, forgive me."

"No, don't worry about it. My father's the type of person … well, you know … we try to hide things … keep it from the public."

"I understand; he has a rep to keep."

"You can't hide everything Dana, especially the horror I suffered being married. I lost our first child." She couldn't help the tears from falling. Dana quickly set down her glass, rushing to her aid, holding Christine in her arms. "He was cheating on me, with some whore! She ran me off the road, and it killed our child!"

"Oh, my God! I'm so, so sorry, Chris. I'm so sorry, honey. Have you taken counseling for your loss?"

"It's not your fault, Dana, these are open wounds and things you can't hide. No, I haven't."

"Maybe it's something you should consider. Look, we're going to hang out a lot more, Chris. We need a girls night out, a girls day out, what the hell! I refuse to let you go through this alone, Chris. Let's do lunch tomorrow?"

"Can I bring my son?"

"I thought …"

"No, I got pregnant again."

"Yes, I would love that. I can bring my nephew, Ryan; he's four."

"That's perfect, Jordan's four, too."

Dana was such a breath of fresh air. They laughed and cried together, bashed men and whoring women, drinking themselves silly.

⊗

Chad woke up with a surprise for Tamara. She remained sleep. He took advantage of her nicely firm body, ravishing every part of her, thinking about Christine. She moaned softly as he thrust harder, giving it his all. Chris's name was on the tip of his tongue as he climaxed. Tamara rolled over, greeting him with a kiss and a good morning.

"You're the best, you know that."

"I try to be."

"I need to talk to you, honey."

"About?"

"I hate to ask Chad, I really do. We need money right away."

"I just gave you two grand, what did you do with it?"

"I paid bills. Look, honey, we're behind on everything. So when I get money, it goes quick."

"How much?"

"Ten."

"Ten what?"

"Ten grand."

"Are you fucking kidding me, Tamara? Where the hell do you think I can get my hands on that type of money?"

"It's within your reach Chad, either that or you can explain to Jordan why we live on the street. Better yet, Christine! Look honey, ask Chris."

"Nope! You leave her outta this mess! No, no, no! No way. No can do!"

Tamara hopped out of bed, pacing back and forth, rubbing her arms.

"I need the damn money Chad! We need the money! Just get me five by this weekend."

"I don't have five hundred!"

"Okay, four. I don't care—two! Something, damn it!"

"I'll see what I can do."

"Oh, thank you, honey."

Tamara disappeared up front. Chad thought about what he needed to say to Chris. A half hour passed. She hopped back into bed, slipping underneath the covers. He felt his heart race into overdrive as she took control. He was almost there. Tamara removed her gown, positioning herself over him. She held his hands down, locking them behind his head, moving up and down, faster and faster. He was out of breath and sexually drained as they lay, laughing aloud.

Forcing sex was the only way Chad would do what I wanted, though Tamara. Trevor was returning next week with his friend and her high stash was getting low already. As Chad lay asleep, she searched his wallet, yanking a few twenties. She tiptoed over toward the middle dresser drawer, reaching in, feeling around the top for her taped-up stash of money and heroin. Stealing twenties was getting her nowhere fast. She had to do something before Trevor returned.

Scandalous mischief danced around her head while lying next to Chad. She only cared about one thing, and that was getting high. Christine had the money; she and her well-off parents had millions. Tamara's plot thickened: their child ... if she could get away with it ... oh, Christine and her daddy would pay big bucks then ... *Jordan's sweet, a sweet boy* ... her inner demons didn't care about that kid... her high needing to be supplied was all that mattered. She didn't want to deal with that nausea, the internal pain in her stomach and hallucinations.

Tamara was like a time clock to Trevor. He always knew when she was coming. The last time, she arrived on his porch on her hands and knees, begging him for a trip. He pulled her in the house. Trevor dangled a needle over her head, laughing like she was a dog. He made her bark, strip nude and drop to her knees and call him God. She promised to do whatever it took. Trevor threw a half filled needle on the floor. She didn't hesitate to scurry nude across the floor. She grabbed the needle, quickly wrapping her upper arm, waiting for a vein. The injection sent her into another world, a world of escape. Her life was in his hands. She paid what little she had; the rest owed was a sexual exchange with another woman watching. If she had to, she'd do it again.

❧

While staring at the ceiling, Christine's first thought was to call Chad and give him a piece of her mind. Who knew if Trish was lying? It would be pointless, but the whole thing about Tamara making her son call her mommy weighed on her. Trisha was the type of person to come to her defense over something like that, but she did it in the wrong way. The road to Christine's troubles was never ending, and they were getting bigger.

Needless to say, Christine never questioned Chad. For a month, she continued inviting him in for sex. She loved every minute spent with him. He never mentioned Tamara and Christine didn't ask. As Chad lay in bed, she sat up, staring at him, wishing he was still hers. "This man has an awful hold on me that I couldn't shake."

She jumped up to a car door slamming outside. Outside the window, Daddy could be seen looking into Chad's car. He tried opening Chad's car door but it was locked. *Oh no, oh no! What the hell am I going to do? He'll kill him if he finds him here!*

"Chad!" She shook him violently, waking him up. "My God, my dad's here! Get up now!" Chad jumped to his feet, ripping the covers from his lap.

"What the hell is he doing here, it's only 6 a.m.!" Chad questioned, throwing on his clothes.

"I don't know, I don't know! My God, what do I say?"

"That I came to get Jordan."

"This early? He's still sleeping!"

"Well, get him up."

"No." She rushed to make up the bed, shoving him out of her room and down the hall.

"I'm not dealing with him, Chris. He'll kill me, especially if he finds out we're still having sex. No, no! You're freakin' thirty-four Chris when are you gonna stand up to him?"

"I can never stand up to him. Just go out the back door, Chad, I'll stall him so he doesn't see you. Jordan's been a little under the weather lately, I'll just lie and say you brought him some meds for his fever." They both listened as the doorbell rang, followed by banging. "Listen for the front door to close. I'll lead Daddy away from the windows, then go."

Christine wiped the fear from her face, yelling out "Hold on, Daddy." Chad stood, waiting for her signal outside the back door.

The door opened. Chad heard Donny's voice traveling closer. He ran toward his car like an escaped convict, quickly getting in. *I hated Chris having to deal with this on her own, but it's her dad.* Chad was able to get five hundred dollars from her, which was a little easier than he antici-pated. He knew since being absent from home all night, the money would instantly shut Tamara up.

Donny traveled through the house without a single good morning, searching every room, invading Christine's pri-vacy.

"Whose car is that out front?"

"What are you doing, Dad? I live here!"

"And guess who pays your damn bills! Whose car is out front?"

"It was Jordan's father, Daddy!"

"Was! Why did you sneak him out the back door, Chris? He couldn't stand up to me like a man! Pussy! Why was he here?"

"Because Jordan has a fever and he brought over some meds about five. I didn't want to leave the house with Jor-dan."

"Keep it up, Chris, he'll be slipping his no good ass back in bed with you! And asking you for money! Has he asked you for money, Chris?"

"No." Tears fell; she felt herself breaking inside.

"That bastard's dick isn't all that! He's scum and will al-ways be scum! You better watch who he's sticking it in and coming back to you, bringing God knows what to you! Wake up Christine, you see what he's capable of doing. Anyone who can screw around with a mother and daughter doesn't care about you! I'll kill that son of a bitch if he hurts you again!"

"He only came to give Jordan his meds, that's all, Daddy!" Donny gave his deathly stare at Christine, reading her like a book as if he knew she was lying. She avoided eye contact, afraid, staring out at the landscape wiping away her tears. "I can fight my own battles, Dad!"

"Oh, yeah? Like the many times before. Trisha came to your damn rescue, and your mother and I! Did you forget Darren? Your ex-boyfriend who left God only knows why and you crumbling so bad we had to get a psychologist!" Christine's dad hammered each painful memory inside her head. She still wanted to know how he knew.

⁂

Parked a couple miles back, Trisha waited in her girlfriend's car, wondering. She hated to, but she had to warn Mr. C. about Chad being at Christine's house alone. Two in the morning to six; she knew just what they were doing. Neither Christine nor Chad was getting away with this one. Donny should be ripping into the both of them right now. Why the hell would she still allow him over? *I told her stupid ass he's married. Chad's not slick! I know he's after Chris for money, he's just using sex to make his way in.* "How could Chris be so stupid!" Trisha yelled at the top of her lungs, gripping the steering wheel. "I told her, I told her and she's still screwing him!"

Trisha ducked down in the seat upon seeing Chad's car approaching. A smile of defeat crossed her face, wishing she could have been a fly on the wall. Numerous devious plots crossed her mind. Trisha rummaged through some papers on the floor, searching for her cell phone. Her fingers itched to phone Chris.

❧

I'm so tired of that damn Donny! Chad said to himself, whipping his car around the corner. *Christine better have stood up to him! How the hell did he find out I was there or does Donny always show up that early? Geesh, this is insane, my hands are still trembling. That damn Donny is no joke, his barbaric voice alone would send anyone into pandemonium. Donny would completely break every bone in my body and devour me if he found out that I'm married to Tamara and still messing around with his daughter.* A growl of anguish escaped his mouth, his body became spasmodic thinking about all the mess he was in, but his adrenaline was too high to quit.

❧

A couple of days had passed. Jordan's fever seemed to fluctuate from day to day. Today was one of his better days. With a toy car in his hand, Jordan raced around the house, making a racing sound. Strands of his curly hair bounced as he leaped from the couch. Things were going peacefully for Christine.

"Jordan, where are Mommy's keys?" Chris ran around frantically in search of her keys. The last thing she wanted to do was be late for her girls' day out with Dana. Excitement gleamed, finally a real friend. They could relate to each other. She wasn't out for money; the only setback was

Dana was happily married. Humph! Christine could only wish for things to be back to normal. Her keys turned out to be underneath the couch and one culprit came to mind: Jordan. She playfully chased him around the house, pretending to be mad. *I love seeing him laugh. I don't know what I'd do if something were to happen, God forbid, or to lose him.* She brushed the horrible thought from her mind, whisking him into the air, attacking him with kisses.

The play date began at the park. Dana waved them down, running toward Jordan and Christine, holding the hand of a little boy. Dressed down in an Adidas jogging suit with matching shoes, she was still gorgeous. Her long ponytail flopped side to side as Ryan giggled, racing her through the grass.

"Hello, Christine. My gosh, I'm not as young as I used to be." Dana exhaled deeply, trying to catch her breath.

"Hello, Dana, come on you're not that old! You look like you're in your twenties." Dana chuckled aloud.

"That's a good compliment, Chris, but not by a long shot."

"You gotta be kidding me!"

"Nope. Late forties!"

"My gosh, I would have never guessed."

"This is what happiness being rooted and grounded in the Lord will do for you, not to mention Jerick. Oh my, is this your lovely son, Jordan?" Dana leaned in pinching his cheek.

"Oh, yeah. Jordan, this is Dana." Jordan shyly whispered hello. What did she mean by being rooted and grounded in the Lord? Christine didn't want to look stupid asking, but Dana seemed to think she already knew what it meant. Chris and her parents were hardly a church-going family. Her father rarely mentioned God. Her mother, on the other hand, her side of the family, they always mentioned God, especially Gram and Aunt Vivien. Christine felt so embarrassed, so avoiding it was best.

"And here's my little nephew, Ryan." He had big, light brown eyes and deep dimples like his aunt. He could pass for her son. Ryan danced around, anxious, as Auntie Dana pinched his cheeks.

"He's so adorable! Dana, he could be your son."

"I know, I get that all the time, but the catch is, my brother and I are twins." Christine's mind went straight to picturing her brother; he had to be fine. "He has a little girl, two months, with his wife, Chana, that I can't wait to get my hands on. I am going to spoil her rotten."

Scratch that thought. She couldn't help staring at Dana's radiant smile. She had a bright aura, like nothing she'd ever seen.

"You boys want to play on the playground?" Dana asked. Jordan and Ryan jumped around, screaming yes. "Is it all right, Christine?"

"Sure." Jordan and Ryan took off running. Dana and Christine followed at a slower pace. They stopped at the fence, laughing together, watching the two kids play.

"I love seeing the children happy. My husband and I are working on a project together for underprivileged children.

We want to give back to the community. You know, God has been so good to us, it's only right."

Christine nodded her head, agreeing, trying to avoid looking stupid again. Dana was so positive; Christine was still sitting in her negativity.

"Do you have a church home, Christine?"

"Oh, no, I mean not at the moment." She didn't want to go there. "I wouldn't call it home, but I do attend sometimes."

"Sometimes?"

"Not as much as I should." Her only way out was a lie.

"He's been too good to your family to leave him out, Chris."

"I just ..." She paused, staring at the ground.

"You just what?"

"I feel like I'm not good enough."

"Are you serious? Christine, look at me."

She stood staring at her, ashamed of all her guilt. It seemed to pour out the more Dana talked about the Lord forgiving, and no one being perfect. There was that inner wall, bringing her back to Chad and all he had done. Dana preached for a while, quickly changing the subject to another sensitive topic.

"So is your ex-husband helping?"

"Huh?"

"You know, helping you take care of Jordan?"

"Umm, not like I want him to."

"Why not? If you don't mind me asking."

"Well, my family hates Chad."

"Chad? Is that his name? There has to be a reason why. Then again, rich people can be overly protective of their children." Dana chuckled. "In their eyes, no one is right for their son or daughter." Dana stood perplexed, pondering over the name Chad and where she had heard his name from, but nothing came to mind.

"You can say that again. Daddy has his reasons. Mom's more laid back but takes Dad's side. Chad's a good father, Jordan loves his daddy. Chad's taking him for the weekend. It's kind of a stretch but I guess I can allow it."

"Why wouldn't you allow it?"

"Ha! His new girlfriend!"

"Yeah, that can be a problem. So your last name is still Crawford?"

"I changed it back. I didn't want anyone knowing it used to be Stone."

"Stone? That doesn't seem to fit his character." Dana's thoughts went to Chad's last name. She stared off into space, thinking where she had heard that name. "You seem to be still in love with him."

"It shows, huh? I just can't help it, Dana. I'm still in love with Chad and I can't hide it! I feel so guilty because we're still sleeping together! But it feels so good when we're together!"

"Chris, you can't put yourself in second place! Stop doing that to yourself! If he can't put you first, then you should be nowhere on his list! I sure pray you're using protection, Chris."

"He's my child's father."

"So that gives you a reason to just trust him? He's sleeping with another woman. Don't you know the more you have sex with him, anyone unmarried, you pick up all that person's demons? This is why it's so hard to break away. It's sexual spells, hexes, bewitchment, a curse. Chris, you have to be smarter than this, you have Jordan."

"A sex spell? It sounds like some fairy tale."

"But it's reality and a serious one! Chris, this is no game! Jezebel, you know her right? Christine shrugged her shoulders. In the bible, King Ahab's wife, she murdered all of God's servants, only Elijah remained. Read 1 Kings 18:22, they all went against the power of the Lord. Jezebel spirits can be in men or women. Understand that when you stand against the principality of Jezebel, even if you resist her lust and witchcrafts, you must guard yourself against the power demons. Fear, discouragement, Jezebel sends these demons. I know this is a bit much. "

"What am I supposed to do? I love him."

"Does he love you?"

"Yeah, I think so."

"You're going to have to figure this out on your own, Chris. It sounds like you need to find your own self-worth. You've been damaged and I hate to say it, he's caused a lot of your pain. If this man is sexing you down and then asking for money, you need to take your blinders off. Neither money nor your sex is going to make him love you. If he does love you, he would find a way to make things right. You're going to have to grow a backbone, Chris. Your demons can't be fought alone. It's not your fight. Hand it over!"

"To whom?" Tears rolled down Christine's cheeks.

"What? Christine, you hand it over to Jesus! You need a true friend in your life and I'll be that friend to uplift you and pray for you."

"It's so easy for you to say let it go, get Jesus! What have you been through? I bet nothing! You don't know!"

"That's where you're wrong, Christine. I was bullied as a child, beaten by my mother who always told me she hated me and wished she never had me. You have parents and you have the nerve to walk around ungrateful. Ha! I wish I had real parents. My father, my father ... wow. He left when my mother got pregnant, stayed out of my life for eighteen years. I finally met him when I was seventeen. We were fine at first, but that's when the emotions started to kick in, especially hearing him speak of his other children. You know, it was always them, not me! He wanted me to respect him! That was a damn laugh. How? Needless to say, he walked out as quickly as he walked in.

"My mom lost herself in drugs, alcohol and men. She was young and beautiful just like you. Grandma raised her well, but my mom didn't listen. She wanted to follow the crowd, but the crowd was too big for her and it quickly engulfed her. Mom passed away. I hurt my grandma. At twelve, I couldn't find the tears to cry, I was numb. I guess God had finally said her time was up but she wasn't listening. My mom's heart finally gave out. One day, she collapsed on the floor while at work. Her breath was taken that quickly. I thought the pain would stop but it didn't.

"I sat countless times in my room, contemplating suicide. One night I almost did. I took a bunch of my grandma's pills. She found me that night curled up on the floor, unresponsive. That was my first suicide attempt." Dana wiped streaming tears from her face.

"I was always known for being beautiful, especially in high school. The girls hated me, Chris. One night, two of them asked me over. I thought 'what the hell, why not?' When I got there, the two girls left me alone in a guest room. I felt abandoned so I decided to leave. When I opened the door, two boys I knew from high school were standing there, blocking the door. I saw the devil in their eyes. They grabbed me, forcing my clothing off. Those damn girls never came to my rescue even though I screamed 'Help, they're raping me!' My virginity was taken from me by a rape, I was gang-raped at eighteen. Needless to say, in court, it was all of their words against mine. They lied, I didn't have a good attorney, couldn't afford one. They were jocks, you know, popular, with money! They got away with raping me!

"That night, I wanted life to end. I slashed both my wrists. Oh, but grandma, she was my lifesaver, she always knew when her grandbaby was hurt." Dana gave a sorrowful laugh. "She found me again. This time, I could hear her praying, asking the Lord to spare me, to even take her! Do you believe that? Grandma was ready to give her life for mine!" Dana leaned over, crying. Christine felt horrible inside. Her eyes widened with pain by Dana's testimony. Chris reached over to hold her.

"My God, Dana, I'm so sorry." Dana's painful memories penetrated her heart like a knife. She had been through hell and back and still standing. Christine listened to her speak about the goodness of Jesus. If her grandma never taught it, she would have been dead. Chris cried, feeling all of Dana's pain. Dana spoke about giving her problems to the Lord, healing, and deliverance from all that she had been through, putting Chris's little problems to shame.

They ended the night cracking jokes at a pizza place downtown. The boys dug into their ice cream, spilling the majority of it on their clothing. Christine couldn't help stare at Dana. She was strong despite the weakness she suffered as a child and teen. Jesus works like that? Christine was so used to giving her problems to man or woman. Her cell vibrated inside her purse. It was Chad, sending a text message.

Chad: Hi Chris, can we get together tonight?

Chris: I'm out with friends at the moment.

Chad: I miss you haven't seen u in 2 days. Can I come over in a couple

Christine: Idk Chad.

Chad: Plz I make it worth your while

No matter how much she wanted to tell him no, something inside wouldn't allow it. She wanted him, too. Chad continued to beg.

Christine: Ok c u in a couple.

She couldn't wait to get home. The entire time Dana

spoke, Christine's mind was on Chad and him running his hands down her body.

Christine and Dana ended the night cleaning the boys off inside the women's restroom. They were antsy and tired. Ryan was already nodding in front of the sink. Outside Dana gave Chris a huge hug, promising to call her this week for another hangout, this time just the girls. They agreed to a good massage in an upscale spa. The name Stone continued floating across Dana's mind as she backed out. There was still a blank.

As soon as Christine got home, she rushed Jordan into the bath, placing him in his bed, kissing his forehead goodnight. She ran to the shower, ripping her clothes off, lathering up in her favorite body shower gels. Quickly she threw on the sexiest lingerie, waiting for the doorbell to ring.

Two hours passed. Furious, she sat watching TV, wondering where Chad was. She dozed off, waking to the doorbell echoing. Christine glanced at the clock on the wall. "Damn it, Chad's two hours late." She leaped from the couch, stealing a glance at herself in the closet mirror, ready to give Chad a piece of her mind. She swung open the door quickly, dripping every thought on the tip of her tongue. Chad stood in a suit, his shirt half open, showing his nicely chiseled chest, with two bottles of wine in one hand. His cologne melted her right where she stood. There were few words as his soft lips greeted hers. Chad placed the bottle of wine on a table, savagely embracing her. Her knees were weak, as she felt herself buckling. Chad lifted her up, carrying her to her bedroom. She ran her fingers down his chest, licking every part of him, removing his pants. They stood naked, wanting each other. Chad forced her down on the bed face down, plunging into her. Passionate moans escaped her mouth; her legs started shaking as Chad took control, moving faster. Her muscles tightened, giving him all she could, screaming his name and how much she loved him. Chad continued telling her the same. Her nails dug into his leg, scratching the skin, as he forced his way harder. They were almost there. They both let out screams at the moment of release. Sweat poured from his chest, dripping onto her back as he stood behind her, exhaling deeply.

"You're so good to me, Chris."

Christine thought back to Dana as Chad continued releasing. Again, no protection, and he was going back to her tomorrow. She had to be getting the same thing if not better. No, no … Christine wasn't going to allow this night to be ruined. As Chad slowly pulled way, she asked him to get the wine and two glasses. Chad returned with the bottle of red wine, filling the glasses. Her mouth was so ready to taste the wine. They did a toast to good sex, laughing it off. The taste of wine hit her mouth. An exhale of relief poured as she continued drinking it down. Before Chad could place down the bottle, she asked for another glass. They drank the night away, making love over and over. It felt like heaven being in his arms. She didn't want this moment to end. They topped off another glass, finishing both bottles. She staggered through the room, naked, laughing at his corny jokes. Chad rushed up to her, pinning her against the wall with a long kiss. "I love you, Chris, you and Jordan."

"Yeah, I know." A drunk laugh escaped her mouth.

"Chris, I hate asking, I really do, but I'm in a bind and I need help."

"What kind of ... of kind ... I mean ... bind, did you say? Is that what you said?"

"Yes, baby, it is. I need ten thousand dollars now!"

"Chad, I ... I ... don't kno ... know." She staggered away from his arms, trying to remain focused.

"Just write a check, Chris. I'm in really big trouble if I don't get it!"

"Tro ... tro ... trouble ... wh ... what kinda trouble, Chad?"

"I'm not going to involve you, Chris." Chad handed Chris her purse, begging and pleading.

I hated to do it but I knew after good sex and wine, it was the best time ever to ask Christine for some money. I took advantage of her vulnerability, watching her write the check. I took the checkbook from her, placing it on the nightstand whisking her into bed.

As Chris lay asleep, her checkbook sat on the nightstand next to her pen. Chad fought to avoid the voices inside his head. He removed the check, shredding it into pieces. This moment was too good to pass up. Chris would never remember what she wrote. Chad sat down, studying Christine's signatures from prior voided-out checks she never removed. Once he doctored her signature, Chad wrote another check for thirty thousand. He tore off the check, ripping out the receipt, stuffing both into his pocket. It was so easy to get thirty, why not more? No, another day. It felt good on the outside, but internally Chad knew it was wrong. Finances outweighed the guilt. Right now, money was needed and the Crawford's had millions. *It's not like Christine is going to miss thirty thousand with all the millions in her account.* Chad laughed it off, leaning back, snuggling next to Chris.

❧

Two in the morning. Christine's taste buds were still yearning for more wine. Slowly she got out of bed, heading for the kitchen, racing for her stash. *Chad's car, oh, no, I have to hide it.* She placed the bottle of wine down, racing outside toward his car. *Just in case daddy shows up, he wouldn't think twice about searching the garage.* Once back inside, she filled her glass several times, gulping them down. She needed more wine and maybe even a pint of dark liquor.

Eight in the morning. It was another day of waking up to reality. She had hoped to make breakfast for their son and Chad, but he was already gone. She peeked into Jordan's room. He was still sleeping; next to him lay a blue dolphin stuffed animal. Chad must have bought it this morning and sat it next to him. She just wanted Chad home. She stood looking at herself in Jordan's mirror, holding the stuffed animal tightly. With each bad thought, she wanted a drink, but how could she go out and get more with Jordan still asleep? Marie, the maid, comes today. *I'll have her pick up three bottles of wine and whatever else I need before she comes at eleven this morning.* Besides, this is the weekend. Jordan's staying with his dad. Who knows if that thing of a woman is gonna be there. She needed something to calm her nerves to get her through the weekend.

⤫

Chad picked up an old friend of his, Heather, and quickly headed to the bank. He promised her a piece of the pie if he could use her name on the checking account. That way, Mr. A'hole couldn't track it back to him. After cashing the check, he paid Heather three thousand plus lunch downtown.

"That's so generous of Chris to give you money, and her agreeing to place it under my name so her parents don't find out. Wow, she really loves you Chad. Are you guys planning on getting back together?"

"Ummm ... I don't know, Heather. Chris really doesn't want you to mention the money. If this gets back to Mr. C., she could get into a world of trouble."

"Oh, my lips are sealed, Chad. Anything else you guys need, I'm there! You know, I heard through the grapevine that she and Trisha were and are more than friends."

"What? That's not true and Christine doesn't even speak to Trisha anymore!"

"That's strange because I saw her with Trisha last week! You know why they don't speak?"

"Why?"

"Trisha's in love with Christine. I'm dead serious, Chad, they have slept together and word is getting out."

"Christine said it wasn't true!"

"Of course, she would, it's probably against her rich family values! Trisha's a very vindictive person. Watch out, and this is coming from her ex-husband. He wasn't cheating on her, she was cheating on him with a friend of his. They had been going strong for about a year before her ex found out from his own friend. Trisha's lie got everyone on her side to believe she was the victim, even told others her ex was beating on her. She sure had Christine fooled." Heather laughed out loud. "She took her ex to the cleaners, you hear me, with lies. She's a very jealous person."

"I witnessed that when she was staying at the Crawford home. Trisha did brag to me about her and Christine that they were in love with each other. No, no, not Christine!"

"Rumor has it she's trying to get you out of the picture so she can move into Chris's and your son's life."

"It will be a cold damn day in hell before I allow some lesbian relationship around my son. Christine doesn't want to mess with me on that one. Especially the way her dad feels about it. I'll tell him."

"And you get your funds cut off, too. You tell and she gets cut off and you get nothing, Chad. So I think you should keep your mouth shut for now!"

"Damn, you're right! Damn it! But I got something over Chris's head."

"Just as well, as she has something over yours."

"What?"

"Remember, she was in the truck with Trisha last week. Duh, you know Trisha told her."

"Told her what, Heather!"

"Come on, Chad! I know you're married to that Caucasian woman!"

"How did you find out?" Chad ran his palms down the front of his pants.

"Word is getting out, that's all I know Chad. I heard it from Peaches at the club. You watch yourself with her. Something strikes me odd about her. What's her name?"

"Tamara."

"Yeah, that! Well, it's been real, Chad. I have to head into work tonight."

He watched Heather walk away, replaying their entire conversation. Tamara had been acting strangely lately. It was always sex, then money, money we could never keep. It was enough hearing about Chris, but now Tamara?

☙

Tamara opened their apartment door, excited, ready to surprise Chad. However, it was Trevor, showing up unannounced with his hand out demanding his money. Time had come and gone so fast she didn't realize it was next week. Most of her time had been spent high, and hiding it from Chad. Trevor forced his way in, shoving her aside. She fell backward against the wall.

"You got my money?"

"I'll have more of it today, I promise! He's out right now getting it!"

"Who, that Chad guy? He better be getting it from that rich bitch!"

"Yes, I believe so." Tamara stood shaking, "I need more Trevor, just a little bit?"

"More! You can't even keep up wit' what's given. You owe me, bitch!" Trevor placed a firm grip around her neck. She felt it tightening, forcing her down to the couch. Trevor tossed the basket of clean clothes onto the floor. He whipped her around, stuffing her face down into the pillows. "You know what you have to do to get my high supplies." Tamara took in several deep breaths as Trevor began to rape her. His belt dangled in the air from her peripheral vision. She questioned what he was doing. A sting on her backside made her scream. Trevor continued hitting her back with his leather belt, demanding his money. Her screams were muffled by him forcing her face into the pillows.

The pain set in across her back. Trevor stood in front of her, snapping the belt in her face like she was some child. He reached into his pocket, pulling out a bag. Tamara wiped the tears from her face. Her heart raced, yearning for a high. Trevor leaned forward, dangling the bag in front of her face. He forced her to look into his devilish eyes.

"I want my damn money, Tam, I don't care how far we go back as friends; you owe me big, damn it! Your sex ain't that good anymore! I gotta dime a dozen like you droppin' down to give it to me! Get my damn money, Tam!"

"Yeah, okay!"

Trevor slammed the bag in her face, quickly zipping up his pants. She didn't wait to see how he got out. The door slammed closed. She ran straight to the bathroom, searching for her needles, burning what she needed. The injection took her to another place. She felt her heart rate pick up, exhaling her relief.

∝⥲৹

Tamara's car was still in the parking lot. *I thought she had to work?* Chad thought. He walked to the apartment and into a mess. Laundry was all over the floor along with the pillows from the couch. What in the hell was she doing? "Tamara!"

Shit, Chad! Tamara slammed the bathroom door shut, quickly gathering her high supplies, stashing them into a plastic bag. "I'm in the bathroom, Chad!"

"What are you doing, and don't you work today?"

"Yeah, I'm not feeling well, Chad. It's some kind of virus." Tamara hurried, cleaning the residue from the counter top, using a piece of tissue and flushing it down the toilet.

"What's with the clothes all over the floor?"

"Huh? Oh, I must have knocked them over rushing into the bathroom. I'll get 'em!"

"I need to speak with you."

Tamara took a brief look at herself, combing her fingers through her hair, exhaling. She tucked the small bag inside of the middle of her breast. *I can do this. Chad better have money.*

Chad couldn't stop feeding into his curiosity. Heather's words remained etched in his brain as he walked into the living room. Chad reached down, gathering up the clothes, and tossing the pillows onto the couch. He picked up a leather belt from off the side of the couch.

This isn't mine. Chad measured it around his waist.

"Hey, honey."

Tamara appeared, looking a little worn out. Panic struck across her face as she zoomed in on the belt in Chad's hand. "I told you I'd pick them up." Tamara lightly took the belt from his hand, tossing it into the laundry basket. She quickly greeted him with a kiss, embracing him tightly, hoping he wouldn't ask. The pain stung as Chad rubbed his hands across Tamara's back. "I've missed you, honey. I tried going into work, but I suddenly got sick." She knew overriding him with questions would deter him from asking about Trevor's belt. "What did you have to see me about?"

"Oh, yeah, I got some money!" Tamara felt her feet come off the floor as Chad held her in the air, excited.

What a fucking relief! Tamara thought. "It better be a lot! How much did you get?"

"Twenty thousand." There was no way Chad was telling her how much he really got. Tamara's eyes widened with excitement.

"Twenty thousand, Chad! Oh, my God, she gave you that much!"

"Yes, yes she did. What are you doing to get it?" Tamara's demeanor changed. "Are you still screwing Chris, because if so, I swear to you …"

"No, no, I'm not! Why would you say that?"

"Cause people don't just do things for nothing! Is she still in love with you?"

"Tamara, she's Jordan's mother and nothing else, I promise you! We have a child together. I don't know if she's still in love with me. What difference does it make? Remember, twenty g's."

A huge smile appeared on Tamara's face. She thought about paying some of the money to Trevor along with more high supplies. "So how much do I get? You know, to pay some of these damn bills down."

"I'll give you three g's."

"That's not enough, Chad!"

"What do you mean it's not enough?"

"I … I mean we have more bills than just three thousand dollars, Chad!"

"How much are you looking for?"

"At least five grand, that's it! That will get us back, Chad! Please."

"Okay."

"You're so good to me. I love you so much, Chad! Thank you." She waited as Chad counted out the money, practically drooling, snatching it before he placed it into her hand.

"I've had a long day." Chad rubbed his body against Tamara, softly sucking on her neck. "You think we can …"

"No, I'm just not in the mood right now, honey, I'm sorry." Tamara shoved him away, preoccupied, brushing past him.

"What? I get nothing for my good deed?" Chad threw up his arms, upset.

"I told you, I'm not feeling well. I've gotta make a run. I'll make it up to you when I get back."

"Where are you going?"

"I'm gonna put some money on a few bills that are due now."

Chad plopped on the couch, watching Tamara gather her purse and keys. Her "I love you" went in one ear and out the other as the door slammed. Discouraged, Chad listened to Tamara's car speeding off.

Tamara dropped a few hundred on some overdue bills, keeping the rest. She sped over to Trevor's flat with one plan in mind. People trafficked in and out. Two guys stood outside as if guarding the house. She moved her stray hairs into place, taking a deep breath. She was a mess - no shower and a jogging suit with flip flops. Trevor appeared on the front porch, his jeans sagging. Tattoos etched his skin, covering his body like a shirt. He leaned over from a distance, peering into her car. *He must notice me,* thought Tamara. Curious, Trevor approached her car. She looked up as he tapped on the window for her to let him in. The locks clicked. Tamara took another deep breath. Trevor sat on the passenger side staring at her, waiting for eye contact.

"What are you doing here?"

"Ummm … I, ummm … brought you something. Reaching into her purse, Trevor's hand stopped hers before she could get it out. Paranoid, he threw her hand out reaching in her purse, grabbing the bag. She watched his smile grow, counting the money, and then suddenly thin out.

"This is only twenty five hundred, Tam. I said I wanted all my money!"

"Trevor, I'm trying. I promised to give you something and I did, didn't I?" Trevor laughed. "Can I get some more? I'm almost out."

"Shit, your ass is already in the hole!"

"I need it, Trevor, please."

"I'll tell you what, Tam, you keep having your man get money from his rich bitch. In the meantime, I have a few guys in need of some."

"Some what?"

"What you do best, Tamara! You do this and I'll knock down four hundred."

"I'm not a prostitute, Trevor!"

"Well, you better consider being one, I'd sure hate to come for that husband of yours."

"You can't!"

"But you know I will!"

"Chad gets the money! Without him, there's none!"

"And you're still behind, hoe, and asking for more!" Trevor yelled. "You do this, I'll knock off today's supply owed, and give you enough 'till next week." Trevor opened the door, flagging one of his boys. A short fat guy approached the car. He commented on how good she looked while Trevor whispered something in his ear. "Do we have a deal, Tam?"

She nodded yes. Her stash was low and she needed more to keep going. Inside, Trevor allowed her to shower. She sat on the toilet, contemplating her decision. Trevor banged on the door, rushing her. She walked into the room with a towel wrapped around her. A bed, TV, money and two guns sat on the table. Two guys stood outside and waited. Trevor stood at the door, lightly shoving her in. She kept her focus on the drugs, feeling the towel being ripped from her body. Trevor stood at the door, watching, smiling, making absurd comments. The two sandwiched her in. It was hard to breathe with all the weight pressing against both sides and she had no control. Five minutes later she fell to the floor, wet and sticky and out of breath. The two guys zipped their pants up, high-fiving Trevor as they walked out. Tamara felt she was sinking lower and lower. Trevor stood over her.

"Who's your God, Tamara?" He knelt down, placing a firm grip on her face, forcing her to look at him. "Who's your God?"

"You are." An out-of-breath plea came from her mouth. Trevor placed a bag in her hand.

"There's more, but only if you're willing to work for me."

"I don't know, Trevor. That really hurt."

"Ha! You'll know when you get low and the real pain sets in. You'll never be without what you have between your legs! Think about it! You'll be back next week, Tam! And it better be with another down payment!" Trevor walked away. She stared into the hallway, listening to them degrade her. *I'll have his damn money. I can't do this! But he knocked off what I owed today.* She headed for the door without speaking.

"I'll be waiting for your call, Tam!"

Tears fell for a minute; her mental block was instantly put up. Right now wasn't the time to feel sorry for herself, she was going to enjoy this high.

⟿

Chad unexpectedly changed his day to keep Jordan until tomorrow. Dana left several messages on Christine's cell, wanting to set up another girls' day out. It was one of those days she just wanted to avoid her, avoid everyone. Her mind was spinning from the hangover. Dana continued calling. Next came a text message. Dana's urgent message caught Christine by surprise.

Dana: Can we meet Chris? It's important we talk.

Chris: Hey, what's up?

Dana: Hello, Chris, I really need to speak with you asap. Can we meet today? I can come to yr house if it works better.

Chris: Oh, ok, can u tell me what it's about?

Dana: Chad!

Chris: My address is 5467 Heartland Drive

Dana: I'll see you soon

Dana made it seem so urgent. What could she possibly want to talk about? She showed up in less time than expected. Christine invited her into the dining area.

"Beautiful place you have, Christine."

"Thanks, Dana. Can I offer you something to drink?"

"Sure, water with ice will be fine."

Dana sat, wondering if this was the right time to expose

what she knew. How was she going to explain it all to her? Chris returned with a glass of water, plopping on the chaise lounge next to her.

"So, what's the urgency, Dana?"

"I really need to speak with you, Chris. It's about Chad." Christine felt her heart skip a beat.

"Okay, about what?"

Dana started in slowly; the real truth couldn't be revealed just yet.

"Have you forgiven Chad for what he's done?"

"Forgiven him? I love him."

"Have you forgiven him?"

"I don't need to forgive; it's a constant reminder every time I see him!"

"So, you're acting out on revenge and bitterness? An unforgiving, vengeful, or bitter spirit will not only affect you and those around you, it will separate you from the blessing of God."

"I'm not bitter, just a little hurt! I love Chad, okay? What's there to forgive? I lost a child!"

"Sooo, that's why you don't respect his relationship? And you keep bedding him 'cause you love him? If you keep inflicting hurt on a person, you don't love them!"

Christine was more than agitated by Dana's questions. *Who the hell does she think she is?*

"You keep throwing this love thing up as your reason to rhyme. Do you know the difference between love and lust?"

"Of course, I do, I graduated from the best damn college! Who doesn't know, Dana?"

"A lot of people don't, Chris. Or they use it as an excuse to say they're in love."

"Lust is purely sexual, love is when you care."

"Agree to disagree, Christine. Lust and love aren't about what college you attended! It's common street sense. You just said it's purely sexual; not true. One can lust after money and material things. Isn't that what you're doing with Chad and he's doing the same with you?"

"No, he's isn't! And I'm not!"

"Come on, Chris! Love is more than caring, honey! And you have to love yourself before you can love someone else!"

"I do love myself! Chad and I are in love!"

"If you loved yourself, Chris, you wouldn't allow yourself to be second or third on a man's list. If you don't start forgiving, you're going to self-destruct."

"I don't need your insults, Dana!" Christine jumped to her feet. "You think because you're all happily married, with a successful husband ..."

"Whoa, Christine, first of all, I'm not insulting you! So you can calm down. Don't you ever bring my husband into what we speak of unless I do!" Dana pointed her finger with a stern look that Chris knew she didn't want to mess with. "The truth is what it is! That's why you're on the defense. I'm not scared of those devils inside of you and they're legions that you have allowed! Because of your personal differences! If you don't get yourself together, it's all coming down on you. You reap what you sow!"

"I don't have devils inside me, Dana!"

"Everyone deals with something Chris, even I do, especially as a Christian! You're so lost in the world, the devil has you blinded and comfortable in shit! I hate to be the bearer of bad news, Chris. When you mentioned Chad's last name, I knew I'd heard it before, but it didn't dawn on me 'till yesterday where I had heard it from. His new wife, Tamara, good hair boo, and yes he's married, Christine. Tamara Lewis, now Tamara Stone, I used to hang out with her. Blonde hair, nice tan, wanna-be black girl!" Christine's eyes shot open.

"It's black."

"She changes it, Chris, a different weave every month. She's a snake; not only a snake but heavily involved with drugs. A guy named Trevor and I can bet you he's draining all of her lemons into sour juice. The bitch couldn't get sweet even if sugar was added.

"What do you mean?"

"Street slang Chris. The bitch is sour and only out to get. Your son is not safe around her. Trevor is also a big dealer around town, supplies her drugs. Tamara's also a whore. I call them how I see 'em. I've seen her do anything for money."

Christine's heart ached; the pain continued crashing in like a huge title wave.

"Tamara tried seducing Jerick before we married. Needless to say, she had sex on the dance floor with one of the guys we knew. She was jealous because Jerick was interested in me, not her. Jerick planned a surprise birthday party for me. Without my knowing, he invited all my friends. You should have seen the outfits worn around my husband. She was out to get him even though she knew the party was for me. Her world came crashing down when Jerick proposed to me. Little did she know it was all a set-up? My cousins and I laughed her out of the party."

Christine felt her world caving in quickly. Her hands started trembling, her stomach turned as she listened. Anxiety set in. The shaking became uncontrollable. A scream of anguish and pain bellowed out of her mouth. She ran out of the room, crying, wishing it was all over. Dana ran after her, apologizing, as Christine knelt over, wallowing in tears. "That explains the rash and sores around my vaginal area I tried ignoring."

"Get yourself tested, and your son, Chris."

"My son?"

"Yes, things spread, Chris."

"No, no, not my son Jordan. This couldn't be happening, not again!" Tears formed a pile on the floor. Dana cried with her, rubbing her back for comfort.

"I can't go through this again! I can't, I can't do this, Dana!"

"I asked my husband if I should tell you. It was hard, Chris. He said if I was a real friend, I would. I hate being the one to tell you this. Tamara hasn't changed, Chris, I'm telling you because you have a son. Chad obviously doesn't know what he's dealing with. Trevor is heartless; he will kill and has killed if he has to. She has sex with him for drugs. This is a drug addict, Chris, who does anything for money and you're sleeping with this guy? She's out for money Chris, a known gold-digging whore!"

The pain was too much to bear. Christine felt her vision going in and out; her body swayed, falling forward.

"Christine! Christine!" Dana sat on the floor next to her, dabbing a cold cloth on her forehead.

"What happened?" Christine touched her forehead, feeling the pain.

"Are you okay? You passed out, Chris."

Christine was weaker than she had expected, collapsing over with the pain. *This is serious, she needs some serious help.* Dana felt horrible for Christine. Deep down, she was a good person but so confused inside. Dana saw so much of herself in her but at a younger age. She helped Chris to the nearest chair, offering to call her parents. She begged her not to. She needed to see a doctor but refused. Dana watched her brush endless tears from her cheeks. Jordan rushed to her side, begging for something to eat.

"I'll take care of him, Chris if you don't mind?" Dana sat him down with a cut apple, a Pb and j sandwich and a glass of milk.

"I'm tired!" Chris struggled from the chair. Dana raced to her aid. "Can you take Jordan for the night?"

"He needs to be with you Chris, he helps you."

"No, no, I don't want him to see me hurt like this. Please." Christine begged.

"Okay, I'll go grab what he needs but first of all, let's get you seated comfortably."

Christine's mind was on nothing but taking a drink.

Dana needs to hurry up. I need to drown out my pain and sorrows. As soon as she and Jordan left, she raced for the cabinet, yanking down two bottles of wine and Hennessy. Drink after drink, Chris polished off one bottle and then the other. She staggered around the house, tipping up the last bit of Hennessy, accidently knocking over pictures and several lamps. The house phone rang; her mother's voice faded in and out. She needed to speak with her and it was urgent. *Who gives a damn! I seem to be in high demand and bad fucking news.* She kept calling. *Stop calling my damn phone!* The bottle smashed up against the wall, shattering, spilling the leftovers on the wall and floor. Christine staggered to the kitchen, yanking down another bottle of wine. Several glasses in the cabinet hit the floor, cracking. The top was too hard to remove. *Damn it! I hate everyone!*

Chris walked to her phone, fumbling through numbers, stopping at Chad's. She pressed "call."

"Hey, Chris."

"You ... you ... you son offff a bitch! I'll ... I'll fucking ki ... ki ... kill you!"

"Christine, is this you?" Chad responded, concerned. Chris screamed her pain into the phone. *Did she find out about the money?* He questioned himself.

"You dirty ba...bas...bastard! I fucking ha...hate you!"

"Christine, what's wrong? What are you talking about? Are you drunk?"

"You ... you always cause pa...pai...pain. I found ou... out you're ... you're married! You ... you ... fucking liar!"

Who in the hell told her? Shit! Chad pulled his ear away

from the phone, searching his mind who could have told her.

"I … I … I hate you! I hate you! That bitch, that b … b … b … bitch is a drug addict, wh…wh…whore! I know, I know everything!" Christine laughed out loud. "You … you married a … a … whore and she's a dru … drug addict! Tamara, Tamara Lewis! You … you dumb ass!"

"Christine! Christine!" She continued yelling. *What the hell was she talking about Tamara being a drug addict whore? How did she know her maiden name?* Her words sent his heart into panic. He paced the floor nervously, denying everything. "Tamara couldn't be!"

"You … you can for … forget about see … see … seeing your son! Never again, never! never!" Christine whimpered. "You wait 'til … 'til Dad … Daddy finds out! He … he's go … gon … rip your ass lim … limb from limb!"

"Christine, it's not true! Please, I'm begging you, don't tell your dad! Please!"

"Too late! There's … there's a rash! Rash … sex … I shouldn't, why? Why? Why, Chad? Oh God, why?" Christine dropped her phone, staggering up toward her bedroom. Echoed cries faded. Chad stood frozen, staring down at the floor. *I'm fucking dead again if any of what Chris said is true! My life is over … the money? Oh God, what have I done? Chris has always been good to me!*

❧

A day had passed as Christine sat polishing off another bottle of wine. Twelve in the afternoon. Dana had called several times. She stood outside with Chris's son, banging and ringing the doorbell. Dana turned away from the door Jordan's little hand clenched in hers. There was no way to tell if Christine was in there. Dana whispered "will try again honey" tucking Jordan into a car seat. She glanced into every window helping to see Chris.

I didn't want him right now; all I want is to drink. Her mother continued calling the home phone and her cell. Christine tilted the bottle up sucking down huge gulps, leaning her head back against the wall. She was a complete drunken wreck, knotted hair, smeared makeup, reeking of alcohol with the same clothes on from yesterday. Trisha sent a text. "Everyone just leave me alone!" She yelled out.

Trisha 12:40 p.m.: Hey, Christine, I've been worried about u lately, u ok?

Trisha 1:35 p.m.: Christine, I need to speak with u

Trisha 2:50 p.m.: If you don't answer I coming over.

Trisha 3:10 p.m.: I'll be over after my shift at 8.

Christine angrily slammed down her cell. Keys jiggled at the front door. She hopped to her feet afraid it was her dad. Quickly she raced through the kitchen, grabbing all the bottles, tossing them into the closet. Her family was a quick way to make anyone sober. *Oh, no, the bottle.* She could still hear the keys at the door which told her it was her mom fumbling with Dad's set of keys.

"Christine!"

What am I gonna do with the mess against the wall? She scanned the room quickly, grabbing a large picture and placing it in front of the shattered glass. Christine raced to the nearest bathroom quickly rinsing with mouthwash.

"Christine!" She turned around to see her mom standing there. She was angry. "Christine Kay Crawford! I've been calling and calling. What the hell is going on?"

"Nothing, Mom!" She kept her cool, refusing to let her know anything.

"You better be glad your father didn't tag along! You look a mess, Christine." Her mother approached but Chris walked away. She followed Chris toward the kitchen.

"Jordan, honey, grandma's here!"

"Ummm … Jordan's with a friend, Mom."

"Who?"

"Dana Russell."

"Who the hell is Dana? I don't approve of my grandson being everywhere! It's bad enough he's allowed at his own father's place!"

"Daddy knows Jerick. He's a business partner, Dana is his wife."

"Oh, wonderful! It's nice to know you've found a real friend. Does she have children?"

"No, she keeps her nephew, Ryan. He and Jordan play well."

"Lord knows that boy needs to be around other children his age before he grows up to be a sociopath."

"Not my son, Mom."

"Look at his father."

"Please, Mom! What's so urgent?"

"I was reviewing your bank statement, Christine. What's this large purchase made?"

"What purchase?"

"Thirty thousand dollar check was written by you to a Heather a day ago. I can't make out the last name."

Christine's heart sank to her feet. Her mother handed over the bank statement. Chris felt her lungs caving in.

"What the hell did you write a thirty thousand dollar check for, Christine?"

She quickly swallowed the lump in her throat. She was without words, and couldn't answer her mom. Her chest heaved up and down.

"Christine, what and who did you write this check for?"

I had only written a check to Chad for five; what was this? She thought. "Excuse me, Mom." Christine felt nauseous feeling the twisting pain circle around her stomach.

"I need an answer, Chris!

"I'm sure I can answer that mom."

She ran to the other room grabbing her purse, ripping through it and pulling out her checkbook. *Check 1100, 1101* she called the numbers silently in her head. *1103. Where's check 1102? Where's the one written for five thousand?*

"Christine Crawford, I'm talking to you!" her mom yelled from the other room.

"It was for an old bill, Mom. I don't understand where the check is. I'm sorry. Yeah, I ran across the bill, I've been trying to avoid it because it cost so much and I didn't want you and dad to be mad. So I finally got the nerve to pay it off."

"A personal check, Christine?"

"Yeah, Heather owns a company. I had purchased a piece of furniture and forgot to pay her."

"Look, Christine, I can hide everything else from your father but when it comes down to his money, Donny wants to know everything, even the damn serial numbers on each bill. He has worked too hard for this, Christine! I'll hide this one from him, but you can best believe the next time it's going straight into his hands!"

Chris just wanted her to leave - now! She nodded, agreeing, keeping her distance, thinking to herself. Chad, it was Chad! Her insides cried. *He had to have changed the amount when I was drunk. That asshole, he used me! They warned me, I hate him! I hate myself!*

"Christine, are you listening to me?"

"Yes, Mom."

"You don't seem yourself, something's off with you. Are you okay?"

"Yeah, just tired. Thanks for keeping my problems from dad, Mom. Are you finished? I have to run out to the store. I'm a little low on a few things for Jordan and me."

Valerie pecked Chris on the cheek, handing over the paperwork.

"Shred it, asap! And get a damn shower, you smell like the boys from the gym."

"Yes."

"Get out of the house more, Chris! I mean it! I'm worried about you."

"Okay, Mom, don't worry, I'm fine."

She slammed the door, sinking to the floor, crying, ashamed and alone, too embarrassed to call anyone to show how used she had been.

Dana: Christine I came by r u ok?
Christine: Yeah, I just need to rest. Can Jordan stay with you again? I promise to get my sweet boy back 2morrow.
Dana: Sure, don't do anything stupid, Chris. Not your fight.
Christine: Yeah I know, thanks Dana.

∽∾

There was quite the discomfort coming from her personal area as she sat on the toilet. It hurt to wipe. She propped her foot on the countertop, lifting her gown. The area was red and itchy with little bumps formed around her inner thigh. She noticed a bump on her lip. *Oh, my God, what is it?* She stripped down quickly, turning the water on warm and hopped in. Water ran down her face, along with tears. *Dana warned me and so did Daddy! How could I be so stupid?* A burning sensation hurt as she ran soap across the area. *It can't be, no, it can't be!*

Christine let the area air out before placing on some boxers, something that wouldn't hug the skin. She needed an appointment now! The doorbell echoed through the house. Shit! Trisha's SUV sat in the driveway. She walked toward the door slowly. "Trisha, what do you want?"

"That's no way to welcome an old friend and ex-love

now, is it!" She rushed in, standing in front of her. "You look horrible."

"Yes. Trisha, I'd rather you not be here."

"Oh, I get it, you'd rather have Chad." Trisha laughed.

"No, I wouldn't. I just wanna be alone right now."

"So you can drink your problems away, Chris?"

"I haven't touched a drink, Trish!"

"That's a damn lie, who the hell do you think you're fooling? Remember, I was there, Chris, lies and all!"

"You don't have to remind me, Trisha, okay? I said I haven't been drinking!"

"So, you're going to keep lying to me, huh?" Trish stormed passed her. Christine grabbed her arm, fighting to keep her back. She opened the closet door. "I told you, you were lying! I told you!"

"Get out, Trisha, just get the hell out! Chris raced toward Trisha, swinging her arms. Trisha grabbed her, tossing her backward. Get outta here!"

"You found out, huh? You found out the truth and, let me guess, it's Chad, the one who loves you, and you love him! That son of a bitch!"

"It's none of your business Trisha, go home to your girlfriend!"

"Not till I mention what I have to say."

"Just hurry up!"

"I have bumps around my vaginal area. Christine avoided eye contact, staring out the window. Did you hear me, Chris, I have bumps, a rash. I didn't have it before."

"So you come here, blaming me. You better check your goddamn new girlfriend!"

"So typical of you! Your ex is the one who can't keep his dick in his pants! She doesn't have it, Chris!" Trish yelled, yanking Chris's face toward her. "Yeah, it's you, look at the damn cold sore on your lip. I never thought you'd allow someone to give you a disease, Chris! And now me! Chad!"

"Fuck off, Trisha! Who knows who the hell you've been with and her!"

"No, you fuck off, Christine! I trusted you! I warned you! You got your head so far up your ass you're not listening, and now look!"

"Get the hell outta here Trisha, before I tell!"

"Tell what Christine? That it was your idea to murder Danielle!"

"No, it wasn't, Trisha it was your idea damn it! You hit her!"

"And so did your drunken ass! Bitch! The nerve of you, all for Chad! Again, that bastard is mixed up in all of this shit! Your dick-whipped ass continued sleeping with him and he's married. Married, Chris! If you ever mention my name in Danielle's murder, be sure to mention your own bitch!"

"They won't believe you!" Christine laughed. I have money, Trisha! It's all going to fall on you bitch! You, not me! You!"

"There's one thing you missed, Christine. Because I'm used to you and your bougey family throwing around money! I recorded you hitting Danielle." Christine looked

Trisha in the eyes. "I also have your text message on my old phone, and how you wanted her dead that night!"

"Your texts read the same! You wanted her dead! You bitch! You bitch!" Christine charged at Trisha, clawing.

Trisha yanked Chris by her hair, slamming her face down to the floor. She lay helpless, whimpering. "You really don't know me Christine, and I can be your worst nightmare. So, go tell it, go! You have nothing on me, bitch!" Trisha let go, rising up from the floor watching her cry. "You disgust me Christine, no backbone, only money." She turned away, slamming the door behind her.

Christine opened the closet; there was no more to drink. She placed on some jogging pants and grabbed her set of keys. Every horrible thought passed through her mind while heading to the store. She wanted them gone.

She headed straight to the counter, pointing out the different liquors, as the cashier piled them on the counter. She rang up the total. It was well over hundred dollars. Christine handed over the cash, telling her to keep the change. She stuffed the bottles into her trunk. The next stop was the grocery store. She ran through, grabbing what was needed, along with six bottles of wine.

～⊗～

Chad's life was in turmoil. Christine's call had him on pins and needles, wondering if Donny was going to come over. Most disturbing was Tamara and she being a drug addict whore. That would explain where all the money has gone. *I have just given her five g's! Oh, God! I got a migraine from all this.* He looked inside the medicine cabinet searching for Tylenol; a bottle of pills fell into the sink. Valac..yclo…vir. *What the hell is this? I can barely pronounce the name!* He tossed back a few pills staring at himself briefly in the mirror. *I'm in so much shit if it's true about Tam.*

The front door opened and closed. Keys were placed on the front table. Chad walked up front as Tamara paced the floor. She seemed more than nervous and shocked to see him standing there.

"Chad, you scared me!"

"Hey, where you been?"

"I told you, I paid a few bills."

"Do you still have money left?"

"Ye … yeah, I do, why?"

"My car payment is due and I wanted it to come out of the money I gave you."

"Why can't you use yours, Chad?"

"Because it's my money."

"You mean Chris's money … I'm sorry, Chad."

"Where else did you go?"

"Why all the questions? I told you, and I stopped by a friend's house."

"I need five hundred to pay off my car, Tamara." Chad handed out his hand.

"It's in the bank Chad. I'm not walking around with all that money! I'll take care of it tomorrow!"

"Do you have any money on you?"

"What? Why are you hounding me about fucking money Chad!"

"You can lower your goddamn voice, Tamara. I'll ask what I please when it comes to the money I've given!"

"I'm sorry, I just don't know why you're asking me all this!"

"You can stop yelling at me, Tamara. You're acting like some damn crack head!" She walked away grabbing her keys from the counter top. Chad stopped her before leaving, yanking her back through the door.

"Let go of me, damn it!"

"What the hell is wrong with you?" She fought him, almost ripping his eyes out, demanding he let go. As Tamara weaseled out of his grip, her back was accidently revealed. As he pulled her shirt down, he noticed the marks.

"What the hell is this on your back Tamara? She stood crying, avoiding the question. What is it?" His forced grip on her arm revealed the inner tracks running down the inside of her arms. His world was spinning. Tamara remained speechless, crying aloud. Where is my damn money, Tamara?"

"I gotta go!"

"You're not going anywhere, damn it! What the hell are these marks on your back and inner arms? I wanna know now!" He screamed angrily in her face.

"Nothing, Chad, nothing!"

"Nothing, nothing! Who was here earlier huh? Trevor, your so-called high school buddy! Was he here, Tamara? That's his damn belt! What the hell is it doing off his pants? You fucked him in our living room, didn't you?" Tamara felt a sting on her cheek. She grabbed a hold of her face before Chad's hand struck again. Tamara remained in denial.

"Stop it, please! I'm your wife!"

"Are you fucking him? Chad gripped her face, wanting answers now. He could see by the look in her eyes it was all true. He shoved her back, knocking her to the floor. "Get the hell outta here!"

"Chad, please!"

"Get out bitch, you been fucking this bastard in my home! Is he supplying your drugs Tam, is that it? I'll kill that bastard!"

"No! Please, he's dangerous, Chad, he'll have his boys kill you!"

"So it's all true, you fuck him for drugs, and you been using my goddamn money to give to him! You dirty bitch! I should have seen it coming a mile away."

"It's no different from you screwing your ex-wife!"

"At least she's not a damn drug addict whore! Get the hell out of here, before I ..." Chad raced toward Tamara with thoughts of strangling her dead but stopped himself. "Get out bitch!"

"I'm sorry, Chad, I never meant to hurt you," Tamara whimpered picking her keys off the floor. His mental block refused to hear her lies.

❦

Trisha couldn't believe Chris had the nerve to threaten her with Danielle's death. She drove through town furious, contemplating stopping by the police station. Now wasn't the time. Chris was already self-destructing and fast.

❦

Dana: Jordan's running a fever, complain throat hurts.
Christine: Ok calling doctor, u can bring him home.
Dana: Ok, gave him Tylenol for fever
Christine: Thanks Dana, c u

❦

Dana stood by Chris's side, helping her keep Jordan calm in the hospital waiting room. She gave that stare like she knew all of Chris's horrible secrets. The nurse called. Dana and Chris followed her to the nearest room. Chris hated this hospital, too many bad memories. "The doctor will be with you shortly." She closed the door. Chris snuggled Jordan close to her; he was burning up. More so, the pain between her legs was growing.

A series of test were run. It was quite alarming when she asked to run a sexual disease test on Chris. She refused. Doctor Vixen said it was the only way to get a quick answer. She begged Chris to perform the test. Dana lowered her head walking over to the door. She looked at Chris before stepping out of the room.

"I noticed the cold sore on your lip, Christine," said Dr. Vixen

"So?"

"Have you ever had them before?"

"No." She marked off some notes on her paperwork.

"That's why I asked to run a test on you."

"Because of a cold sore? What about my son?"

"It appears to be the herpes simplex virus."

"What? No ... no way!"

"Have you had unprotected sex with multiple partners, Christine?"

"What about my son?" Christine cried.

"Answers in your son's condition lie with you, Christine, but only if you're honest with me."

"I'm so embarrassed." Doctor Vixen took Jordan from Christine's arms, placing him on the chair next to her. "Yes, I've had unprotected sex, but I know him!"

"Christine, it happens all the time, you never really know a person. Any vaginal discomfort, rashes, pain?"

"Yes, I noticed them today. Please don't tell me this was passed to my son?"

"We don't know yet, Christine."

"Oh, no! How?"

"Well, touching something infected with the herpes virus, such as infected dishes, towels, razors, and other shared items. If you've shared a drink with your son it can be transferred. Please get on the examining table."

Christine sat back with her legs up, feeling the pain, mentally and physically. Another nurse stood on the side of Doctor Vixen handing over the utensils. *I never thought I'd be in this situation.* The test was over. Doctor Vixen tapped her on the leg and asked her to get dressed.

Okay, Christine," she sighed. "From the red blistering bumps on your vaginal area, I can tell you now that it's herpes type 2. This is the one that occurs around the vaginal area."

Christine placed her hand over her mouth crying. Her hatred for Chad burned out of control.

"This isn't the end of the world Christine, there's medicine to help make it easier, which I'm going to write you a prescription for. As for your son, I'm also writing him a prescription for herpes simplex one. Sorry, but Jordan has all the signs."

Christine's cries became louder as she felt alone again. *Not my son!* Dana rushed in, quickly rubbing Chris's back. She helped her off the table, grabbing a hold of Jordan's hand.

"The doctor says I have herpes two, and Jordan herpes one."

"I'm so sorry Christine. Do you know where it came from?"

"Yes, him, Chad!"

"And he more than likely got it from Tamara! My gosh, if I wasn't saved I'd send my girls to whip her butt and his too. Vengeance is mine, saith the Lord. Christine, I hope you have thought long and hard about what we talked about."

"I'll never forgive that bastard! Never! I wish he was dead!"

"Christine, don't speak like that! Don't ever wish death on someone; you wouldn't want it done to you or your son!"

"I don't fucking care anymore! I don't care about anything!"

"You should care! When we act carelessly in life we suffer the consequences! I know you don't want to hear this but there are consequences for everything we do, good or bad Chris! You have a beautiful son, who loves you regardless. You allowed Chad in Christine. Again, choice, you made yours!"

Christine hated to admit that Dana was right. She had been fine for three years with him out of her life. Yeah, she had missed him, but it wasn't this bad. She had made a horrible mistake of thinking lust was love.

My only hope was to pray silently for Christine as she vented out her pain, Dana thought. Jordan slept through it all; he must be used to it. The vilest and wicked words poured from Christine's mouth sending chills down Dana's spine. Her inner demons were rising and out of control.

Once they arrived at Christine's home, Dana stayed an hour helping her around the house, cleaning, putting Jordan to bed. Her mind drew a blank seeing all the empty alcohol bottles in the pantry. She didn't know how to even approach her. *Chris can't be drinking like this?* She wanted to stay but she had her own household to attend to, and besides, Jerick was calling.

Dana said her goodbyes, insisting Chris call on her if she needed her. She gave Chris a pamphlet, telling her to read it: that her only way out was accepting Jesus as her Lord and savior and repenting.

Chris studied it for five minutes but her mind was distracted. She needed something now. She placed the pamphlet on the bed, heading straight toward the kitchen, grabbing her keys. Her mouth watered, staring into the trunk. Carefully she toted each bag of liquor into the house placing what she needed on the counter and some in the pantry. She placed the rest in a large box, flipping it closed. She rinsed out her favorite glass and quickly cracked the top off several bottles. Inside her pain she sucked in a few deep breaths, bringing every painful thought to memory. She filled her glass with the best wine, gulping it down, smiling in relief. Another glass brought satisfaction but not enough. She continued refilling her glass until the bottle of wine was gone. Her pain still existed. She opened another bottle, Czar's Golden Snow, and added a mixture of Twenty Grand Vodka Cognac. She sipped slowly as the hours passed laughing, feeling her pain dissipate. Half a bottle of Cognac sat beside her on the kitchen floor.

"Th … tha … that jack … jackass Chad!"

Christine's head swayed from side to side. She focused her blurred vision on two tables; there were two of everything. Slowly she continued sipping, making her outrageous comments about everyone.

"Daddy!" she screamed, curling into a ball. "Hel … hel … help me!" Chris whispered, knocking over empty bottles of liquor all over the floor.

"I ha…ha…hate…h … him! I ha…ha…ever…y…one. Myself…I hat…ha…hate it, hate it!"

Christine felt her heart accelerating; she placed her hand over her heart, gasping as she stumbled to her feet, tripping over the bottles. She exhaled deeply walking through a distorted house. Vomit shot from her mouth onto the couch as Christine dropped to her knees, crawling toward the front door. She grabbed her chest, trying to fight her slowed breathing. Blackness floated against her eyelids. Her body slumped forward head first, slamming against the floor.

◈

Marie had arrived early to clean Chris's home. She didn't know what Chris was going through but the house was in need of a lot more cleaning than the usual twice a week. She was here the majority of the week. She rang the doorbell just to make sure she wasn't near to let her in. *She's probably still sleeping.*

Marie wiggled her keys, placing it into the keyhole. She entered. Her cleaning supplies hit the floor. "Chris!" Her body lay face-first on the floor in front of the couch.

Paramedics raced through the streets, responding to an urgent call from Marie who said she had arrived to clean and found her boss collapsed on the floor.

◈

Dana rushed home, and told Jerick about Christine's alcohol bottles, and urged him to phone Donny and explain what she had witnessed. It was a tough nut to crack. Donny denied it, and even threatened to cut his business deal with Jerick. His daughter wasn't a drunk. Valerie burst into the conversation, asking questions. Once Jerick mentioned Chad, the phone got silent. Jerick explained that Dana was just with their daughter at the hospital. Donny's demeanor quickly changed, demanding to speak with Dana. Jerick muffled the phone.

"He wants to speak to you."

"No, no, no." She quickly gave him the cut throat signal.

"He doesn't believe me, Dana! You know, you were there!" Dana sucked in a few deep breaths, slowly placing the phone up toward her ear.

"Hello, Mr. Crawford."

"What the hell is going on? What's this about my daughter drinking? What, are you trying to get some rumor started?" Jerick hopped to his feet pacing the floor.

"Mr. Crawford!" Dana couldn't get a word in.

"Was this your intention to get close to her?"

"Mr. Crawford, please." He continued babbling as if Dana was a liar. "Mr. Crawford, please hush and listen!" The tone of her voice overrode his, giving her a chance to speak. Paranoia sat on her husband's face. "Please stop with all the accusations! I asked my husband to call you, not to start a childish rumor, or whatever you might think! I asked my husband to call because I am concerned about Christine! I don't care if you don't want to hear it or not, sir! But your daughter is hurting. I was with her tonight at the hospital."

"Hospital? How come we didn't know?"

"I don't know sir, she called me and she had been drinking. To make a long story short, Christine asked me to keep Jordan. It was no problem; I did, for longer than expected. I should have known something was wrong when Christine didn't open the door. Jordan was running a fever. That was the only way I could get her to respond! I drove her and Jordan to the hospital. The news wasn't good, sir." *Why the hell do rich people always defend their children and refuse to believe that their children can do no wrong?* Dana thought.

"What was the news?"

"I'd rather you discuss it with Christine. She's been drinking! A lot."

"My daughter is not a drunk! How dare you!"

"You can sit in denial all you want, sir!"

"My daughter is not a drunk!"

"I know what I saw sir!" One thing Dana hated was people who didn't listen. She didn't have a problem with standing up to them. "If you were to go over there, you would see it in the pantry, the empty bottles!"

Valerie's screams echoed through the phone. Dana heard her screaming Christine's name, the maid finding her on the floor, paramedics rushing her to the hospital. Suddenly, the phone went silent.

"Hello, Mr. Crawford! Mr. Crawford!" Dana placed her hand over her mouth, bursting into tears. Jerick rushed over quickly taking her in his arms.

"What's wrong honey, what happened?"

"I don't know. Tears continue falling. I guess his wife got a call from someone. Oh, my gosh, Christine! The maid found her on the floor! I don't know, I don't know what happened, the phone went dead!" Jerick and Dana instantly went into prayer for Christine; she needed it.

Donny and his wife ran frantically toward the garage. Donny placed a call to the hospital, demanding answers about their daughter. There wasn't a Christine Crawford admitted yet. The receptionist ran across her name on the computer that she was coming in as a new arrival.

"What did they say? What did they say?"

"She said Christine's is being rushed there now, they can't give any damn information!" Donny hung up the phone furious, squealing out of the driveway.

❧

I promised Sandra I'd be home two hours ago, I was more than late, though Trisha. Christine's threats had her distraught but more so pissed off. She wasn't about to let Christine throw her under the bus about Danielle! No way in hell.

Inside their apartment, Sandra sat at the dinner table, sipping wine. Trisha's quick apology did nothing; she had this evil smirk on her face, barely speaking two words. Sandra watched her walk into the bedroom. *I just hope I haven't infected her with herpes.* She searched her dresser drawer for her old phone. She felt around for it in the normal place she had left it, wrapped tightly in her t-shirt. Panic overtook her. *Where is it?* She tore through her clothes. *Maybe I put it in a different spot? No, no I didn't.* Freaking out, she searched her entire side of the dresser, ripping through her nicely folded up clothing. *Where is it, damn it?* She paced the floor aimlessly, thinking. Every thought brought her back to when she had placed the phone in the t-shirt. She was keeping the memories of Christine and her. *Oh, God! I know I put it here.* She didn't have enough nerve to ask Sandra; there was so much from photos, texts between Chris and her that Sandra didn't need to see. Oh, no, and worst of all? *Damn it, where is that phone?* Heavy knocking at the front door startled her. Sandra silently got up from the table.

⌘

Curiosity and Trisha's lying had opened Sandra's eyes to her games. She knew she was still in love with that bitch, Christine Crawford. Most of the time she claimed to be late. *Ha! I knew where she's been.* Payback's a bitch.

⌘

Trisha dropped her pride, heading out to ask Sandra if she had seen her phone. Through the hallway, she could hear two unfamiliar voices echoing. "Sandra hav ...?" She blanched at the sight of two police officers standing at the front door. Sandra still had that devious smirk on her face.

"Your phone?"

Trisha's heart sank to the floor. She was speechless. *What did she know?*

"The one with you and Christine plastered all through it! Damn photos, oh, and better yet, old text messages of how you and Ms. Crawford murdered Danielle Rivers!"

Trisha shook her head in denial, feeling cornered by the walls. *She betrayed me!* "Sandra, that's not true, I just never got rid of it!"

"It's all in the phone Trisha! You guys murdered an innocent woman!"

"Innocent! You don't know what the hell you're talking about! No, it was Christine!" The two officers approached her, one scrolling through her phone. "It was Christine! I swear to you, it was her idea! He was cheating on her, her husband, with that woman!" Tears rolled down Trisha's face, her voice became hoarse from all the yelling. "Chad, Chad Stone, she wanted him dead 'cause he was cheating! Please, you have to believe me!" Sandra's smirk told it all. Trisha's arms were tugged behind her back, cold clamps gripped tightly around her wrist. "Sandra, how could you do this to me? I didn't do it! I swear I swear I didn't do it!"

"Ma'am, you have the right to remain silent. Anything you say can and will be used against you in a court of law. You have the right to an attorney." The rights being read floated in one ear and out the other. "With these rights in mind, do you wish to speak with me?" the woman police officer continued to ask.

"No, I have an attorney."

"I'll have all your stuff out this weekend. So I hope you have somewhere to put it!" Said Sandra. If Trisha's looks could kill, they would have knocked Sandra dead on the spot.

"Yes, I will."

The neighbors stood in the hallway watching. It was the walk of shame being ushered out in handcuffs by two police officers. Trisha could hear the whispering, and the obvious pointing of fingers made her lower her head.

If I am going down, she is too. Trisha sat back thinking of all the mess she had allowed herself to get into. One of the officers mentioned Mr. Crawford while talking to her partner. *What was that all about?* She looked back at Sandra, quickly shutting down the conversation, leaving her curiosity on high alert.

⌘

Donny and Valerie arrived at the hospital. It was a moment of anticipation, wondering why their daughter was rushed to the hospital. Donny rushed out of the doors, pulling Valerie to his side, in search of the nearest desk.

"May I help you, sir?" The receptionist asked.

"Christine Crawford." Donny waited as she entered Christine's name.

"She appears to be in with the doctors right now."

"What? For what, does she have a room?"

"Sorry sir, from what it looks like she was just brought in by the paramedics. My computer is not giving much info."

"I … we need to know something now!" Donny slammed his fist down on the desk. This is our only daughter! I want the best doctors helping her! Only the best, money is no object!"

"I'm sorry sir until we're confirmed with a room you two are going to have to be seated in the waiting room."

"Are you serious?" Donny stormed off angrily. A call came through at the receptionist desk.

"Hold on, sir!" Donny and Valerie quickly turned around. They waited for the receptionist to finish her conversation. "Okay sir, sorry about that. Doctor Spindel is on duty tonight, he's familiar with Christine. He wants you two to wait in the smaller waiting room, away from everyone else."

"Did he say how she was doing and what she's here for?" Valerie questioned.

"I'm sorry no, he didn't."

Valerie sighed wiping her tears.

Donny and Valerie were pointed in the direction of the smaller waiting room. Donny paced the floor periodically glancing at his watch. The door opened. Doctor Spindel stood there, holding a clipboard. Donny extended his hand giving a firm handshake.

"What's going on, Doctor Spindel? Why is our daughter here?"

"Well, Mr. and Mrs. Crawford, it won't be the best news coming from my month," Doctor Spindel sighed.

"What? What the hell is going on?"

"Right now we're pumping Christine's stomach."

"Pumping her stomach! From what damn it?"

"Alcohol poisoning! She was drinking, heavily drinking. Does Christine have an alcohol problem?" Donny lowered his head, replaying Dana's conversation.

"What? No. No, she doesn't."

Valerie slumped over, placing her hand over her mouth, bursting into tears.

"Christine is way over the alcohol limit. She has too much alcohol in her system. Her vital signs are extremely low and she is unresponsive. Does she have a drinking problem?"

"I don ... I don't know where all this is coming from."
Donny ran his fingers across the top of his head.

"This type of drinking isn't something one just picks up.
It's a long-existing problem."

"You're saying our daughter's an alcoholic?"

"Mr. Crawford, that's something you, your daughter and
your wife need to discuss. I'll let you know when Christine's
in a room."

The room went silent. Donny stood with a perplexed
look, gazing down the hallway. Dana's word's replayed
again.

"Grandpa, Grandma." Jordan's little voice called from
the opposite end of the hallway. Valerie stepped into another room, quickly wiping her tears.

"Mr. and Mrs. Crawford." Marie flagged them down,
waving her hand. "I'm so sorry." Donny reached down,
boosting Jordan into the air. "I'm so sorry; I have never been
so terrified in my life!"

"What happened, Marie?"

"I don't know, Mr. C., I walked in and found Chris's body
on the floor. I rushed over to her. Her breathing was shallow
and she had a light pulse. I called the paramedics first, kept
them on the line, then Valerie on the land line. If I wouldn't
have shown up!" Marie wiped her tears. "There were bottles, so much liquor; she reeked of alcohol, Mr. C. One doctor asked if Chris had a drinking problem. I told them no, I
don't know!"

"Grandpa, where's Mommy?" Jordan interrupted.
Donny looked at his grandson, unsure how to respond.

"Mommy will be here soon hun," Marie spoke. "Here, I'll take Jordan to get a snack, sir. Please keep me posted. You can call me on my cell phone when you feel it's safe for him to return."

"Thank you, Marie." Jordan cried, calling out "Mommy" as Marie comforted him, walking him the other direction.

The news Dana spoke of and now Marie was devastating. *My little girl, a drinking problem, alcohol poisoning? Where did all of this come from?* Donny walked back toward the room, engulfed with thoughts. He paused between the door structures. "Chad freaking Stone! That damn Chad!" Donny blurted out.

"Honey, what is it? What about Chad? He's been out of Christine's life for years now!"

"I'm not so certain about that!"

"Yes, he has!"

"Val, a week ago I received an anonymous call at four in the morning. The caller said Chad had stayed the night with our daughter! I rushed over furious, ready to kill that asshole! When I got there, a car was there." Donny laughed. "She hid it, him, Chad. That pussy ran out the back door, she helped him. Christine mentioned something about him bringing medicine for Jordan!"

"I hope that's all it was because Chad is married!" Donny whipped his head around shocked.

"What? Married! What the hell was he doing over there at the house that time of morning?" Donny's anger ignited as he paced the floor.

"I sure hope Christine isn't that stupid." Valerie reflected back to the thirty thousand dollars missing. Pieces were coming together; the money was withdrawn from the bank account last week. Valerie lowered her head. "Oh, God!"

"What?"

Valerie stood, hesitant. *I swear I'll have that punk bastard killed if he's is remotely involved! I swear on my life!* Now was not the best time to tell Donny, maybe never. Donny made it adamant about his hatred toward Chad. "Honey, please calm down, please don't make a scene."

"Calm! I'll show you calm!" Donny dialed a number on his cell, quickly placing it up toward his ear.

"Donny, please."

"Not now, Valerie!" He knew Chad wouldn't answer. He made sure to leave the most hateful and threatening message ever. If he was any way involved with Christine's being in the hospital, he was dead! Chad was going to get the message one way or the other. His fingers wouldn't stop texting. His marriage, sleeping with his daughter… he made known.

⚜

Chad's phone continued to blow up and just when he thought life couldn't get any worse. Reading and listening to Donny's threats had him trembling in fear. Word was out and Donny knows he was married. Christine was in the hospital due to alcohol poisoning? Oh, my gosh! *Donny will kill me if he finds out about the money. What if Chris already told him? Donny has the power to strip me and my family of everything.* One problem had led to another. His phone continued ringing. He refused to answer his calls. *I need to get out of here! I need to leave! Donny has me feeling like a criminal on America's Most Wanted.* Chad called his boys, Travis and Marco, with the only suitable solution he could think of.

❧

How did I get here? How did I allow people to dictate my life? I'm in control, not them! Trisha, Chad all of them, no one could see my pain. Rich people don't go through this! I've always got what I wanted, I've always held it together! I've always fixed the problem damn it!

"Humble yourself." The voice floated across her subconscious mind. "Pride and arrogance I hate."

"Who are you, speaking?"

"You're reaping what you have sown."

"Huh? Who are you?"

"Let go, my child! Your demons are too big to battle. Humble yourself."

"Humble?" *Daddy, Mommy where are you? I hear voices but they're not yours. Jordan! Baby, where are you? Why is it so dark? I hear you talking, who are you people and why are you touching me? Where am I?* Lying there, parts of her life were revealed, good and bad. It was horrible: lying, cheating, pride, arrogance, devious nature. Assisting in a crime over revenge, threatening Trisha. *My God, I felt used, abused like someone else was controlling me. I wasn't in control! I'm lost and afraid, Lord, please help me!* The darkness continued to claw at her, trapped by chains and legions of demons too big for self-battle. *Help me, I am lost! Dana was right! Money wasn't going to save me, nor mom and dad.* Grandma Denis and Dana's prayers were being revealed to her. *Daddy, you can't solve this one with money.*

For two days, Christine's vital signs remained a mystery. Doctors told Donny and Valerie that she was brain dead. *"I'm here! Can't you hear me?"* All her strength was gone, there was no movement in her body. Donny continued demanding the best doctors. They came and went, still the same results, disappointment. *I don't wanna go to hell!* Christine's screams became louder, afraid and alone; things in a world she knew existed but never taken seriously were shown to her. *I don't wanna go, please save me! The Lord revealed to me what I needed to do in order for Him to let me out of this. If not, He would surely let me die and go to hell. I give in, please save me!* The darkness disappeared. She could feel her fingers move. Several doctors rushed in, checking her vital signs. In their perplexed moment, they all wondered how Christine recuperated.

I can see grandma praising God. Daddy thanked the doctors; they instantly took credit for something they didn't do. Mom's voice echoed in my head as she leaned over, calling my name. I am still out of it. Grandma rubbed my fingers, leaning closer. I continued whispering "Thank you, Jesus. Thank you, Jesus!"

"What is she whispering, Mom?" Valerie asked.

"Praise God!" Grandma shouted. "She's whispering 'Thank you, Jesus!' It wasn't your money or those knuckle-headed doctors. You heard them say it. That they couldn't do anything else for her! Get your head outta your butt,

Donny! You spent all this money! For what? For a mystery work of the Lord that no man could take credit for! Instead of thanking Jesus, you thanked man! I'm appalled at you, Valerie Kay! You better pick up your old roots! It's a shame her friend and I had to come lay hands on her, anoint her with blessed oil. This is something you should be doing! Donny and Valerie, you will learn, 'cause this battle is far from being over. Jesus is in control now, not these damn doctors! And Chris better walk the walk! You'll see, some things are going to happen that money and pride will not save!"

Momma was right, thought Valerie. She felt horrible. She didn't realize she'd strayed so far from Him. Money, the money. Donny stood arrogantly with his usual unbreakable look. Tears fell to her face as Chris opened her eyes. *Thank you, Lord! I know momma's a prophetess; when she let you have it, she never held back. Donny didn't like it because she could read him like a book.* Valerie thought.

"Hi Mom, Grandma, Dad," Chris whispered. "I'm sorry, everyone."

"It's okay honey, just get some rest." Valerie held on for dear life. *Momma was right. Christine has major issues, the help a parent could not provide.*

❧

My life is over! Trisha thought. *I can't believe Sandra went through my things and called the police. So much incriminating evidence was on my phone. Three police officers brutally interrogated me, accusing me of murder. I didn't say much.*

They switched things up, and I was confused. Her attorney arrived; by that time Trisha was in tears, overwhelmed and scared.

☙⸱

Two men dressed in suits unexpectedly appeared outside Chris's hospital door. Mr. Crawford did a double take, wondering what the hell was going on. Valerie looked down at her daughter, gazing deep into her eyes. By her sorrowful expression, there was something Chris was holding on to. Valerie felt Chris's hand tighten as she watched Donny race for the door. Questions ran rampant through his mind why the detectives from Danielle's case were outside. Detective Marsh extended his hand briefly introducing his partner Detective Johnson quickly stepping aside.

Donny's handshake was nothing like the usual firm, confident grip; it was loose. Unsure, he stood, periodically glancing back at Valerie and Christine, his merciless voice lowered almost to a whisper.

"What brings you, gentlemen here?"

"Mr. Crawford, I'm sorry to bother you and your family at this time, but we have some questions we would like to ask your daughter," spoke Detective Johnson.

"Is this a joke? About what?"

"We have some new evidence in the murder of Danielle, and it involves you daughter Christine."

"What?" Donny stepped forward, filling in his gap of uncertainty. "Are you two joking?"

"No, sir! Trisha was arrested and we have new evidence proving …"

"Proving what, damn it!" Donny pointed his finger in Johnson's face. "What did that damn Trisha say? Now you're accusing my daughter of being a murderer! The nerve of you!" Donny moved closer, whispering out his frustration. "My daughter will not speak with you without our attorney present!"

"I expected you to say that, Mr. Crawford. Here's my card."

"I don't need your damn card!" Donny rudely shoved it back into Johnson's hand.

"Fine, but you'll need that attorney. We have some heavy evidence linking your daughter and Trisha at the crime scene of Danielle. I should have just come and arrested her, but by rights, since you're so well-known and people respect you, I thought it would be best to question first. Keep down the ruckus, you know."

"You mean to keep from gettin' your ass sued! What in the hell is going on, Marsh?"

"I'm just going by what we have, Mr. Crawford. I don't like it anymore than you do. You'll be seeing a lot more of Detective Marsh and me. Good day, sir."

Donny stood frozen, angered, watching the two detectives walk away. He took several deep breaths before returning back into the room. Valerie stood by Christine's bedside with curiosity written all over her face.

"Donny, why was detective Marsh and the other man here?" Valerie approached Donny. "What was that all about?

I can see something's got you uptight." Donny pulled Valerie into the bathroom.

"Detectives Marsh and Johnson just arrested Trisha!"

"Oh, my God, for what?"

"They said it's about Danielle's murder."

"No way, not Trisha!"

"That's not all of it, they wanted to question Christine!"

"About what Donny?"

"They said there's evidence linking Trisha and Chris to Danielle's murder!"

"Bullshit! Valerie whispered. "What? No way Christine and Trisha were at the house. I don't believe this, Donny!" Valerie cried. "What are they trying to do to our baby?"

"You mean what has your baby done to herself? Momma's voice spoke from around the corner. I told you earlier, Christine had a lot of things she needs to do, this is one of them."

"What are you saying, Momma! That she's involved?"

"No, you said it! If Christine doesn't do what's right, Jesus will make her pay. He saved her life for this very reason."

"You're talking crazy Mom! You're as bad as those damn detectives!"

"You can lower your voice when speaking to me, Valerie Kay! I told you the battle was far from being over! I love my granddaughter with all my heart! But what's right is right and what's wrong is wrong!"

"I don't get what you're saying!" Spoke Donny.

"Are you saying your granddaughter, the one you so

love, has something to do with a murder? Huh, momma?"
Valerie raised her voice. Donny walked away furious heading over toward Christine. "If you think that, Momma, get
out! Get out and never come back!" Valerie whispered,
pointing her finger toward the door.

"You think it's that easy to shove your problems under
the rug? Remember, you always trip on them! I don't have
the time of day or night to argue with you. I won't waste
my time! You can throw me out all you want to. Your sis
said it would happen soon. But just remember, you can't
throw Jesus out of your life, you're going to need Him more
than ever now! It's the money! You and Donny remind me
so much of the woman in the Bible with the issue of blood.
Payin' all your damn money to doctors, never focusing on
Jesus!" She chuckled. "It's Christine that is reaching out to
touch the hem of His gown, not you two!" Grandma remained self-assured never looking back, exiting out the
door.

"Where's Grandma going, Daddy?" Christine quickly became agitated releasing her paranoia. "No! No, Grams, I
need you, please don't go! Momma, what did you say to
her?"

"It's okay, Christine," Donny spoke.

"No, it's not okay, I need Grandma!" Christine cried.

Valerie avoided the question, trying to calm Christine as
she fought to get up.

"Let go of me! You always interfere! I know why those
detectives were here!" She blurted out. The room went
silent. Christine's face was flooded with tears.

"I don't want to hear it! You only speak unless you have an attorney, Christine!" Donny stormed out of the room.

"I know why!" Christine yelled.

"Sedate her, she's talking crazy!" Several doctors rushed in. Donny stood at the door, waiting for the injection, refusing to listen.

"I know why!" Chris continued fighting. "I know why, damn it! You two never listen to me! Never!" Christine's voice lowered, her body sank back into the bed, drifting as the injections began to take effect.

⚮

Things became even more chaotic after Chris was released from the hospital. Her mom and dad constantly argued. Donny was so pissed off about the lies Trisha told, and momma was at wit's end with grandma and her Jesus talk.

Her parents refused to talk or ask Christine about that night. Donny's best attorney was already preparing for the case. Between daddy and their attorney, Christine was forced to not speak a word to anyone. Every time she went to her mom, asking to talk, she boldly told her to go talk to her father. Chris knew her mom was avoiding. At no cost, she would carry out Donny's demands. *The pressure, I need a drink, just a sip! No, I can't, just a little that's all, to feel better.* Christine knew her own family was enough to cause her to a relapse.

Everything in her home had been removed. Donny was selling the house. Her momma found her stash of alcohol.

She trashed everything. Again, she was back at home with her parents, but this time with her son. Word had gotten around town about Trisha and Christine seeing each other. Just when she thought things couldn't get worse, her daddy bombarded her with questions, speaking his mind freely about homosexuals. She couldn't tell him right now. *Lord, forgive me.* Donny cut her allowed spending down like she was some sort of kid. Three thousand a month from the unlimited was barely enough. He had taken all her credit cards away.

To make matters worse, her mom found Jordan's prescription. She researched his meds online. Christine sat in her room, trying to block her out as she yelled at her, wanting to know why her grandson was prescribed this type of medication. Her mom kept yelling out "Does Jordan have herpes?" Chris's mind felt crippled. *Alcohol, I need a drink to escape the pain. No, if I go back ... I can't, I can't! Where's my willpower!* Her mom grabbed her arm, asking the question over and over. Chris was breaking inside. "Yes! Yes, damn it, Jordan has herpes one, I have herpes two, Momma, are you happy, damn it?" Valerie was appalled and speechless. She couldn't believe Chris had just yelled at her. *Deja vu,* just like Valerie did to her mother. Relentless tears fell down her cheeks. "I'm trying, I'm trying ... to be a good mother!"

"Where did you get herpes from?" Christine looked up to see her daddy standing in the doorway. Where Christine, where did you get it from?" Tears floated down her face;

she felt weak in the knees. I said where!" Valerie yelled violently yanking her arm.

"Chad!" His name shot from her mouth. Her daddy disappeared. His footsteps echoed through the house.

"I warned you, Christine. I knew he was the one who wrote that check for thirty thousand dollars. It all makes sense. You were so convinced this man loved you! Your father's going to kill that bastard. Every time he's around, trouble brews, and now Trisha! Those sons of bitches won't get any money if Donny and I can help it! How did Jordan get infected?"

"Drinking after me, towels, my open sores. I don't know."

"Or maybe that low life cunt, Chad!" Valerie stormed out of the room, slamming doors wherever she went. Chris could hear her calling for Donny.

"I'll kill that bastard! Enough is enough!" Donny grabbed his keys, avoiding Valerie's calls, heading for the front door. He paused on the porch to a face he didn't want to see. Sally made her way up the front steps wearing a sleazy black dress and heels.

"Get the hell out of here, Sally!"

"Well, hello to you, Donny! And your nosy ex-wife, who I know is somewhere, listening!"

"What the hell do you want?"

"You shouldn't be so rude Donny, especially when your daughter is up for murder charges!

"That's a damn lie!"

"Actually, your ass should be bowing down and licking

my feet!" Sally removed her shoe partially lifting it in the air.

"That will be a cold damn day in hell, bitch! And I sure don't see Danielle with a cold glass of water yet, just a pair of gasoline thongs!" Christine stood listening through her open window.

"I'm suing the piss stains out of you for your daughter murdering my daughter!"

"Bitch, you won't get a damn dime, you money-hungry hoe! Suing for what? What type of mother are you? Not like you cared that Danielle is gone, it frees your time to trick around and screw whoever you want! You still screwing Chad?"

"Fuck you Donny, and that high horse your ass is riding on! Imma knock you off and you'll be licking dirt after I get through with yo' ass!" Two security guards placed a firm grip on Sally's arm, yanking her back.

"Get this low life trick bitch out of here! And if I see your face again, I'll shoot and ask questions later!" Donny zoomed by, getting into his car, taking one of the guards with him. He sped off as Sally was rushed off the property.

"Chad Stone. Find out where the bastard lives!" Donny demanded his security guard. A few calls were placed and in a matter of minutes, a positive address was provided.

"He's leasing an apartment in West Bloom."

"Not too far from where Christine was living! That doesn't surprise me!"

Donny merged his Benz onto the closest freeway and accelerated. They quickly arrived at West Bloom apartments.

Outside, he scanned the driveway, searching for a car like the one that was parked at his daughter's house. No luck. Donny quickly followed behind a young lady entering the locked apartment, pretending to be a tenant, parading around like a teenager dressed in a black and gray Nike suit with matching shoes. Donny and his guard climbed up to the third floor.

"You knock. I'll stand out of sight." Donny stood against the wall, rubbing his hands together, waiting, counting each knock.

"I don't think anyone is here." The guard placed his head against the door, listening. "I don't hear anything."

"You two looking for a guy who lives here? Her voice came out of nowhere. A short Asian lady stood before them, holding a large set of keys. "You two know them?"

"Not really, ma'am," spoke the guard.

"They were gone! Gone! Owe me two months' back rent!" She angrily fumbled around with her keys, trying different keys in the keyhole.

"Damn it! When did he leave?" Asked Donny.

"He owes you money, too?"

"His damn life."

The apartment door flung open. The Asian lady stood with her hands on her hips, shaking her head. The apartment had been ransacked; the belongings which had been taken were simply what were needed. The living room was cleared out. The dining table with five chairs was left. Dishes were left piled in the kitchen sink. The refrigerator was partially open, a mess and empty.

"Gone! Just left! Left mess, big mess! Mr. Stone and wife will pay for this!" She continued through to the back, complaining.

"Looks like Chad hopped up and moved sir." The guard laughed.

"That bastard knew I was coming!"

❧

Christine had never really taken a look at all the mess she'd caused, 'till now. Dana and Jerick invited her to attend church with them on Sunday and for the Thursday Bible study. Chris was so excited until her momma refused to allow her out of the house. She said it was nothing personal, that Chris created her own mess and she needed to lay low until court. *Daddy would blow a gasket if he knew I was out alone. I need help.*

Christine: Dana plz pray, going thru hell right now. I really need Jesus!

Dana: Are you ok? My husband and I will pray, u need to pray yrself Chris in spirit."

Christine: idk how?

Dana: Call on Him read the book of Palms, it's long but it will help you.

Christine: Is He listening?

Dana: Yes, imma call u so we can pray aloud 2gether."

Dana and Jerick always knew the right words of encouragement to use. A partial weight was lifted off Christine's shoulders. *I'm so happy God has placed them in my life and grandma.* Christine secretly texted her grandmother asking her to pray, she never had a problem with that. She told Chris she needed to confess, it was one of the three things she needed to do to be released. Christine remembered the voice, telling her there were things she needed to clean up; Grams just confirmed it.

The morning sunshine was radiant, beaming through her curtains. Two birds sat on her window sill, chirping. It all seemed so peaceful. Jordan's little body lay next to hers, curled up in his usual fetus position. Gently she stroked his soft fluffy hair, tearing up. Christine couldn't imagine life without her boy.

Reality echoed from a nearby vent. Her mom and dad were arguing again about Trisha lying, which quickly sent her back into a depression. Her body rocked back and forth. Pictures of alcohol passed. *Just one drink.* She sneaked out, tiptoeing to her dad's study. She knew where he kept it - behind a small bar next to the sink. *No, I can't!* Temptation overthrew all her bad thoughts; her breathing increased as she approached the bar. *Just one.* She grabbed the finest, quickly pouring a glass, running her nose across the scent of alcohol. Each sip sent her into a bliss. She poured another, gulping it down. More! She grabbed two large bottles of cognac, tiptoeing back to her room. Her mom's and dad's voices were silent. She carried the bottles into her bathroom, locking the door behind, and quickly hiding the other up under a bunch of towels inside her closet. Inside the bathroom she poured another, sipping slowly until it was gone. It was such a relief, the escape. She sat next to the tub, filling another glass.

"Christine."

Oh, no. She hopped to her feet, spilling a bit, staggering toward the sink. "Yes, Daddy."

"I need you out here." She could hear her mom waking up Jordan. She listened as they left the room. She gulped down the last bit, filling another. *I don't wanna talk to you guys!* Silent tears fell down her face as she continued polishing off one bottle of cognac. Her head was spinning; drunkenness had overcome her.

"Christine!"

"Go … go aw … away, Mom!" Her mom's footsteps quickly left her room. Her daddy's voice approached.

"Christine, open this damn door!"

"N … n … no, Daddy! Jus … just go away!"

"Is she drinking?" Valerie asked. "Christine, you open this damn door!"

"Stand back!" Donny took a step back. He lifted his foot, slamming it into the door. Chris lay on the floor next to an empty bottle. Valerie rushed in, kneeling down next to Christine.

"You're going to drink yourself dead!" Donny rushed behind them grabbing the empty bottle off the floor. "She's blasted, Donny! How the hell is she supposed to meet with them? Can you hold them off?" Cried Valerie.

"They're not willing to wait!"

"Get her dressed; I'll see what I can do! Some damn reporters are already behind our gated fence! Nice job, Christine! You better be glad that bastard skipped town because we were on our way to whip his ass! Do something with her, damn it!" Donny turned around with his finger pointed in Christine's face. "How can you be such a total disgrace to the Crawford's in this short of time? What happened to you, Christine? What happened! I'm so disappointed in you, and hurt!"

Her daddy's words went straight to her heart. Christine could almost see tears forming in his eyes, but he held them back, storming out of my room.

"I'm sorry, Daddy! I'm sorry! I'm sorry, Mom." All she could do is whisper out her pain, apologizing.

"We're hurting right now Christine! It's tearing your father and me apart! Don't you give a damn?" Valerie forced Christine's jeans and shirt on. "Stop wallowing in your damn sorrows! Pick 'em up and keep damn moving!" Valerie wiped tears from her eyes. "Your shit has everyone fighting, your grandma and I, Donny! Get the hell over that bastard already!"

Christine felt horrible. The pain she put her family and her son through, over a damn man who cared nothing about her! She had been played worn out with deeply embedded scars, scars of revenge her parents were soon to find out. How much more pain could she cause them? *I was no better than Danielle.*

The detectives didn't wait for her to get well. Two of them picked her up from her parents' house and hauled her off to the police station. Valerie and Donny fought tooth and nail, threatening to sue the station and put everyone out of work. Christine remained humble, consumed in drunkenness, with her head lowered, ashamed of all the mess she had allowed in. The news was out. A few reporters waited behind the gate, swarming the police car. Ten of Donny's best security guards held them off, allowing Valerie's and Donny's car to follow behind the police car.

When they got to the station, two detectives escorted Chris down the hall.

Their eyes meet for a second. Trisha, her parents and some little black guy who must have been the attorney sat in one of the rooms. Christine could already hear her dad accusing Trisha of lying. Detective Johnson forced Donny to be quiet or leave. Mr. Leonardo, the Crawford's attorney, entered the room.

"You're not questioning our daughter when drunk!" Donny demanded to the police.

"Not my fault she's drunk, but no! I'll give her time to sober up. She's got plenty of time, Mr. Crawford," Spoke Detective Johnson.

"How can I be sure you won't question Christine?"

"Ummm…your attorney's in there with her. You and your wife can wait by the door if you want. Like I said, we will give her time to sober up."

Christine didn't know how long it had been. Her head finally stopped spinning as she came to, realizing where she was. Black coffee was pushed in front of her by Mr. Leonardo.

"Welcome back, Chris."

"This is not a welcoming place, nor do I want to be here."

"I don't think anyone does. Please, drink up, we have a

long day. I don't know what evidence the police have, Christine, but since you've been home, I pretty much briefed you on what you need to do. Do you happen to know what the police might have?"

"I don't know, sir."

"Can you think of what it might be? Mrs. Trisha Laney is claiming it was all your idea. Christine, I can better represent you if I know the truth. Did you murder Danielle?"

The question replayed over inside her head.

"No." *I couldn't believe I just said that!*

"So you didn't have anything to do with Danielle's murder?"

"You're confusing me. I didn't murder her."

"Again, did you have anything to do with her murder?"

"Yeah," Christine whispered. Mr. Leonardo seemed shocked.

"Okay, well, Mrs. Laney is saying it was all your idea, and that you're the one who threw the head blows."

"That's not true! It's not true, sir! I swear to you it wasn't me!"

"They have proof."

Christine was speechless. Two detectives flooded the room quickly grabbing a seat. A tape recorder was placed in front of her.

"Would you like anything before we proceed, Ms. Crawford?"

"No, thank you."

"We're going to run an alcohol test on you to make sure you've sobered up." Detective Johnson approached with a plastic-covered tube, placing it her mouth, pressing a couple of button on his Breathalyzer. "Okay, great." Detective Johnson leaned over showing, Mr. Leonardo the results. "Print these results off and hand them to the attorney, please." Detective Marsh left the room, quickly returning with copies.

Sweat quickly built up around Christine's armpits and the palms of her hands. For some reason, her breathing picked up. *What did Trisha say to them?*

"Can I ask a question, sir?" Mr. Leonardo spoke.

"Sure."

"Did Ms. Laney turn herself in?"

"No, no she didn't. Sandra, her girlfriend, did."

Christine's heart sank. Trisha did mention something about a phone. She stared at the dim white walls inside the interrogation room, thinking back to how she got here. Only one name came to mind, Chad. Her heart was heavy. *I have to take responsibility for my own actions. Trisha wasn't just going to pin this on me.*

"Wouldn't that be a conflict of interest? A jealous girl-friend?"

"Possibly, but the proof is in Ms. Laney's old phone. Regardless of conflict, texts and photos don't lie," Mr. Johnson smugly spoke pressing the record button.

"Share the photos with me and the so-called text!" said Mr. Leonardo.

"I'm not at liberty to do that."

"But you're at liberty to threaten my client with information pertaining to this case without me seeing it! That's bullshit and you know it!"

"Call it what you want, Mr. Leonardo!"

"I will Johnson, its Ms. Laney's word against Christine's until proof is revealed. Only certain questions will my client answer."

Johnson leaned forward in his chair placing both elbows on the table. "State your full name for us, please and the date."

"Christine Kay Crawford. Ummm... it's Thursday, August 15th 2013."

"Thank you, Ms. Crawford."

It didn't take long before Christine was in tears. The questions kept coming; some made her confused to what she said and what they were asking. She could see why some admit to something they didn't do.

"Did you murder Danielle?"

"My client will not answer that," Mr. Leonardo interrupted.

"Trisha says it's you, and it was all your idea."

"That's a lie!" Christine's eyes swelled up with tears. She could imagine the pain and disappointment on her parents' faces hearing the dark secrets come out.

"Just tell us the truth, Ms. Crawford. We have the murder weapon and confession from Mrs. Laney! You did it, didn't you!" Christine cried, feeling badgered.

"That's enough, goddamn it! I know nothing about a murder weapon! My guess is that you're lying to my client to get a confession! Not over my goddamn dead body! Show proof! My client's not going answer that question!

Has my client been arrested or are you two playing your normal interrogation games?"

"Here's her arrest warrant." Johnson slapped some papers on the table.

"Murder charges!" Leonardo laughed. "With what proof?" Johnson uncovered several papers, sliding them over. Leonardo studied each document, word for word. "I'm requesting bail for my client." Mr. Leonardo hopped up, furious, gathering his folders.

"Bail has been set for one million dollars."

"Is that the same price for Ms. Laney or just the Crawford's?"

"Are you insinuating that the force is biased?"

"I need money! Christine's bail will be paid up front. Don't let me find out you are! Let's go, Christine!"

"Don't leave town! We'll be seeing you two real soon!"

"I know what the procedure is Johnson, you just make sure you stick to yours!"

Once Christine and her attorney left, Johnson shot up angrily from his seat, tossing his chair back.

"I thought we had her!" Spoke Marsh.

"We did! Ms. Laney lost the damn photos she said were on her phone! All we have are text messages! Damn it!"

"What about the phone company? Can't they retrieve photos?"

"Not without the Sims card. We need more, and I'm going to get it. Get me the Danielle cold case box and all of her files. Someone is going to break in this case."

When the bail was paid, Christine walked out feeling

worse than before, heavy and weak, weighed down by an unseen force. Donny quickly pulled up coming to a screeching halt, beckoning their security guard, Valerie, and Christine to get in. The entire ride home, Donny cursed Chad and Trisha, and he was going to see to it that they paid.

Once they arrived home, Donny and Mr. Leonardo disappeared into his study. Christine ran straight to the play room. Jordan sat, having a ball, without a care in the world, whooshing his toy plane around in the air. It was a joy to see him happy. He brought so much life to her.

"Mommy!" Christine leaned over, lifting him in the air, holding him tight. Valerie stood in the dining room, staring. How long had she been there? Christine's heart accelerated. Why was she giving that unsure look? Christine loved on her son's cheek, Valerie disappeared in the blink of an eye.

Valerie camped out in the den, relaxing with a cup of black coffee. She reached over to grab a letter opener sitting on the table. Valerie anxiously tore open the top, slowly sliding out a stack of paperwork. She gazed up at the ceiling, wondering if it was the right thing to do. Memories replayed and now this. Valerie refused to second guess herself anymore. With the pen held in hand, she started filling out the paperwork.

Christine walked past her daddy's study pausing shushing Jordan quiet, where she briefly overheard Donny laughing about knowing some of the jurors and giving them a small payoff. Her heart sank. Mr. Leonardo uttered a loud laugh, right along with him. Mr. Leonardo stated it was in the bag, regardless of the truth, he would keep it sealed up.

He was going to blame everything on Trisha; they brought up things in her past they knew she wouldn't be able to handle. What about Christine's past? What kind of questions would she be asked? The pain shot through her chest. The thought was there … No, no, no drinking! Mr. Leonardo stated he would keep her from taking the stand, by all means necessary. *They're going to rip her to shreds! What if Trisha's attorney mentions the relationship between us? There's that pain again, shooting through the heart. Oh, gosh! If mom and dad find out! Grams?*

Jordan was getting antsy. Mr. Leonardo's voice moved closer toward the door. The door knob twisted. Christine ran to the next room, muffling Jordan's mouth, hiding behind the door. Donny and Mr. Leonardo passed by laughing. The bottle crossed her mind. She raced upstairs and down the hall, quickly stopping Marie. She handed over her son. Dana's nephew, Ryan, was coming over for a play date in a few minutes. Christine just needed a minute to escape, just a minute.

"I'd get it together Chris. Your parents are talking about placing you in rehab after all this, Christine!" Marie said, holding Jordan's hand.

"What? What are you talking about?"

"Oh, shoot! Said too much; come on Jordan." Marie turned to walk away. Christine quickly yanked her back.

"What are you talking about?"

"Chris!"

"Tell me, now!"

"Please, promise me you won't mention my name? I need this job, Christine."

"I promise. You've kept secrets for me, remember?"

"Yes, ma'am, lots. Mr. C. would have my head if ... I overheard your parents saying they were placing you in rehab. Somewhere in Mexico for four mouths."

"What? Mexico?" Christine yelled.

"Shush, shush, please, Christine! It's not that bad, you have him you need to think about. The first thing to sobriety is admitting you have the problem."

"I'm not a ... I don't have a problem! I can quit when I want to without being shipped to Mexico by my damn parents!" Christine stormed off, pissed.

"Christine, please, wait!"

Her bedroom door slammed shut. She paced the floor aimlessly, furious with her parents. She stared at the bathroom door, wanting it. It was calling her. *No! I don't have a problem, I don't damn it! I can quit!* The voices were getting louder inside her head, her thirst for one drink saturated her entire mouth. She burst into the bathroom door, uncovering her stash. She could feel her mouth-watering staring at the cognac bottle. She cracked the top, lifting it up toward her mouth, taking a large gulp. It was the beginning to her escape she took another gulp. The knock on her bedroom door startled her.

"Christine, Dana's here!"

Oh, shit! "Okay, hold on, please!" She placed the top back on the bottle hiding it, quickly racing for the toothpaste, brushing, and gulping down mouth wash.

"Christine, it's Dana, open up."

"Oh, gosh! Okay, Dana, I'm coming." Dana greeted her with a strange look and a hug. Marie stood at the door giving the same look.

"Your parents said it was okay for Mrs. Russell to come on up."

"Please, ma'am, call me Dana." Marie nodded.

"You ladies have fun."

Dana walked in, shutting the door behind, still having that I-know-what-you-were-doing look on her face. An unexpected poke with her finger to Christine's side forced her mouth open. Dana leaned in close, sniffing her breath.

"Ouch!" Christine yelled. "What did you do that for?"

"Saying the word "ouch" brings up the deep smell of your breath, you know, the one you're trying so hard to hide!"

"I'm not hiding anything, Dana! That hurt!"

"I wanted it too. Christine, I've dealt with an alcoholic mother! I know the smell of mouthwash over alcohol! Plus the poke was to make you feel the pain you're making family and friends go through, especially Jordan! You practically bit Marie's head off denying your use, and look what you run to! Don't you see? Christine, I've been there! Hiding myself behind suicide and sex, sex from men who cared nothing for me. I was looking for love from the world, only burning myself and hurting everyone in sight! Yes, I sat in denial, but you know what I had to look at? The scars left on my wrist. You see these, Christine?" Dana lifted her sleeves, revealing her cut wrists. "It's a constant reminder of where the Lord has brought me from! But I had to admit it, I had to stop denying it and running away!" Christine stood crying, listening to Dana.

"They want to send me away!"

"Who?"

"My parents, to a rehab!"

"What's so wrong about that?"

"They didn't talk to me about it! They just took control of my life like every other time!"

"Christine, you have to start acting like an adult, and drinking yourself to oblivion is not the answer! I agree they should speak to you about it before planning but you've allowed them to take control over so much, you panic when the world comes crashing down and don't know what to do! Your dad controls all money and your mom everything else! Where's the bottle?"

"What?"

"The bottle of alcohol, Christine." Dana held out her hand waiting.

"I ... I ..."

"Don't you lie to me? See that question was a test, to see if you would admit to your addiction."

"Addiction's such a harsh word."

"You didn't think that when you were addicted to having sex with Chad."

"That's different, Dana!"

"No, Christine, it's the same but a different addiction! You need to learn how to forgive yourself and Chad!" Christine walked to the opposite side of her room. "By your actions, you still haven't. It's not going to be easy, but it's your release, Christine! Jerick asked me was it wise to still be around you with murder charges pending. I told him the Christine I know now doesn't dictate her future. Regardless of what you may have done in your past, I have to forgive you. You need to forgive yourself."

Christine walked into the bathroom, turning to Dana with the open bottle of cognac. She stared at it briefly.

"You're really trying to kill yourself, Christine!" Relief set in watching Dana pour it down the drain. For the first time, Christine felt like she had control.

"Dana, thank you for not judging me."

"Who am I to judge?"

"Well, my parents are doing enough of it, especially dad. There's so much dirt floating around! Daddy knows everyone! You know I could walk away from this."

"What do you mean?"

"In court, I could get away with it all! They're planning on blaming it all on Trisha."

"Where would your conscience lay, Christine? I hate to ask but …"

"Yes!" Christine burst into tears, allowing the pain to run freely down her cheeks. "It was her idea! She planned the whole thing, I swear! I hit Danielle in the head two times. She wasn't dead. I was too weak. Trisha took the pipe and started beating her head. I backed away, feeling sick to my stomach, seeing the blood splatter on the walls! I know it wasn't right! I was so mad, she caused me to lose my baby, and Chad was cheating with her! My own stepsister!"

"Stepsister?" Dana covered her mouth, surprised.

"Dad's ex-wife's daughter, Sally's daughter, Sally slept with my husband, too!"

"Oh my gosh, Christine. Geesh! Lord forgive me but that's some low down shit! Oh, my God! I can't imagine what I'd do, Christine, so I can't judge you. Right now my blood is boiling just from you talking about it so God only knows how I'd react with the short temper I used to have."

"I wanted them all to pay, especially that whore Danielle! Chad allowed her to destroy our family!" Dana rubbed Christine's back, crying along with her.

"I hate to say it, Christine, but we still have to forgive those who have hurt us. You can't walk away from something of this magnitude and expect to get away with it. Well, you could in the world, but God sees all! Don't play with God, Christine. You were supposed to die that night! He left you here because there are some things you need to do. No matter what the outcome, He's going to get the glory.

"As for Chad, forgive him and let God have his vengeance! Don't let your parents send you to hell in a handbag! You know what you need to do and what's right. If Trisha's lying, allow God to reveal it, but first you have to let go and allow him. Therefore, submit yourself to God. Resist the devil and he will run away from you. Read the book of James, Christine. Come close to God and He will come close to you. Humble yourself in the Lord's presence and He will exalt you. See, God opposes the arrogant but gives grace to the humble. Your family is very arrogant. That devil's brew is not helping. Leave it alone! It takes you far away from God. Besides, your parents want rehab, but I know Jesus can wipe that taste clean out of your mouth quicker than rehab."

"It's not that easy, Dana," Christine whimpered.

"It's not easy because you won't allow it! I know those voices speak, telling you to drink. You have to fight them, and you can't do it alone. I have your name on the prayer list at our church. I've specially asked three of the elders to pray for you."

"Why the elders?"

"Where there are three or more in prayer, Jesus is in the midst. Yes, He is in the midst of those praying alone too; we have to make it personal with Him. Cry out. The Bible says call upon the elders of the church and Jesus, not rehab. But if it's needed so be it. See, we've become too complacent in the world where we're leaving out the very One who has the power to deliver us. We are in the world but not of the world."

"What's that mean?"

"Just what it says. As saints, we don't do everything the world does. Whoever wants to be a friend of this world is an enemy of God. No one is perfect, Christine. Don't get me wrong, we all have faults and failures, but we also have victory over every adversity, but it's a choice. I'm a work in progress and so are you. Yes, I have cracks in my foundation that still need work! I can't do it myself, my strength comes from Jesus."

"You've made mistakes even as a saint?"

"Oh, my gosh, yes, Christine! And I still make mistakes daily but I repent."

"God won't forgive what I've done!"

"If you repent, He will. 'At that time it will no longer be necessary to admonish one another to know the Lord. For everyone, both great and small shall really know me then, says the Lord, and I will forgive and forget their sins. Jeremiah 31–34.

"I really didn't know God would forgive me."

"But here's the catch. If God forgives us, the one who created all things, everything, Christine why can't you forgive yourself and Chad?"

"You know, you put all this in a way that makes sense. I even feel better taking about all this, and my confessing it and you not judging me lets me know that you're a true woman of God and a good friend. I'm going to work on forgiving myself and yes, Chad, along with my parents. You know, when Grams and I used to talk and pray, I felt so much better. I didn't worry as much. Yes, we rich people have worries." Christine chuckled. "I used to attend church with Grams, but I just didn't get it. My parents used to attend; that's where I met Chad."

"As you see, the devil can be sitting right in church with you!"

"Amen to that one! I can't believe how great I feel right now! I just have to fight, fight my addiction off. Wow, I just admitted it!"

"And the devil is mad right now. He's going to come at

you in every direction, Christine, but remember, you already have the victory."

"I don't know if I'm … I mean I'm …"

"Shush, don't you let that come out of your mouth! You fear God, not the devil! You know Satan has to ask God if he can attack us?"

"No way! You know, I've heard that but it sounds so different coming from you. Why does He allow it?"

"He's the father of us all! It's like a tough love thing. If God allowed us to continue sinning, doing what we wanna do, we'd all be going to hell! Jesus died for all of our sins to be forgiven. That's how much God loves us that He gave His only begotten son. He has to send the devil to wake us up from sin or else we'd keep doing it. Would you allow Jordan to keep hitting another child, or are you going to discipline him before it grows to be something much worse?"

"You're right Dana. Imma beat his little behind, but that's another thing, my mother doesn't want me to whip him."

"Spare the rod, spoil the child.' We wonder why these kids are heartless and prisons filled, revenge, anger, hatred, you name it! The Jesus foundation is not being rooted and grounded in our children so they're runnin' ramped and out of control. The Bible says there's going to be a great fallin' away. Read 11 Timothy. It will explain to you how and what people are turning into. Fight the good fight, finish your course and keep the faith. We suffer from hardship as an evil doer, even unto bonds. We imprison ourselves from the sin we live in, spiritual chains like a criminal, but the word of God is not bound."

"Yeah, I remember what a lot of it says about people. I know pieces of it. For men shall be lovers of their own selves, covetous, boasters, proud. The disobedience to parents, unthankful, despisers of those that are good, heady, high-minded, lovers of pleasure. Where I saw myself. And something about leading captive silly women loaded with sins. Wow."

"Isn't that the world we're living in? Hell has enlarged itself! So you know what that means!"

"So many don't believe that hell is real."

"Do you? I do!"

"Yes. I tell you it was shown to me when I was unconscious in the hospital bed. God showed me if I didn't change … I don't even want to think about it."

"Maybe that was the wakeup call you needed, to slap you on the right track."

"Yeah, I don't wanna go to hell. I want to do right by God and my son. Promise me something, Dana."

"Sure, Christine."

"That whatever happens in court…" Tears fell down Christine's face. "Whatever happens, you'll still be my one and only true friend. I wanna do what's right, I'm tired of being tired! And I know in my spirit it's the sin. I felt His present heavy in my spirit walking out of the jail. Mom, dad were so proud, haughty-like can't nobody touch them! I didn't feel it was right. Please, even if they lock me up! Don't give up on me, visit me!"

"I promise you, Christine. I believe there's a miracle for you. In Jesus's name, only if you do what's right."

Dana brought so much light into the darkness in Christine's room. She felt so many burdens being lifted from her heart. After Dana left, Christine apologized to Marie, her dad and mom, Grams, and then her son. Marie praised God, walking away; it was a joy to see. Christine was going to fight this addiction with the help of Jesus. Inside her room, she rested a pillow underneath her knees. *I'm going to be here a while.*

The devil always found a way to creep in. Christine asked her momma to lock up daddy's study and to keep the key with her. Her alarming response of "you should have more willpower" threw Christine off. She refused, making every excuse that daddy didn't have time to lock and unlock his study every time. *But you had time to lock it when he was married to Sally and you were screwing him,* Christine thought thoroughly disgusted. *What's happened to her? We used to be so close. I know I've hurt them, but I just apologized. One thing for sure, Momma was getting extra close with my son.*

Nearly a week had gone by, Christine embraced her sobriety. Even with all the court pressures and the newest one about Sally's attorney suing for 3 million dollars. Christine literally saw her daddy's head spin like the exorcist. *How could she? I didn't do it! How much was she suing the Laney family? Probably nothing!*

Strangely, Valerie spent most of the week in and out. The most bizarre thing was seeing her waiting outside by the mailbox. *She waited for something very important, but what?* Christine thought.

Words about the case and trial had been squelched by Donny and Mr. Leonardo. The Crawford's arrived at the courthouse. People and reporters who knew about it piled the parking lot of the courthouse; other reporters, from all over, were in search of a story. Tony, their 6'3" 240-pound security guard, and Angela, aka "Secret Ninja" who was an expert in countless martial arts skills, warded off the media with no problem. Trisha's attorney stopped to give his statement. Christine overheard him lying that it was all Christine's idea to murder Ms. Rivers. *I have to remain repentant,* thought Christine to herself. She recited a few scriptures in her head, blocking out the negative. Donny caused a scene yelling calling everyone money hungry liars. *There was no time to wish I'd never done what Trisha wanted. Dana and Jerick were coming and so was grandma. Through it all, they still were coming to support me.*

Inside one of the courtrooms, Defense Attorney Leonardo repeatedly briefed Christine on what and what not to say. Her mind was in and out of oblivion, overwhelmed, hearing him say the Whitengales, Trisha's parents, have a good attorney. Donny paced the floor, spilling out every bad word possible. Christine just wanted it all to end.

Mr. Leonardo walked close by, holding Christine's arm. She glanced up at his salt-and-pepper hair. Deep wrinkles were carved into his olive-colored skin. Behind his smile of confidence, he gave Donny a firm handshake, releasing

Christine to her family in front of the courtroom doors. Donny embraced her, whispering that everything was going to be all right. She didn't feel secure hearing that. Next, her mom gave a snug hug and light kiss on Christine's cheek with no encouragement. Her heart rate shot up seeing her grandma. Her grandma's embrace was ever so soft with her normal light smell of Chanel perfume. Grandma asked everyone to grab hands and bow their heads. As she prayed that His will be done, chills shot down Christine's spine. She felt herself shaking. "Favor," she cried, "favor, gives us favor in this courtroom! Favor with God forgiveness! In the Name of Jesus!" Christine's hands were still trembling. Grams held her tightly, whispering "I forgive you" into her ear. She knows; of course she does; Grams is a prophetess.

Christine's name echoed from the other end of the hallway. The Russell's waved before entering the courtroom. Sally brushed by, upon her face a revengeful grin, along with putting on her best acting, wiping her face with a tissue, as if she cared. Oh, what one will do for money!

Trisha's attorney, Fortmeyer, and family kept their distance, subdued behind the evil glares exchanged. The silence spoke a million words. Trisha and Christine were being tried together.

❧

"All rise and give your attention. Honorable Judge Watkins, Justice of the Supreme Court, presiding." Judge Watkins appeared from behind a door, slowly taking a seat. Her black hair was tucked into a tight bun, with graceful lines of age in her stern look as she gathered her paperwork. All of the players in the court drama were in their right places, ready to be seated.

"Please close the doors, this court is now in session. The Chief or Presiding Justice of the Court will announce the case."

"Is the counsel for appellant ready?"

"Yes, Your Honor."

"Please be seated."

"Is the counsel for respondent ready to proceed?"

"Yes, Your Honor."

"Please be seated."

"Will the first defendant please rise? Trisha Laney, you are charged with first-degree murder on the 28th day of March 2010. How do you plead?"

"Not guilty!"

"Will the second defendant please rise? Christine Crawford, you are being charged with murder on the 28th of March 2010. How do you plead?"

"Not guilty!"

"Please call your first witness, Mr. Fortmeyer."

Trisha slowly approached the stand, raising her right hand, repeating the sworn oath.

"Ms. Laney, how long have you and Ms. Crawford been friends?"

"About twenty years. We're not friends anymore."

"What would cause you two not to be friends anymore?

"Because of what she did!"

"What did she do?"

"She murdered Danielle!" The court burst into an up-roar. Christine shook her head from side to side, feeling out-raged.

"I didn't do it!" She whispered softly.

"Objection! Objection!"

"Ms. Laney, please tell us what happened the night of March 28, 2010."

"Well, it was late. Christine and I had just finished din-ner. She was a mess, distant. Her husband Chad, was cheat-ing on her with Ms. Rivers and God only knows who else. Christine was so angry; all she talked about was revenge. I watched her plot out switching the cameras and stuffing the beds to make it seem like we were sleeping. She said we were only going to scare her, that's all. I should have seen through her anger that it would turn for the worst when she grabbed a steel pipe from her dad's workplace. We waited for Danielle to come home, secretly following be-hind. Christine shoved her way into her apartment. She closed the door to keep out the sound. That's when she began to strike Danielle several times. Blood splattered on the walls. I begged for her to stop. I couldn't believe she was beating her," Trisha cried.

"She's lying, she's lying on me," Christine whispered.

"No further questions, Your Honor." Mr. Leonardo raced toward the bench, handing over a piece of paper to the Mar-shall.

"Records show that you used to work at a spy camera place. Weren't you the one who altered the cameras?"

"No, and so what if I use to work there?"

"Wasn't it a two-way conversation about revenge?"

"No, it was her!"

"That's not what the phone records show, Ms. Laney. Permission to approach the bench, Your Honor."

"Granted."

Mr. Leonardo handed over a piece of paper. "In your text messages, they clearly state you wanting revenge for Christine's pain. Quote: 'I wanna kill that bitch for the pain she caused you.' "

"Objection, Your Honor!"

"Overruled! Pass this document over to Ms. Laney's attorney.

"If the murder was Ms. Crawford's idea, why didn't you stop her? Isn't that what friends do?"

"She was determined."

"But you had to go with her?"

"I wasn't going to hurt her. It all changed!"

"You also mentioned that Christine shoved her into the apartment and started beating her. How is that possible? Was Miss Rivers fighting? Better yet, what were you doing at that time?"

"Nothing, watching. I was scared!"

"Objection."

"Sustained. Get to the point, Mr. Leonardo!"

"Never mind, she knows my point. She watched! Ms. Laney, wouldn't you say after twenty years of close friendship, that you were ready to do anything for Ms. Crawford?"

"No sir, I was not."

"When Ms. Crawford had her accident, weren't you living in the Crawford home, and taking care of her hand and foot?

"Yes. I was but ..."

"You were doing anything for her."

"That's different!"

"Ms. Laney, you had other motives didn't you?"

"What do you mean?"

"Quite the jealous streak. In Exhibit C there's a letter dated a day before Ms. Rivers was found dead. Ms. Laney wrote to Ms. Crawford expressing her love for Ms. Crawford and she would do anything to make her happy, including murder!" Trisha's eyes shot over toward the judge and back to her attorney.

"Objection."

"Sustained."

"That letter is old!"

"Order! Order!"

I'm so embarrassed, they know, thought Christine.

"I'd like to present Exhibit D. It's covered for a reason." The Marshall placed the unknown object on the table.

"Objection!"

"Sit down, Mr. Fortmeyer."

"Your Honor, if you would please read past the second paragraph written 'I love you so much, I will do anything for you, hate seeing you in pain,' Ms. Laney, isn't it true you were the mastermind behind Ms. River's murder?"

"Objection!"

"Overruled!"

Mr. Fortmeyer lowered his head.

"Because of your love for Ms. Crawford! You knew you could have her once everyone was out of the way!"

"No! No, that's not true! She did it, damn it! Christine hit her!" Trisha wiped the tears from her face.

"Order! Order, quiet in my courtroom!"

"That brings me to Exhibit D. You should recognize these well, Trisha." Her mouth gaped open, seeing printed photos of Danielle's apartment. *I thought all that stuff was lost, Sandra,* she thought to herself.

"Order! Order!"

"You hated her husband?"

"Who didn't, so did her father!"

"Your Honor, I have no further questions."

"Witness, you may step down." Trisha's knees were trembling. She didn't dare look at Christine.

"This courtroom will adjourn for a fifteen minute recess."

Heated words were exchanged by both attorneys in the hallway outside the courtroom. Trisha stood, wiping fake tears from her eyes. Grandma softly rubbed Christine's shoulders, putting her at ease. After fifteen minutes, Court was back in session.

Christine listened to witness after witnesses testify on her behalf, that even if she thought of murder, she wasn't capable of carrying it out. Detective Johnson didn't have much. Trisha never revealed where the murder weapon was hidden. She also knew they didn't have much without it and she could blame it all on Christine.

"I'd like to call my next witness to the stand: Christine

Crawford." She prayed on her way up to the stand, trying to calm the nervous jitters in her stomach after being sworn in.

"Ms. Crawford, in your own words, can you tell the courtroom what happen the night of March 28th, 2010?"

"Yes, sir. Well, it started with me being upset, I was quite upset. I had found out my husband was cheating. Trisha was always there to comfort my open wounds, she hated seeing me hurt and likewise I hated seeing her hurt. We grew up together. I did leave the hateful text about wanting Danielle dead! But they were only words! That night, I couldn't stop shaking from all the pain. Trisha came to my room with an idea: her well-hatched plan of scaring Danielle. I laughed about it, agreeing to her idea. We dressed in all black, gloves on our hands, stuffing pillows and extra blankets in our beds to make it look like we were still sleeping. Yes, we talked about how much we hated Danielle and her mother all the way to her apartment. Trisha knew what car Danielle drove, even her apartment number; I didn't know it. We waited for Danielle to pull up. All the while, Trisha kept telling me that Danielle was probably out screwing my husband and she was going to pay! I told her this was a bad idea. Maybe we should leave. Danielle arrived. Trisha nudged me out of the car, sneaking up behind her. Danielle was at her door. Trisha snuck up behind her, pushing into the apartment. I did shut the door. Danielle started screaming and fighting. Trish hit her over the head and shoved a piece of clothing into her mouth. I backed away, scared! She just kept hitting her!"

"Objection!"

"Overruled!"

"I begged Trisha to stop, the joke was over!" Christine wiped the tears from her face. "That's when she came to me, forcing the pole into my hands. 'Do it! Do it now!' she yelled. 'Look at all the pain she's caused you!' I focused on all the pain, slowly walking toward Danielle. I struck her once on the side of her face. Trisha shoved me closer, demanding I hit her in the head. I did! I hit her, but she was alive! She tried crawling to the door. I was wrong! She cried."

"Did you murder Danielle Rivers?"

"No! No, I didn't! Trisha walked back over striking Danielle two more times. Danielle wasn't moving anymore."

"No further questions, Your Honor."

Trisha's attorney rose to cross-examine Christine.

"So, Christine, it is your word against my client, and you're blaming her for the murder? I'd like to present Exhibit B. If you notice, Your Honor, Christine's hateful texts of wanting Danielle dead and she didn't care how it was done!"

"I admitted to that already."

"Objection!"

"Overruled. Continue, Mr. Fortmeyer."

"Thank you, Your Honor! Weren't you the one who gave Danielle her final blows, Ms. Crawford?"

"No, I didn't!"

"Didn't you state to Trisha that your money would cover all crimes and that you would get away with it?"

"Yes, I did, but I was drunk when I said it."

"But you meant it. Your Honor, I'd like to ask you to remove jurors 5,9,10."

"On what reason, Mr. Fortmeyer?" Whispers floated around the courtroom.

"Order! Order!" Judge Watkins slammed down her gavel. "Silence! Court is still in session!"

"Money." Mr. Leonardo turned toward Donny, whispering. Christine held back her tears of frustration, becoming angry at her father. The Whitengales pointed their fingers in Christine's direction.

"Jurors 5, 9,10, please exit the courtroom."

"Isn't it true, Ms. Crawford, those jurors were paid to take your side?"

"No. I don't know what you're talking about, sir." *Daddy and his game of money. Now he probably messed everything up. How could he? Why can't he just leave things alone?* Christine thought. The Whitengales and Trisha sat smirking.

"Aren't you the one who masterminded the whole plan because of your husband cheating? It wasn't Ms. Laney's husband! It was you who got the murder weapon, car, and your hands to commit murder!"

"No! I didn't do it!"

"Objection, Your Honor!" Mr. Leonardo shouted. Daddy pointed his finger in Mr. Leonardo's face, demanding he do more.

"I said I helped, damn it! It was meant to be a scary joke! I didn't kill her! Trisha Laney served the last blows! I don't care if you believe me or not, my God knows!"

"No further questions, Your Honor!"

"Ms. Crawford, you may be seated!"

The courtroom was in an uproar. Judge Watkins slammed down her gavel, demanding silence in her courtroom.

"Quiet in the court! Are there any more witnesses?"

"Yes, Your Honor. I'd like to call Sally Crawford to the stand.

This should make the Crawford's look even more guilty, Fortmeyer thought to himself.

"I'm not supposed to testify!" Sally sat up from her seat. "What the hell is going on?"

"I don't know!" Mr. Link, Sally's attorney, answered.

"You're my damn attorney, you should know something!"

"You were the last resort, in case they couldn't prove who the murderer was, that you would have to take the stand."

"I wasn't expecting to take the stand!"

"Sally Crawford, please take the stand!" Judge Watkins called.

Sally slowly approached the witness stand, confused. She tucked down the pieces of her wig, putting them in place.

"Raise your right hand and place your left hand on the Bible."

"That Bible should ignite into flames with her hand on it," Donny whispered to Valerie.

"Sally I have Danielle's medicinal paperwork. Sally shot

a quick glance at the judge and back to Mr. Leonardo. It states here that she suffered from Schizophrenia and Bipolar. Was Danielle medicated?

"What does her mental state have to do with the murder?"

"Answer the question!" The judge ordered.

"Of course, she was."

"We have a record that Danielle was not taking her meds and she had not been to her therapist in ten years. So how was she medicated?"

"Danielle is a damn grown woman! I can't follow her everywhere!"

"But you knew that Danielle's behavior was out of control. Right?"

"Objection!"

"Overruled!" Fortmeyer flopped down in his seat.

"No, I had my own life!"

"Had, so Danielle was never causing problems?

"I don't know what you're talking about!"

"Records also show that Danielle was institutionalized throughout her life. Records also show that you refused to lock her up as her Doctor requested. It states here that Danielle is dangerous."

"Objection!" Fortmeyer yelled as the people in the court whispered aloud.

"Order, order in the court! Get to the point Mr. Leonardo. The judge yelled.

"Sally, how long were you and Mr. Crawford married?" Mr. Leonardo asked.

"Umm, four years I do believe."

"Would you say it was a good marriage?"

"Yes, that's before his damn ex-wife kept coming around!"

"Was Danielle ever around the family?"

"No, no really."

"Why not?"

Sally sighed. "Danielle was different."

"Different like a trouble-maker?"

"No!"

"You sure about that, Sally?"

"She was young, and someone killed her!"

"Isn't it all about money with you, Mrs. Crawford? That's why you're here?" Mr. Leonardo asked.

"No, she murdered my daughter!"

"She? You seemed to be focused on one person. Weren't you planning on that one yourself, Sally?"

"Objection!"

Judge Watkins ruled. "Mr. Leonardo, stop badgering the witness!"

"I never! Never!"

"Was your daughter having an affair with Christine's husband, and you knew about it?"

"No. That's not true!"

"You lying whore!" Donny rose out of his seat, yelling.

"Order, Order! Quiet in the courtroom! This is the last warning, Mr. Crawford, or you'll be waiting outside!" Donny plopped in his seat, fuming.

"It's a shame that you raised your hand under oath,

swearing not to lie, Sally Crawford. Weren't you the one who screwed Ms. Crawford's husband?"

"That's a lie!" Sally jumped up! The court was in an uproar. Judgmental fingers of disgust from people in the courtroom were pointed at Sally.

"Order! Order!"

"No further questions, Your Honor."

"Mrs. Crawford, you may step down."

"I'd like to call my last witness to the stand. Guards, will you please escort him in." Sally slowly sat back down, with her eye glued to the doors. The courtroom waited, anticipating who it might be. Christine turned around in her seat, waiting, shrugging her shoulders at her parents asking who it might be.

"Your Honor, I would like to call Chad Stone to the witness stand."

"What?" Christine whipped her head around, watching the guards walk him in. Chad kept his head down. Donny stood with a grim expression, wanting to kill him.

"What?" Trisha looked back, surprised.

"What the hell is he doing here?" Donny leaned over, furious.

"Mr. Stone is your daughter's best defense, sir. It had to remain a secret or you would have decided against it, and we need him."

Christine could barely look at him. Was this some kind of joke? His suit fit nicely around his thick muscle-built body. Chad's voice sent a mix of emotions, one thinking about all the good times, the other all the pain. *Hold it to-*

gether, Christine, let it go! She watched him get sworn in. This could be good or it could be bad. Butterflies swarmed in her stomach.

"Mr. Stone, how are you today?"

"I could be better, sir."

"Please tell us how you know the defendants?"

"Well, I've known Trisha since my ex-wife, Christine, and I were married, maybe four years or so."

"Do you remember the night of Ms. River's murder?"

"Vaguely. The next day, Trisha threw in my face that she was going to be with Christine. That she could treat her way better than I could! Trisha said she was in love with her!"

"Why would she do this?"

"All the mess I've caused! My cheating, lying, the loss of our child. I hurt everyone in my path."

"Did Sally know that her daughter was sleeping with you?"

"Yes, she did!" Whispers floated around the courtroom.

"Order in the court!"

"You liar!" Sally yelled.

"Quiet in the courtroom! Mrs. Crawford, you're on your way out the door if you keep it up!"

"Sally came to me several times after knowing about our affair for months. She told me that none of this could get back to Donny because it would ruin her marriage and she wasn't going to allow her daughter or me to mess it up! She was going to take it to her grave. Sally made it clear she didn't want the Crawford's to find out or she would lose out on the money."

"Did you have an affair with Sally?"

"Yes sir, I did! Once. She wanted to continue, but I couldn't."

"He's lying!" Sally leaped up.

"You nasty bitch!" Valerie screamed.

"Valerie Crawford, no more outbursts!"

"Was Danielle violent?"

"Yes, she was, she had a mental disease Sally also tried hiding, schizophrenia."

"Police records show that on February 9th Ms. Rivers ran Ms. Crawford off the road, resulting in the loss of her baby. I have no more questions."

Fortmeyer rose up and approached Chad. "Why are you here today, Chad?"

"If you must know, for all the wrong I've caused."

"So you suddenly feel bad?"

"Yes, sir, I do." Chad held back his tears, clearing his throat.

"Would you say that your ex-wife is capable of murder?"

"Never!"

"She was upset by what you did. Would she murder for you?"

"No sir, she wouldn't."

"Did she stress to you how much she hated Danielle?"

"Yes, she did, but she would never kill."

"For someone you hurt, you sure have a lot of faith in her."

"I know Christine."

"There is another side of your ex-wife you didn't know about, isn't there?"

"I'm not sure what you're talking about."

"Her drinking. So you really don't know your wife after all, do you, Mr. Stone? No further questions."

"Court will be adjourned until tomorrow morning at ten A.M. for final deliberation."

Before Christine could even look Chad's way he was gone. She really wanted to thank him for testifying. Two guards pulled her away into another room. Donny and Valerie followed close behind, blocking off unknown camera people.

"That son of a bitch Donny's not going to get away with this, calling me on the stand, undermining me like I'm the bad person. It was his daughter that murdered my child!" Sally spoke, blocking out everyone else except her as being in the wrong.

"Trisha seems to be more at fault, Mrs. Crawford! Testimonies prove it all and so do the documents," Spoke Chad.

"So why are you standing up for them? Murderers!" Sally yelled. "The nerve of you!" Judge Watkins shook her head, disgusted.

"Calm down, Sally, and stop making a spectacle of yourself! I'm not the damn judge nor the jury if they let someone go. The murder points to one person! If it's money you're after, then you've lost. I'll tell you now the Crawford's will go to hell and back to prove you and everyone else wrong! So she admitted it! It doesn't make her the murderer!" Mr. Link spoke

"I've had enough of this shit!" Sally walked outside the courtroom into the hall. "Donny, you won't get away with this!" Sally screamed outside the courtroom. "You're going to pay for my daughter's death!"

"What the hell are you doing? You're making matters worse for yourself, damn it! Everyone is looking at you!" replied Mr. Link

"I don't care, Christine murdered my daughter!"

"You keep saying Christine; I think this is more personal then you caring about your daughter." Sally slapped her attorney.

"They're not getting away with this!" Security guards rushed up behind Sally, dragging her away from the courtroom.

"Find yourself another attorney! Your bill will be in the mail for what you owe!"

"I don't need you, damn it! I can find a damn attorney anywhere!"

Valerie poked her head out from the courtroom door. "Was that Sally making an ass of herself? What did you ever see in her, Donny?"

"Sex."

"How are we looking with the case, sir?" Christine inquired.

"I'm a lot disappointed hearing you admit to things I told you not to. Why?"

"I'm not a liar and I'm not a murderer, sir. You wouldn't understand my new relationship."

"Christine, you're not ready to see anyone," her mother interrupted.

"There you go again! Dictating my life, His life and my relationship with the only man who can save me! Jesus! He's around me all the time Mom, at night and in the morning! What are you going to do to stop that? You stopped me from attending church."

"Watch your mouth, Christine!" said Donny.

"No, Daddy, it's about time I speak my mind and stop running to hide behind you two! You guys and your damn money can't save me! Your lies, games, thinking you're better than everyone else! Jesus saves me! Do you two ever wonder why I am this way, gullible, naïve, stupid to the world?" Christine laughed. "Because you never let me fall! It sounds crazy, but you never let me hit the ground!"

"Why would we allow that?"

"To wake up, Momma! So I can learn on my damn own!" Christine burst into tears. "Ever since I was a child, I could never fall, even when I wanted to! Daddy's always there to bandage open wounds that never heal, like Chad and many others, setting me up on new damn dates with open wounds! Yes, I caused a lot and I'm sorry, but I can handle myself."

"Like the herpes?"

"Valerie."

"What, Donny?"

"There you go again, Mom, there isn't an ounce of forgiveness in your heart 'cause all you do is throw up the past. That wasn't Mr. Leonardo's business! You think I don't know about your past? But who am I to throw it up even though … never mind. My God has forgiven me so why are you still condemning me? You catch me, but you continue burning me at the same time with damn ridicule and hatred! Daddy, you know I asked Mom if she could lock your study up?"

"No, I didn't know that!"

"Your butt is going to rehab!"

"Oh, you can't wait to send me away!"

"Valerie, please!"

"Are you taking Jordan from me, Mom? That's it, isn't it?"

"No one's taking your son away, Christine!"

"You might wanna speak to my so-called mother about that!"

"You watch your damn mouth! He doesn't need a drunk mother!"

"Nice going, Mom. You know, you remind me so much of Sally, maybe that's what dad sees in you."

"Don't you dare compare me to that whore! You were the one sleeping with dad and he was married, just like I was with Chad."

"Christine! Valerie! Enough!"

"Dad, I just wanted her to lock your study to control my temptation. You know she refused? She wouldn't do it! She made every excuse about it being a problem with you having to unlock your doors!"

"Honey, that wouldn't have been a problem. Valerie, why would you say that to her?" Valerie turned away, avoiding the question.

"You're not getting my son. I already have the paper-work in place for Grandma to take him when I go away, someone that's going to raise him in church and not rich money trash!"

"You're not going anywhere, honey."

"Yes, Daddy, the Lord already revealed it to me. I have to pay for my crime and I'm okay with that. Grandma said she'd bring Jordan to visit me every weekend." Valerie blatantly rolled her eyes. "Roll 'em again, Mother, I don't care!"

"Is my daughter going to serve time?" Donny rushed over toward Mr. Leonardo.

"I'm trying my best, sir. If it's what she feels she needs to do."

"It's not a matter of what she wants, it's what I want!"

"No, Daddy, it's not! Let me fall, damn it! Let me fail!" Christine cried. "There you go again, it's not about you! It's about me and God! Stay out of it!"

"What? What are you saying?" Donny yelled.

"What am I doing? This is my daughter who I love dearly!" Valerie stood in the corner, crying, and disappointed at herself.

"Stop it, please! You're causing my destruction! Stop it! Please, Daddy, let me fall; let me fail at something, so I can come out better with my Lord. He's going to protect me. You can't save me! Stop trying to be God! My God is way bigger, richer than you! Stop it!"

Chris had finally gotten her word across by standing up to her parents. Donny wrapped her tightly in his arms. It was a side she had never witnessed: her dad's tears soaking her blouse. He apologized. Valerie joined in, asking Chris to forgive her. She explained that she only wanted the best for Jordan. Out of fear she reacted the wrong way. Out of fear and anger, thinking she was going to lose her daughter. "I forgive you, Mom and Dad, please forgive me?" floated from her mouth. Out of all these years, this was by far the best moment. *God gets the glory even though the devil's trying to stop me. I had my family back who the enemy was trying so hard to destroy.* "I love you guys so much, but let God work. Stop getting in the way. He doesn't need help, you two know this."

"You're right, baby, I'm so sorry, I was so angry at you!" Valerie cried. "You know I really do love you and my mother."

"I'm sorry too honey, for not letting you fall. Forgive me, please," Donny cried. It was an unforgettable moment seeing him this way.

"I do, I forgive both of you. I love you guys."

"We love you, too. I promise to stay out of it," Donny spoke, overcome with guilt.

"Thank you, Mom and Dad."

❧

Chris stood proudly in the courtroom. So many barriers were finally broken. Her parents had a better understanding of her needs. *I'm truly blessed and grateful, even though I'm sitting in a courtroom, facing possible murder charges. God knows my story.* Chris felt the presence of the Lord was all around as she stared at the ceiling, praying.

Mr. Leonardo made several valid points in his closing statement. She was shocked to hear him mention how parents can sometimes hinder their children. "My client was forced to make a decision at her weak point by a monster only out for revenge. The evidence clearly states that Ms. Laney would do anything, including murder, to wipe away Ms. Crawford's pain, and she did. She plotted the entire crime on motives to gain her rightful spot in Ms. Crawford's life as her lover. Altering the cameras, fabricating the real reason to head over to Miss Rivers apartment, knowing her intentions all along were to murder Danielle Rivers. It was only meant to be a prank, pranks are not good, but my client felt threatened by Trisha's behavior. Two hits, jurors, Danielle Rivers was still alive … and out of those two hits, Ms. Laney was not satisfied so she filled her head with Christine's ex-husband cheating, forcing her to hit Danielle Rivers again. When the job was not completed … that's when Ms. Laney became outraged … outraged by Ms. Crawford's weakness, her incapability to make the final blows to Danielle Rivers head. Ms. Laney snatched the pole from my client's hand … and let's face it, people … she was angrier now because of Ms. Crawford's failure. In my closing statement, Trisha Laney administered the final blows to Danielle Rivers head, not Ms. Crawford, which leads to her death!"

After each closing statement, the jurors left for deliberation. Christine wiped endless tears from her face as everything soaked in and the guilt surfaced. Hearing Mr. Leonardo speak of what transpired that night made her feel horrible inside. For one to even plot killing someone over a stupid man or woman was complete foolishness.

Each one of the jurors reappeared. A short female from the jurors passed the verdict to Judge Watkins, who read it and handed it back. Christine glanced back at her mom and dad, smiling. Grams and the Russell's gave the "okay" signal.

"Will the defendants please stand?"

"Jurors, how do you find the defendants?"

"We find the defendant, Trisha Laney, guilty of first degree murder." The courtroom went straight into an uproar. Trisha leaned forward on the table, crying. Her family was disgusted.

"No way in hell!" Sally blurted out.

"Order! Order! One more outburst, Mrs. Crawford-the-Second and you're out of my courtroom! You should be happy justice is being served on behalf of your daughter!" Sally sank down in her seat, filled with disappointment.

"We find the defendant, Christine Crawford, guilty of accessory to the crime."

"No! Damn it, no! She can't get away with this! She's a murderer!"

"Get that woman out of my courtroom! The court is adjourned. Sentencing will be in three days!"

Christine fell to her knees, praising God for His many miracles. *He didn't let me down! Thank you, Lord! Thank you, Lord!* She could hear Grams praising aloud. Her mom and dad lifted her off the floor, embracing her, praising God with her. Through all the pain, there was a huge light at the end of the tunnel. The Russell's, Grams, even Mr. Leonardo, huddled together in one big hug.

"Follow me to the restroom, Christine."

"You can't use the restroom yourself, Dana?" Christine laughed, as they walked through another room, avoiding the people. Dana paused in front of her. Her height blocked the view of the person standing in front of her.

"I thought we were...."

"I'm sorry, I had to." Dana moved aside, allowing Chris to move forward. Chad stood leaning against the wall with his hands tucked into his front pockets. Christine didn't feel that anger. He approached slowly.

"Hello Christine. I'm sorry, I asked Dana if I could see you. I figured she'd be the best one to ask." Christine remained speechless. "I wanted to apologize, sincerely, from my heart, for all the pain, heartache, and turmoil I put you through."

He was serious.

"All because of my selfish needs of wanting to please me Christine." Chad handed her an envelope. It was over twenty thousand dollars. She was speechless. "Please forgive me, for everything."

"I have already, Chad. Here, you can keep the money."

"No."

"I insist, Chad. I am so over all of this. Take it! I had to forgive you to get to this point in my life. My hardest thing is letting you go, to stop hindering myself from God's blessings. With the help of God, Dana and Grams."

"The warrior, huh?"

"Yes, you remember, Grams is no joke. I don't know where I'd be, Chad. I was so angry at you, I was becoming a different person and I ask you to forgive me, Chad. I had no business sleeping with you out of revenge or anything else when you're married."

"I'm sure you know about Miss Tamara by now," said Dana.

"Yes, I do, and it's over! I've prayed and asked the Lord to remove my feeling for you. I want you to be in our son's life, but only on friendship and as a good parent."

"I thank you for still allowing me to see him. You really have changed Christine. I need the Lord to work on me. Well, I'm going to get out of here. Thanks again for allowing me to keep the money, Christine."

"Thank the Lord not me, Chad. Oh yeah, I finally stood up to Daddy." She could hear Chad laughing, saying "Finally, and good job." She hated seeing him walk away, but she had to let him go for her own peace of mind.

❧

The Russell's arrived at the house. Jordan and Christine were attending church service for revival week. She really needed it. Donny stood next to Jerick in one of his nice suits, engrossed in a full conversation about business. Valerie, her voice echoing, yelled: "I'm coming." She appeared in a conservative dark-pink suit dress with matching hat.

"Are you two going out?" Asked Christine.

"Yes, we are, dear." Valerie chuckled.

"Where?"

"To revival week with you, our grandson and the Russell's."

"Praise God!" Dana yelled.

"Oh, my gosh, this is awesome! Mom and Dad, you're the best!"

That night the Holy Spirit continued to hit Christine. On altar call, she couldn't stand still. Her hands shook and her legs danced on their own. She rededicated her life back to Christ, promising to try again. Her daddy whispered in her ear about how proud he was. Her heartfelt overjoyed.

❧

Day three, sentencing date. Christine wasn't really nervous. She glanced over herself in the courtroom bathroom mirrors, taking several deep breaths. She leaned forward, dousing her face with cold water. The door opened and slammed shut. Trisha stood behind her, wearing a deceitful expression. Christine backed away. Trisha followed as Christine moved closer toward the doors.

"So Ms. Christine! You got daddy to win your little case! All lies to make it look like it's all me."

"No, Trisha, I didn't! You heard me: I confessed to what I did!"

"You lied!"

"No, I didn't Trisha, you know I didn't lie!"

Trisha kept moving closer, blocking out every word spoken. Christine could feel her tension and anger. Trisha's voice became louder. Christine was afraid. In silence, she stood refusing to argue. It was pointless.

"I have to go, Trisha." As she turned to walk away, she unexpectedly felt a tight grip around the back of her hair. "Let go, Trisha!" Trisha slammed Christine's face against the wall, punching the back of her head with her fists. "Help me! Stop it, Trisha! Somebody, help me!" She screamed, praying someone would hear her.

She overheard a woman yelling "She needs help!" Two guards burst into the restroom, wrestling Trisha down to the floor, handcuffing her. Valerie and Donny rushed in, with obvious looks of wanting to strangle Trisha.

Donny pulled Christine out into the hallway, asking if she was okay. Valerie followed, brushing Christine's tangled hair back in place. "My head, it hurts, Mom, she kept punching me."

"I can't believe she just attacked you," Valerie said. "Somebody needs to lock that monster up! You sure you're okay, honey?" Valerie checked the back of Chris's head. She dabbed her lip with a tissue, catching drops of blood from Trisha slamming her face against the wall.

"Yes, Mom, just a little startled."

"The judge is going to hear about this!" Donny yelled.

Christine couldn't believe Trisha had just attacked her in the restroom. Her parents and Mr. Leonardo were furious, but they kept their cool.

Christine sat next to Mr. Leonardo, still taken aback at Trisha's outrageous behavior. Judge Watkins gave a brief statement. She also threw in knowing about Trisha attacking Chris in the restroom. Trisha stood silently, waiting for her sentence. Twelve years with no probation brought Trisha to her knees. Judge Watkins blurted out that if Trisha wanted a longer sentence, she could pick fights inside the prison.

Next was Christine's turn. Sweat began to form around her hands. Her heart was relieved upon hearing her sentence set at two years. Her arms went straight to the air, giving praise like never before, grateful, because it could have been worse. Her family rushed over, exchanging hugs and thank you's. Trisha slandered Chris's name while being handcuffed and dragged out of the courtroom by police officers. Two marshals approached. Donny stepped in front blocking their way.

"You two take care of our baby," he cried, moving aside, allowing the officers to pass. Long hugs were exchanged with wailing of tears. "It's going to go by fast, guys, you'll see." Her mom and dad promised to visit this weekend.

Christine was sentenced to a correctional facility for women. Living quarters were a lot different than what she was used to, but it made her more humble. Her roommate, a thirty-year-old Caucasian woman named Sara, was serving time for Vehicular Manslaughter, a mistake she often vented about. Five years ago after leaving a party and one too many drinks, Sara got into her car to drive home. She was headed down a one-way street with the headlights to her car off. The lights up ahead were blinding until a loud crash startled her. Sara staggered from the car to find out she had been the cause of an accident. Sara dialed 911 on her cell, crying into the phone about what she had done.

Chris could see the pain on her face of taking a child's

life. An eighteen-year-old girl died. Chris told Sara she was-
n't here to judge her. She couldn't cast a single stone. She
admitted it took years to forgive herself for what she had
done, but it was her step toward healing. Sara was humble
like Chris, into God and praying all the time. She even had
a small ministry inside the correctional facility. Sara invited
her. Chris was so exhilarated and honored. Everything Sara
spoke was powerful. Chris wanted in. She helped Sara and
the others start up another ministry for women and forgiveness. They taught women how to forgive molestation, as
well as teaching how to eliminate anger, pain, and rejection.
It was shocking to see so many who know nothing about
forgiving. Chris had gained so much favor; her work in
Christ made her feel like she wasn't in prison.

Chris and Sara were both on work release for a local
church two hours a day. What better place to be? They
scrubbed that church from top to bottom, leaving it
sparkling clean. The pastor had nothing but good words to
say about them. *God is so good! What the devil meant for
evil, God turned it to good!*

Eight months had passed. Chris received a letter from
Chad. He stated he thought it was a trick when Valerie
asked him if he wanted to see their son. He was seeing Jordan every other week and her father allowed it. Chad was
getting his life together. He moved out of town and started
to work for a large company. Guess who helped him get the
job? Chris was so overjoyed about her parents.

Her mom, dad, Grams and her son came to visit every
weekend. She got to enjoy playing with her son. The Rus-

sell's would often pop up. Amazingly, Sara and Chris were both up for early release with good time.

There was something Chris had to do. She felt in her spirit it was time. She asked Sara if she could give her testimony. Sara was delighted. No matter how much the devil tried telling Chris she had lost, she only gained Jesus, peace of mind and sobriety. No matter how much money one has, they must still face the wrath of God.

There I stood in front about thirty women ranging from young to old. Some I wondered how they ended up in a place like this until, looking at me, they were probably thinking the same thing. Standing there, shame started to creep up... their hungry eyes waiting for me to speak. That's when I realized I was no longer that same person. I took in a long inhale, and then exhaled deeply.

"I'd like, to begin with, a short prayer, if everyone can please bow their heads. Lord, I thank you for this opportunity to speak to your people, people that have been hurt and maimed by society. I ask you to surround this room and fill all of us with you grace and mercy, give a listening ear and caring heart to receive. Remove the hurt, pain, envy and allow your glory to fill this place. I ask you in thy Lord and Savior's name, Amen.

"Hello everyone, my name is Christine Crawford. Most of you I know already, Natosha, Jenifer, Pooh and some faces are new to me but I welcome you all. I guess most of you are wondering how I even ended up here." Christine chuckled. "Probably one of the many reasons why most of you are here ... not being able to forgive myself for what I had done … it would have prevented most of the pain and suffering I put myself and family through. I allowed a man, my ex-husband, to destroy my life. He lied, cheated, used me for money and sex, but I allowed it all. I had warnings, but I refused to listen or look at the signs flashing red. I was comfortable but growing miserable with myself. I am not putting blame on him … I ended up cheating when he re-married because I still wanted him … I couldn't let go. I con-tinued wearing a mask to hide all my pain inside."

Christine wiped her tears. "The anger built up from his lies and cheating … I lost my first child in a car accident … his jealous lover who intentionally drove me off the road … I lost a child I wanted so badly. To make matters worse, the jealous lover was my stepsister."

The women in the room were surprised, their eyes widened, some crying. "All of this, behind my back, my ex-husband was sleeping with my stepsister, one I hated at the time. My gosh, we never saw eye-to-eye, she thought I was too bougey and I thought she was too ghetto. Needless to say, I tried to get pregnant again … through numbness, pain. I started drinking to suppress the pain. I didn't care, I wanted my baby back. It was successful; I got pregnant. That's when I found out my ex-husband was cheating. My world was crumbling fast… when I found out it was my stepsister I … I allowed that anger in when I should have left him alone … listened to my dad's warning about him destroying me.

I didn't … like many of you. I wanted him to love me. During the suffering and my drinking, a friend of twenty years fell in love with me … I didn't want it … it's wrong, and that's how I felt about being with another woman so please don't chase me down saying I'm against ho-sexuality or I'm anti-gay, please save it! I'm not here to argue! God's word is His word and I'll leave it at that! It's not the moral of the story. My testimony is about me! We as people like to focus on one thing, one trigger point when it's plainly about me being confused and hurt by family and society. I thought I needed that comfort, my alcohol and someone to fill the void of me being afraid of being alone.

"To make a long story short, my stepsister was murdered. I allowed my good friend to trick me and seduce me with anger to carry out her devious plan to end someone's life over revenge. I'm here on accessory to murder charges." Christine cried aloud, pausing. "Because I allowed the enemy to deceive me through my ex-husband, friends, and family, but the biggest one, I allowed myself to deceive me. I tried drinking myself to death … almost did. Through all my selfishness I caused my family horrible pain and suffering, even my child. I cheated and lied just like the person I wanted at the time to be murdered … all because I wanted him to be mine … and he was remarried. Who am I to want someone's life to end … no one in here can cast a stone! I was just as deceitful, willing to remain comfortable in misery for a man.

"How many of you are here because of a wrong decision, with a man or anger?" Christine watched ten women raise their hands, each of them sobbing uncontrollably. "All it took was us forgiving right then, not waiting, contemplating whether we should forgive. That gives time for the enemy to whisper hatred. We have to forgive early on, walking away, allowing Jesus to fight battles."

Sara smiled; everything Christine mentioned was true. She was touching their lives and hers.

"Forgiveness is a full-time job, and most people are being handed the pink slip. Don't get me wrong, people, you cannot forgive in the carnal mind, the flesh is weak, doesn't understand, but the spirit does. You can't forgive without Jesus. I battled that for years when a friend told me I needed to forgive. I looked at her like she was crazy, a damn fool. In the state of mind I was in, it wasn't possible. She gave me her testimony; I thought what I'd gone through was bad! Nope! But she forgave … and yes, you have to forgive yourself. Everything starts with you.

"I realized that I needed God to move forward, that without Him, I was on my way to Hell. He showed it to me the night I drink myself silly. From what I witnessed in that short time He showed me, Hell is not a place I want to go. I'm not standing here because I'm perfect—I have flaws, no one is flawless, don't get it twisted … but I've made horrible mistakes and I can admit it … and I still make them. Only one perfect person walked this earth, and none of us can be compared to Jesus. I'm standing here because I'm not ashamed to tell my story because someone out there needs to hear my story, the whole world needs to hear my story."

The women in the crowd rose up out of their seat to applaud Christine, all of them crying, hearing her powerful testimony. Several hugs were exchanged, as some of the women revealed parts of their stories. Christine felt the power of God around her, embracing each moment.

⬥

A year later, Chad and I remained distant but good parents to Jordan. It was best. To be honest, my feelings had completely disappeared for Chad. God had removed the film once covering my eyes. I had given men a break to solely focus on God. My spirit man still needed to be built. Daddy still had that "if you cross me look" in his eyes when seeing Chad.

I joined the Russell's' church in faith, believing in a brighter future for Jordan and me. My parents remarried. Sara and I kept close ties, mentoring, praying and encouraging each other often. She was blessed with a husband and a new start.

Every so often I'd cross paths with Sally. She remains a bitter woman, still causing a scene. Sally would scream out "murderer" in front of large crowds. Just the other week she begged daddy for ten thousand dollars. Daddy told her to go bungee jump and forget the cord.

I tried writing Trisha, to ask for her forgiveness and to apologize for my actions. Each letter was returned unopened. Trisha wasn't willing to let it go. Well, spiritually, I did what I needed by letting go of the ball, the game is on her. However long she decided to remain bitter and unforgiving, that ball was left in her court. For now, I remain focused on God and my family.

⬥

The End

False Love Addiction

False, real or my unconscious mind
Is this reality or me running from my fears
All of the wasted years lost I can't believe I was so blind

To fall for a shadowed figure I wanted so much to be true
But you played the game while my eyes wide shut that's nothing new
Applaud me for being so foolish
My life has been choked right out of me, how could you do this

I was new to the things of the world until you came along
A predator in disguise I ended with the sad song
For things I should have known were all wrong

I never thought I'd end up down this road
The reality is my mind has me captive in fear
A junkie trapped in an illusion whose heart has turned cold
The drugs have seized my thoughts and ripped away my soul

False love addiction is it you or me
Hidden behind pain and sorrow I just can't seem to break free
From the poisonous pleasures and self-denial carried so deeply
I'm drowning in a wave of water that has covered these scars
completely
Can anyone see

Addiction causing sickness to my health
No more bridges to cross with family and friends,
my disbelief has destroyed all of my wealth

False love addiction I have to leave you?
You've created a monster so great inside my color has
changed into a sinister hew

Finally after years of doing my own personal examination
I am no longer weak to temptation, I am out for salvation

Chase

www.ingramcontent.com/pod-product-compliance
Lightning Source LLC
LaVergne TN
LVHW051449080426
835509LV00017B/1708